Pope John and his Revolution

Pope John

AND HIS REVOLUTION

by E.E.Y. Hales

DOUBLEDAY & COMPANY, INC.

GARDEN CITY, NEW YORK

1965

Nihil obstat: Joannes M. T. Barton, S.T.D., L.S.S.
                  Censor deputatus

Imprimatur: Patritius Carey, Vic. Gen.
                 Westmonasterii, die 8 martii 1965

The *Nihil obstat* and *Imprimatur* are a declaration
that a book or pamphlet is considered to be free from
doctrinal or moral error. It is not implied that
those who have granted the *Nihil obstat* and *Imprimatur*
agree with the contents, opinions or statements expressed.

Library of Congress Catalog Card Number 65-23924
Copyright © 1965 by E. E. Y. Hales
All Rights Reserved
Printed in the United States of America

Contents

Preface   *page* xi

PART I · ANGELO RONCALLI   I

PART II · WHAT HE TAUGHT   25

1. A new kind of Papal teaching   27
2. About personal rights and social security   40
3. About world order and peace   61
4. About the Vicar of Christ   82

PART III · WHAT HE DID   95

1. In the first two years   97
2. In his lead to the council   121
3. In his final effort for unity and peace   141

PART IV · HIS ATTITUDE TO ITALY   161

Epilogue   193

Bibliographical Guide   207

Index   215

Abbreviations

AAS   Acta Apostolicae Sedis
CTS   Catholic Truth Society
DC   Documentation Catholique

Acknowledgements

My thanks are due to many kind friends abroad, especially in Rome, Milan, and Bergamo; in New York and in San Francisco. Nearer home, I would like particularly to thank members of the staff of St Edmund's College, Ware, who have always been willing to help me and to let me have the use of their library; my friend Mr S. E. Gunn who read my typescript; and Mrs David Miller and my wife, who were both kind enough to read the proofs.

The frontispiece photograph is reproduced by permission of Nuova Editoriale S i A, Venice.

E. E. Y. H.

Preface

What did Pope John want?

We are told, on high authority,[1] that he didn't feel very sure himself.

His own phrase to describe his aim was *aggiornamento*: to bring the Church up to date. But he spoke even more about Peace, and about Unity, his favourite text being Our Lord's prayer in St John's gospel: *ut unum sint*, "that they all may be one".

And how might this be achieved? A suspicion is beginning to grow that Pope John, though good as gold, was a sentimentalist, without strength of intellect or practical realism, a benevolent parish priest.

After the adulation, after the grief of the whole world when he died, the reaction. Were they, then, but a dream, those extraordinary few years when the Church met the world, and the world met the Church, and the world thought that perhaps after all the Church could guide mankind through the fearful tangle and towards the prevention of war and the relief of want and the restoration of sanity? Those years when odd things happened, when curialist cardinals were called prophets of doom, and men were told they had a *right* to worship God (in public, as well as privately) as their conscience dictated, and the *New York Times* printed *Pacem in Terris* in full, and the Pope won a peace prize, and Catholics were allowed to vote for Communists, and Mr Kruschev was expected in Rome? Had the Pope merely been straying away from his proper place? Is it rather the business of popes to stick to their job, governing the Church, and only to move out into the world when they have to take up defensive positions to protect her rights? Successors of St Peter, who guards the gate, should they not stay on guard?

Before we resign ourselves to the view that Angelo Roncalli was not capable of serious constructive work, that his achievement was only to open the window and let others get on with the job, we ought to face a few facts. One is that no pope, in the whole of papal history, has ever

[1] Archbishop Heenan's view is discussed below, pp. 3-5.

xi

made so many specific and practical suggestions in the realm of social organization as Pope John made in *Mater et Magistra* and in *Pacem in Terris*. Another is that no four years of papal history have seen such major policy changes as Pope John made. During his short reign he reversed both the international and the Italian policy of the Papacy. It may be true that he had no blue-print for the reform of the Church; he left that to the Council, after showing the bishops where to look for it. A General Council, not the Pope, is the right body to reform the Church. Pope John's aims were wider. He wanted to give a lead to the world, which was something the Council proved more reluctant to do.

And the world responded. She had been looking to Rome for a lead and now she was given one she could recognize. Since the end of the Second World War the western world, and many too in the emergent countries, had begun to look towards Rome with an altogether new interest and attention. There were many reasons for this. World war is a solvent of sectional feuds and Christians from all countries, and some non-Christians, acquired a new interest between 1945 and 1950 in that centre of spiritual unity which had emerged strengthened and serene amidst the ruin of the governments of Europe. It was not merely that a large ruling majority of Christian Democrats, in Italy and Germany, and a leading political party in France consisted mostly of men who owed spiritual allegiance to the Pope (though for those who could remember the anti-clerical past this was startling enough). It was rather that a Europe disillusioned by the works of a narrow nationalism and a savage racialism was looking for leadership. Many turned to the Communists. But those who rejected the Communist alternative looked afresh towards Rome for light on how to live, and how to act in accordance with justice, liberty and charity, and how to rebuild peace.

Nor did Pius XII fail to respond. He told men that the many disasters which had befallen them in modern times were the bitter fruit of their great apostasy, that these things will, in the end, happen if the world deserts the Church. He told them that they must oppose the Communists resolutely, everywhere, and must work for the liberation of the peoples of eastern Europe. He warned them that their new organ of international understanding, the United Nations, would be of little service so long as it was rooted in injustice, allowing much too much influence to Moscow. He reminded them to pay careful attention to the social encyclicals of Leo XIII and Pius XI. And so on.

Many of the faithful applauded but the world, though generally respectful, was unresponsive. The political Right liked the anti-Communist advice and came to regard the Church as a reliable ally. The Communists said the Pope was a warmonger. And the uncommitted remained uncommitted. The fact that the response was poor does not, of itself, mean that the advice was wrong (the rich young man who asked Our Lord what he must do to inherit eternal life seems to have responded poorly to what he was told, though the advice was divine). But it is undeniable that the advice given by Pius XII in these matters made a limited impression, not merely because his language was so philosophical, but because Justice – his top priority – was too evidently to be Justice, first, for the Church. This was logical, but it was not everywhere acceptable.

The return to religion which followed the Second World War was not confined to Catholicism. Christians as a whole shared in it, and the outlook of most of them was more ecumenical than it had been. In Germany, especially, there was a quite new spirit of co-operation, different denominations sometimes sharing those Church buildings that survived the bombs. The separated brethren were better disposed towards Rome, hoping that Catholics would soon come to share in the ecumenical movement. But Pius XII did not relax the ban placed by his predecessor upon collaboration of this kind, and Pius XI had been very specific: " . . . this Apostolic See has never allowed its subjects to take part in the assemblies of non-Catholics. There is but one way in which the unity of Christians may be fostered, and that is by furthering the return to the one true Church of Christ of those who are separated from it. . . . Let our separated children, therefore, draw nigh to the Apostolic See, set up in the City which Peter and Paul, Princes of the Apostles, consecrated by their blood. . . . "[1]

A surprising number of these separated children did in fact do just that, by going to Rome in the year 1950, which was Holy Year. In his

[1] *In Mortalium Animos*, 1928. CTS (*True Religious Unity*) pp. 21, 23. AAS, XX, pp. 14, 15.

address inaugurating the Holy Year Pius XII spoke of the lead which he hoped it would give to mankind; and the world watched with growing attention a massive demonstration by more than two million pilgrims of the hold exercised by the See of Peter. It was the high-water mark in the pontificate of a Pope whose lofty intelligence commanded respect and who had many claims upon the gratitude not only of the eternal city but of refugees, political exiles, and prisoners.

As Holy Year moved towards its ceremonial close it became known that the Pope had an important pronouncement to make and the world awaited it with curiosity and with hope. But when it came, in the form of the Apostolic Constitution *Munificentissimus Deus*, which defined the dogma of the Assumption of Our Blessed Lady into Heaven, it did not seem to the world to meet the need of those who were looking to Rome to give a lead. Though Pius expressed his "fullest confidence that this solemn declaration and definition of the Assumption will greatly help towards the advance of society" it required the eye of faith to see how that might be. To some it seemed that Catholics, having been educated in the Rosary, must already believe in the Assumption, while the separated brethren would not find this belief easier to accept than others which they had already rejected. Those with ecumenical aspirations at heart feared that the appearance of a new dogma, whose acceptance the Catholic Church would regard as necessary to salvation, might not prove helpful. For the most part the attitude of the world could best be described as one of respectful incomprehension, as though it were looking in, from outside, on a mysterious rite. In what sense could it "greatly help towards the advance of society"? The world outside tended to turn away sorrowful, because it was baffled. It had hoped to be told how to act. It had been told, instead, something more to believe.

Pope John said there had been enough definitions and condemnations. It was also possible, he thought, to pay too much attention to social philosophy. Approaching the problems of the world more empirically than his predecessor he had less to say about the primary requirements of Justice and more practical suggestions and policy changes to propose. And the world, which could understand him, and which loved him, rose in response. He told men that they must have a more confident faith and a wider love. He told them that their laws and institutions must enshrine a wider equality and a fuller social justice. But he told them, above all, to seek after peace, not merely as a consequence of a Justice which might as yet be unattainable, but also empirically, bit by bit, as opportunity offered, by co-operating with all men, in whatever way possible – even with ideological enemies. And in his own political policies he showed the way.

This book then is written in the belief that Angelo Roncalli did know what he wanted; that – as a papal policy – it was original; that it is already becoming obscured; and that it is important to recapture it before it passes out of our brief memories. For the notion that Roncalli's only lasting achievement would prove to be his summons of the Council seems to me wrong, and the belief that his peculiar spirit would be perpetuated in that body optimistic.

E. E. Y. Hales
Sawbridgeworth, Herts.

PART I
Angelo Roncalli

In his monthly message in the *Westminster Cathedral Chronicle* (July 1964) Archbishop Heenan wrote: "Pope John was the old-fashioned 'garden of the soul' type of Catholic. He read his Faber and no doubt regularly recited the litany of the Sacred Heart. He was not an original thinker. It was Pope Pius XII, not Pope John, who allowed married pastors to become priests, revised the rules for the Eucharistic fast and introduced Evening Mass. Pope John was no innovator. He was responsible for no great reform. His great achievement was to teach the world of the twentieth century how small is hatred and how great is love." And later on the message spoke of "This pastoral Pope with his childlike devotions."

The Archbishop was exposing that myth-making which had "built up" Pope John "into a man which phenomenal perception . . . conscious of his destiny to become the Liberator of the Church held in bondage for centuries by his small-minded predecessors."

"The Pope I knew was not in the least like this mythical John. My Pope John was more like a benevolent parish priest. I doubt if he had read many of the books of contemporary theologians. He made scholars smile when he told them the name of his favourite bedside book – Father Faber's *All for Jesus*."

One of those who helped to make the myth about Pope John was Robert Kaiser, author of *Inside the Council*. To Mr Kaiser, the Pope was "a political genius". "Behind his actions, with their political resonances, there lies an intuitive grasp of the geopolitical situation in our world."[1]

Between these two estimates lie many others, with only one element in common, their acceptance of the fact that Pope John was *sui generis*, an unique phenomenon, and his brief reign cataclysmic.

Where does the truth lie?

The question can be answered with rather more confidence since the

[1] Kaiser, *Inside the Council*, p. 49.

publication of the diary which Angelo Roncalli kept from the age of fourteen until his death. It is called the *Giornale dell'Anima*,[1] and it tells the story of his long spiritual struggle. It lends more support to the garden-of-the-soul-Catholic interpretation than it does to Mr Kaiser.

But the difficulty about the Archbishop's interpretation, and the reason why it came as a shock to many, was that manifestly Pope John did remarkable, earth-shaking things, things not generally associated with "benevolent parish priests", and much more remarkable than the changes in Catholic discipline introduced by Pius XII. Benevolent parish priests, even when they happen to be popes, do not command the attention of the world, sponsor encyclicals of a revolutionary character, set up the machinery for ecumenical *rapprochement*, summon and give a lead to a General Council of the Church, or begin to thaw the ice in the cold war between Catholics and Communists. Especially do they not do things of this sort when they are eighty years old. But they *could* do them if they were possessed of the peculiar spiritual power which sometimes belongs to saints, and sanctity of that kind *might* be attained by fidelity to garden-of-the-soul spirituality. No doubt such achievements are not to be expected, even from saints; the personality so sanctified must be a powerful one to begin with, and the simplicity, the fidelity, the openness to grace, must far transcend that of most followers of the path to perfection. But a Roncalli of this kind is imaginable; whereas the alternative explanation, Mr Kaiser's "geopolitical genius", is not really imaginable because the kind of things Pope John achieved are not achieved by geopolitical geniuses, but by prayer and fasting. Nor did Roncalli in the least resemble a political genius. In the usual sense of the word he was not really a genius at all.

Our problem then is this. Pope John was indeed, spiritually speaking, a garden-of-the-soul kind of Catholic. But he also achieved something, on a world stage, which was original, compelling, and revolutionary and had not even been attempted by his predecessors since the medieval unity had been broken. The veil which hides his character is only partly lifted by saying that he "taught the world of the twentieth century how small is hatred and how great is love" because his predecessors too had loved, although they chided. The difference between

[1] *Edizioni di Storia e Letteratura*, Rome, 1964.

him and them was that he *accepted* and *welcomed* the modern world (as a working partnership, not in the sense of accepting its beliefs) and they did not, they mostly censured and rebuked it, frequently, and even sometimes angrily. Here Mr Kaiser's diagnosis comes to our aid. For if Pope John was not really a geopolitical *genius*, possessed of a profound understanding of the people of the world, or of the conditions that governed them, he did nevertheless have a very wide knowledge of human beings in a varied range of countries (a much wider range than that of most popes) and this was certainly a factor which helped to make him a world influence of magnitude.

One can be a garden-of-the-soul kind of Catholic in the sense that that simple and devoted priest St Pius X was and it may lead one, as it led him, into distress and indignation at the spectacle of so many presumptuous intellectuals sowing tares of error, so that it becomes a matter of prime concern to weed the garden, even to weed it ruthlessly, to keep the dangerous people out. Roncalli was not like that. Though he kept the garden of his own soul wonderfully well weeded he felt little compulsion to go weeding elsewhere, but rather a great desire to foster any good growth. He was a conservative, but he was not censorious. He was no innovator, having none of the fashionable desire, often attributed to him, to introduce the vernacular into the liturgy, or to 'emancipate' priests from their devotional duties so that they would be free for a more 'practical' life amongst ordinary people; but at the same time he did not allow himself to become preoccupied, as Popes Pius IX, X, XI and XII did, with the 'advance of error' or the 'evils of the age'. His reluctance to criticize or to condemn was matched by his lively interest in every sort of person and every sort of undertaking.

In order to understand him we have to try to understand the mainspring of his own peculiar religious spirit, in short to understand something, if we can, of what his religion meant to him, beginning by recognizing that he was not just a warm-hearted, friendly, good-humoured man, naturally kindly, whose innate good nature expressed itself in an easy tolerance and an unceasing smile of enormous dimensions. Let any who suppose such a thing consult the pages of his *Giornale*, his Diary of a

Soul. There they will find no easy *bonhomie*, no general geniality, but the slow and painful striving after God of a man to whom God alone mattered and who knew that He was to be found only by the path of self-conquest, and by a tireless obedience to the precepts of the Church and to the guidance of spiritual advisers. The Pope whose simple goodness won all hearts had achieved that simplicity and goodness only at the cost of a ceaseless struggle with himself. It had started, in earnest, when he was fourteen years old – indeed, for all we know, earlier. We know that it had started by the time he was fourteen because that was the age he had reached when he began to write his spiritual diary. The first notebook opens with a list of 'Rules of Life' which he had been given on entering the Major Seminary of Bergamo. These 'Rules of Life' were only given to those who had shown special seriousness of purpose in the Minor Seminary. Laboriously the boy copied them all into his notebook, undertaking to devote fifteen minutes to mental prayer, on getting up in the morning, to attend Mass, to do his spiritual reading, to make 'particular' examinations of his conscience, as occasion arose, and general examinations every evening, to confess himself and to communicate every week, and so on.

In the light of his future the most interesting part of this first exercise was his undertaking to honour St Francis de Sales, "imitating him in his gentleness, by being cheerful, peaceful, joyful with everybody – with proper control and modesty – and especially with those who have done us some harm, with those who are uncongenial to us, those who are impoverished, in trouble, or tempted, seeing whether by any means we can lead them to God".[1]

Later on he would thank God that his religious formation had been according to the genial precepts of St Francis de Sales and not in one of the more austere systems of spirituality. Even so, those not in the habit of reading the spiritual writings of souls in search of God are likely to be impressed more by the rigour of the young Roncalli's self-discipline than by the geniality of his education. Under the guidance of his spiritual director he wrote in his diary, at the age of sixteen: "I shall be careful to mortify my feelings severely, keeping them within the limits of Christian modesty; especially shall I discipline my eyes, which St

[1] *Giornale*, p. 9

Ambrose called insidious snares and St Antony of Padua thieves of the soul, avoiding as far as possible the crowds that gather for festivities; and when I cannot avoid being present behaving in such a way that nothing which could lead me to the vice which is contrary to holy purity strikes my eyes which I shall always keep, on such occasions, fixed upon the ground. . . .

"With women of any kind, be they even relatives, or saintly, I shall be especially careful, fleeing from their friendship, their companionship, or their conversation, especially if they are young; nor will I ever look them in the face, remembering what is taught by the Holy Spirit: 'Let not thy eyes linger on a maid unwed whose very beauty may take thee unawares' (Ecclesiastes, 9, 5). Never will I confide in them at all, and when I must needs speak with them I will be careful to use speech that is firm, brief, prudent, and upright."[1]

Such resolutions, made at so tender an age, tell us more perhaps about the seminary at Bergamo in the eighteen-nineties than they do about Roncalli. Later on he would smile at some of these youthful entries in his diary, and he hesitated, before his death, whether to allow them to be published with the rest. But he did allow their publication, believing that some readers might find them useful even though, as he remarked in the last pages of his diary (which he wrote as Pope), temptations against purity had not been his own particular difficulty.

His own spiritual battle, to which he returns over and over again in his diary, was against the sin of pride. The sin was fostered by the circumstances of his upbringing. He was the "bright boy" who had been selected from a peasant family of thirteen children in the village of Sotto il Monte and sent at the age of eleven to study, as a boarder, at the seminary in Bergamo, seven miles away. But he used to return home in the holidays and there, like so many youths in a similar position, he had the utmost difficulty in readjusting himself to his home environment, and his mother found it hard not to spoil him, thus arousing occasional sparks of jealousy amongst the brothers and the sisters and the cousins. It cannot have been easy for him to secure the necessary quiet for his studies, his meditations, or his devotions, or to avoid being marked out as a boy destined for a special kind of future; on one occasion his

[1] *Ibid.,* p. 15.

cousins prevailed upon their parish priest to lodge a complaint at the seminary at Bergamo about what they called his "airs". He longed to be back at Bergamo:

"Only three days of the holidays have passed and already I am weary with them. At the sight of so much unhappiness, in the midst of so much mistrust, oppressed by so many fears, often I sigh, sometimes I weep. What humiliations! I only try to do good, to love sincerely even those who seem to me not to wish me well, and perhaps they think of me as a wretched blackguard. Sometimes it seems to me that even those who care about me, those in whom I confide everything, now look upon me with mistrust...."[1] And elsewhere he refers to "those cursed holidays!". His devotion to his parents, who were worthy people and devoted to him, was never in question, nor his affection for his brothers and his sisters. But, as the eldest son (he had two older sisters), and marked out by his abilities and his sense of vocation for the priesthood, he could not but seem "singular" and he may sometimes have made the mistake of giving advice: "... as regards the trials of family life" he writes when he is seventeen "renewed especially in these days of holiday, I have offered them all up to the Blessed Heart of Jesus, who is my love. He knows that I do not seek for my dear ones riches and pleasures but only patience and charity. He knows that, if I grieve, I grieve only for the lack, in them, of these virtues."

Life was not easy; sometimes he could not write his diary for lack of a candle to see by, sometimes for lack of ink. "To my beloved family" he wrote in his Will "from whom, indeed, I have received *nothing* ..." – then corrected his manuscript to read "from whom I received no material wealth".[2] His sense of obligation to his parents, and his devotion to them, indeed to all his family, was unchanging, and later in life he loved to spend his holidays at Sotto il Monte. But he kept them in their place, and he tried to improve them. When he first reached Rome, as an advanced student at the age of nineteen, he wrote firmly to his family imploring from heaven no material benefits for them, but only that they might be "good Christians, virtuous, resting in the loving arms of divine Providence and in peace with all men.

"What profit would it be to possess all the gold in the world if

[1] *Ibid.*, p. 26.   [2] *Ibid.*, p. 352.

8

one were to lose one's soul? Keep this truth well in mind and never forget it.

"We ought never to pity ourselves for the poor conditions in which we are placed, but to have patience, to look on high and think of paradise.

"Paradise, paradise! That is where we shall rest, do you understand? . . . "[1]

When he had become Patriarch of Venice he wrote, in 1955: "I owe love, in the Lord, to my relatives, all the more so because they are poor, are most worthy Christians in every way, and I never had anything but respect and consolation from them; but it is important that I always live apart from them, as an example to the good clergy of Venice who, for various reasons, some of them excusable, have too many relatives around them, who become no small hindrance to their pastoral ministry in their life, in their death, and after their death."[2] And after he became Pope he wrote to explain to his family that he would not now be able to correspond with them, nor they with him, but they could explain anything they wanted to his secretary, Mgr Capovilla, who was very well disposed towards them. They must strive to keep themselves humble, as he was striving to keep himself, and not be deceived by the gossip or suggestions of the world. "The world is only interested in making money, in enjoying life, and in imposing itself at all costs. . . . At my death I shall not be denied the praise which did so much honour to the holiness of Pius X: born poor, he died poor."[3] When Angelo Roncalli died he was, in fact, able to leave his family just 10,000 *lire* (about £6, or $17.50) apiece.

Hagiography has hidden the real significance of Roncalli's home background behind some sentimentality, exaggerating wilfully, to the distress of the Pope, the degree of his family's poverty. "We had the necessities of life" he would explain. This is what one would expect of the family of an able-bodied tenant farmer, in the Bergamesque country, who worked for a good master. Though the house in which the future Pope was born had only two rooms (besides a kitchen-dining-room, shared by others) the parents had moved to a larger house before most of his brothers and sisters were born and their

[1] *Ibid.*, p. 335.   [2] *Ibid.*, p. 292.   [3] *Ibid.*, pp. 342, 343.

9

condition was not penurious. But it was naturally without culture, and its real significance in the upbringing of the boy Angelo was the sense that it gave him that he was an exceptional being; both his vocation and his education inevitably set him apart from his family. It could not be otherwise when, from the age of eleven, he was living at home in the holidays, but in term time was in the wider world of Bergamo, studying history, philosophy, and theology, subjects quite beyond the ken of his family. Hence his spiritual struggle against pride, against thinking well of himself, against talking too much, against cutting a figure, also against a certain over-exuberance, a kind of impishness into which his sense of humour and enjoyment of life led him. "It shall be my special study to mortify myself, to quell, above all, my self-esteem, my besetting sin, avoiding every occasion on which it can gain a hold over me."[1] "I have greater need of humility than of love in as much as humility is the safer way towards love."[2]

When he met the village curate he talked too much – a form of showing off. He wasted time gossiping in the kitchen, for the same reason. Curiosity leads him into minding other people's business. "This evening occurred again what I have deplored before, I have remained talking for too long, making futile gossip, instead of withdrawing myself. And do I not know for this, too, I must render account to God?"[3] But next day he is able to bless God for a victory over his desire to "cut a good figure and put on the airs of a *savant*". He blames himself for being too merry, but then reminds himself that it is better to be merry than to be sad: 'Let us rejoice in the Lord.' " I am nothing, and imagine myself a great man; I come from nothing and pride myself on those gifts which belong to God. I ought to serve my Creator, but instead I forget about Him, I ignore Him, I serve my own ambition and my own pride. . . . All the men alive on earth bear in themselves the image of God; they cost him an immense sorrow. Yet so many do not love God, do not serve Him, even despise Him, and very many do not know of Him at all. Here is the thought which ought to arouse my compassion. . . . "[4]

In due course, it did so, most conspicuously.

[1] *Ibid.*, p. 12. [2] *Ibid.*, p. 27.
[3] *Ibid.*, p. 53. [4] *Ibid.*, p. 67.

A 'garden-of-the-soul' kind of Catholic. This is apt, provided we remember that a powerful personality, such as Pope John, having made that spiritual conquest over self, could become thereby a channel of grace, able to move mountains, able to alter the course of the Vatican itself and face the Church outwards into the world. But the spiritual battle was a severe one, bringing suffering and tears. That simplicity, that devotion to the well-being of others, which would later amaze the world, was the fruit of victory in a hard-fought struggle, as it has been with so many of the saints. They were a reward, which came unsought, in the course of that search for God which he never abandoned throughout his life.

How marked were these intellectual gifts of which, as a young student, Angelo Roncalli was sufficiently proud to disturb his spiritual progress?

They were not really so very considerable. His superiors thought well enough of him to send him to the major seminary at Rome, known as the *Apollinare*, to complete his training for the priesthood, which was a distinction, but did not require a very exceptional talent. He had done well in Latin and theology and philosophy, but only outstandingly well in history, which remained his favourite subject. Later he would devote much energy to editing the records of the visitations of St Charles Borromeo, Archbishop of Milan, to Bergamo, an effort which would attract the attention of Achille Ratti, the future Pius XI, who was able, as Librarian of the *Ambrosiana* at Milan, to give the young researcher some help. He wrote a life of the Bishop of Bergamo, Mgr Radini Tedeschi, to whom he was attached as secretary, and to whom he was greatly devoted, but this bulky book cannot be said to make very lively reading because it fails to escape from those clichés of conventional hagiography which come readily to the pens of biographers of bishops.

His most interesting writing is his essay on Caesar Baronius, which he first delivered as a lecture at Bergamo in 1907. He had been moved, while studying at Rome (1901–3), by Baronius, that attractive seventeenth-century cardinal, friend of St Philip Neri and the saint's successor in the care of the Oratorians. He liked the story of Baronius's daily pilgrimage, shuffling along on foot to St Peter's, where he gave a penny to each of the begging boys outside the great doors before entering and kissing the bronze foot of the apostle, to whom he murmured *obedientia et pax*. As a consequence Roncalli took *Obedientia et Pax* as his own motto. When later he became a bishop he embodied it in his coat of arms.

Baronius was the historian of the early Church, in the *Ecclesiastical Annals*. He had a feeling for history and wrote it well, which further endeared him to Roncalli, whose own taste ran likewise to ecclesiastical history, but also to the local history of Bergamo. Intellectually, Roncalli was both conventional and antiquarian, with that peculiarly Italian sense of tradition in which Cicero (whom he quoted constantly) and the Old Testament, and the early fathers, and Dante, and later saints like St Antony of Padua or St Charles Borromeo were brought together by the alchemy of piety. He loved Latin, he loved to trace the medieval origins of philanthropic institutions, he had a keen eye for feast days and local anniversaries, and in general his mind was a nice blend of classical and medieval *pietas*.

Such interests were common enough amongst the more intellectually awake of the seminarians of his time and it is unlikely (as Pope John was the first to admit) that his writings would have been rescued from the oblivion which descends upon most of this *genre* of historiography, or would have been reprinted in half-folio editions, had he not happened later to be elected Pope.

A pleasant, open manner, good health, a true zeal for the salvation of souls – both his own and other peoples' – together with fair intellectual ability, and a steady adherence to *obedientia et pax,* were qualities which might be expected to carry an Italian ecclesiastic some way in his chosen walk of life, but not to the top peaks which Roncalli eventually scaled.

How did he get there? This was a question the professors of the Bergamo seminary must have asked themselves, later on, as they entered into their Staff Register the successive steps in the career of their sometime pupil and colleague. In the earliest of their entries (1906) he appears with the title of Professor of Ecclesiastical History. Next year the entry is Professor of Apologetics; in 1910 it is Professor of Dogmatic

Theology. By 1919 he is entered as Spiritual Director. After that it is noted (1920) that he has left Bergamo and has become President of the General Council for Italy of the Congregation of Propaganda (Missions). Unlike some Staff Registers, this one at Bergamo went on recording what happened to members of the staff after they had left the seminary so that, opposite Roncalli's name, we read how in 1925 he became Apostolic Visitor in Bulgaria; in 1934 Apostolic Delegate to Turkey and Greece; in 1944 Apostolic Nuncio at Paris; in 1953 a Cardinal, and Patriarch of Venice; and finally (in small writing, since the space available on the page was by now becoming limited) in 1958 Pope.

How did it all happen? It was a question Roncalli often asked himself.

As is so often the case, he was given the necessary start to his career by his happening to meet the right man at the right time. In the year 1905 he was working in Rome for his doctorate in canon law when he was invited, merely because he happened to come from Bergamo, to assist in the consecration by Pope Pius X of the new Bishop of Bergamo, Mgr Radini Tedeschi. Soon afterwards the new bishop asked him to become his secretary. It was in this post, which he combined with his professorial duties at the Bergamo seminary, that Roncalli was introduced not only to diocesan work but to the whole range of pastoral, social, and charitable endeavour in which his bishop was more fully engaged than any other prelate in Italy. For Radini Tedeschi was the leader in Italy of that progressive social Catholicism which had helped to give birth to Leo XIII's *Rerum Novarum* and which, in its turn, had been encouraged by that encyclical. In this way, at the bishop's palace in Bergamo, while he was servicing meetings of Catholic Action, he was brought up against a constant consideration of the principle which should govern a Catholic society. *Mater et Magistra* must owe much to what was happening under Radini Tedeschi, at Bergamo, between 1905 and the outbreak of the First World War.

The bishop died in 1914. In the following year Italy entered the war and Roncalli went into uniform, serving as a sergeant in the medical corps and as an army chaplain. But in December 1920 a personal contact again changed his career. Pope Benedict XV, who had been a friend of Radini Tedeschi, and to whom Roncalli had sent a copy of his life of that bishop (together with a suitable inscription), invited the author to Rome to take charge of the Italian regulating body for the missions. Another four years, and another friendly contact with a pope sent him as Visitor to Bulgaria. It was Achille Ratti (Pius XI) who did this, Ratti having met the young priest at Milan and helped him in his plan to edit the papers of St Charles Borromeo.

Humanly speaking then Roncalli owed the advancement of his career into the papal diplomatic service to good fortune in his personal contacts. There is nothing about this which calls for comment, but we may wonder how far, or in what sense, his various moves up the ladder of success were welcome to him.

About a month after Radini Tedeschi's death, in 1914, he was writing in his diary:

"I was born poor and I ought to and wish to die poor ... woe betide me if, even in the smallest degree, I become attached to the goods of this world.

"As for the fantasms which my pride may depict for me, such as honour, position, etc, I shall be very careful not to harbour them, indeed to discountenance them altogether. They disturb the calm of the spirit, make labour exhausting, and take away every true joy and everything that is worthwhile and meritorious from good works. For my part, I ought to concentrate on keeping myself humble, humble, humble, leaving to the Lord all other concern."[1]

The man who wrote these words, and so much else in the same vein, was evidently not impervious to the *douceur* of honour and position; it would have been strange, indeed, if he had come so far in life, had already been so praised, without experiencing the pleasures of approbation. Had he *not* enjoyed the good esteem of others, had he *not* been open to the temptations of ambition, could he have won the spiritual victory that became his? Sanctity, we have been warned, is only attained by prayer and fasting, by sacrifice, that is, and by surrender. If Roncalli attained to sanctity, as many believe, then we may suppose that he did so by overcoming his self-regarding tendencies and achieving that surrender of all things to God which he sought so

[1] *Giornale*, p. 195.

strenuously and for which he never ceased to pray. "What are my riches, my property, my capital?" he had asked himself at the time of his twenty-first birthday. "Disobedience, acts of pride, negligence in my duties, little control over my feelings, numberless distractions, pride in my thoughts, my words, my deeds; sin after sin; – there are my title-deeds, those that are really mine.

"And with this miserable inheritance I think to cut a figure, to make a name for myself, to hold my head high, to be stuck up. And I think myself an upstanding young man, a good cleric, and ignore the reality. It is the height of folly, of unreason, for anyone who reckons to be reasonable.

"Ah, good Lord, am I then, even I, destined for Hell? The poor and ignorant man in paradise, and the Turk, and the savage; and I, called at the first hour, brought up in your family, even I destined for Hell, amongst the demons?"[1]

Some will say that he suffered from scruples, others that he had a streak of morbidity. But others, again, will recognize the authentic language of those who, seeking truly after sanctity, are horrified by their own imperfections. All will be able to see what was the nature of the temptation with which he battled. Nobody can read his diary and still suppose that his simplicity, his selfless generosity, his freedom from airs of superiority were his inheritance in the order of nature. Evidently they were his by right of spiritual conquest.

When Pius XI sent him to Bulgaria, in 1925, he had behind him those four years of work for the Congregation of the Propaganda, helping to co-ordinate the missions, during which he had become known to Church leaders in many European capitals. With this new move to the Balkans he was entering the diplomatic service, although as Apostolic Visitor, and later Apostolic Delegate, he was not an accredited diplomat at Sofia (1925–34) or at Istanbul (1934–44) but only the personal representative of the Pope. It was arduous work because the Catholics, whether of Latin or of Oriental rite, were not numerous, either in Bulgaria or Turkey, and his task was to encourage them and hold them together while at the same time trying to smooth their relations with the Orthodox Church and to inspire confidence and trust in the minds

[1] *Ibid.*, p. 89.

of the secular rulers – King Boris in Bulgaria and President Mustapha Kemal in Turkey.

He was remarkably successful. At Sofia he managed to survive a crisis of the first magnitude when King Boris, after marrying a Catholic Italian princess, at Assisi, and making all the required promises, proceeded to repeat the ceremony in the Orthodox cathedral at Sofia and to have his daughter baptized and brought up in the Orthodox Church. Pius XI's reaction to these events was both sharp and public, and Roncalli found himself in an embarrassing position. But he managed to convey the Pope's rebuke without losing the friendship of the King or his own position at Sofia. Everybody there loved him, and he was given a tremendous send-off when he left to take up his post at Istanbul.

There were plenty of difficulties in Turkey, though more in Greece, where it was equally his business, from Istanbul, to keep in touch with the Catholics. It was in Greece that he learnt how strong was Orthodox suspicion of Rome, amongst the higher ranks of the clergy, how deep was the sense of historical grievances, how hard the road to reunion must be. He was happier at Istanbul, where the government was strictly secularist. He liked the Turks and tried to learn their language. He was at pains to try to convince them that the Catholic (mostly Italian) communities at Istanbul were good citizens of Kemal's secularist republic and he pleased them by adopting the Turkish language for some of the prayers in the Catholic Churches – a move which made a poor impression, however, upon the department at Rome to which he was responsible, namely the Congregation for the Eastern Churches.

His life in the Balkans was lived in varied circumstances, sometimes – in the mountain villages of Bulgaria, or in a Greece overrun by the Nazis – circumstances of physical hardship. One of the advantages which he gained from it was an emancipation from the atmosphere of Italian clericalism and the discovery of real spiritual goodness in all sorts of men, of all sorts of belief, Christian and non-Christian. He notes in his diary that the Bulgarian peasants live in the same way as the peasants he knows in the Bergamesque country, and have many of the same virtues; and he constantly repeats his admiration for the Turks. Because of his sympathetic understanding he was popular wherever he went.

Vogliamoci bene ("Let us wish each other well") they called him, repeating his own favourite phrase.

But he often found life a struggle. He was not, in the conventional phrase, 'always happy in his work':

"The prolongation of my life as representative of the Pope in this country" he wrote in Bulgaria in 1933 "often brings to me severe personal suffering which I force myself to hide. But I endure everything, and endure it gladly, for the love of Jesus, to imitate Him as closely as possible, to fulfil in all things His holy will, for the furtherance of His grace amongst these people, who are simple, and good, but so unblessed! – and in the service of Holy Church, of the Holy Father, and for my own sanctification".[1] And it was worse in Greece. "My mission in Greece, oh what a burden! Yet for that very reason I love it the more and intend to carry it on with fervour, forcing myself to overcome all my repugnance. To me it is an assignment, so I obey. I admit that I would not suffer if it were transferred to somebody else, but while it is mine I want to do it worthily at any cost."[2]

Nor was he freed, yet, from his struggle against his own habitual temptation: "[Thoughts about] honours and advancement of an earthly kind do not greatly disturb me; I have the impression that I am holding them in control. Lord, help me, for the temptation can easily arise, and I am weak. The Church has already done too much for me."[3] Two years later, in November 1939, he is careful to contain his joy at the recognition he has received on a visit to Rome: "A short holiday, and disturbed by the thought of having to return soon. By way of compensation, I was received in an extremely kind and encouraging way at Rome by the Holy Father, the Secretary of State, and the Oriental Congregation. I give thanks to the Lord. This is more than I deserve. But I do not work to gain the praise of men. 'The Lord has given.' If this is to be followed, as it easily may be, by 'the Lord has taken away' I would continue to bless the Lord."[4]

Pius XII, himself a diplomat by training, and called to rule over the Church in the year when the Second World War broke out, was bound to appreciate the diplomatic qualities which Roncalli had shown in the

[1] *Giornale*, p. 226. [2] *Ibid.*, p. 238.
[3] December, 1937. *Giornale*, p. 233. [4] *Ibid.*, p. 238.

Balkans. Without any disloyalty to Rome, Roncalli had managed to present the Papacy in a new and more attractive light to the people to whom he had been assigned. Nor had he been living in a backwater; during the war years, not only was Greece an invaded, a belligerent, and a conquered country, in which Roncalli's task was to organize the Pope's efforts for relief, but Istanbul, as capital of a neutral country surrounded by belligerents, provided a unique observation-post where agents from all the warring states could meet and spy on each other and where Roncalli, himself much spied upon, could learn about the diplomatic underworld.

So it was not really surprising – though Roncalli seemed surprised – when Pius, at the end of 1944, confronted by a difficult diplomatic situation for the Church in France, and one in which discretion and good will would need to be exercised by the Holy See's representative, decided to send this well tried servant from the east to be his Nuncio at Paris.

The particular and urgent problem in France arose with the liberation in that year, when de Gaulle's provisional government was formed in Paris, the forces of the Resistance came out into the open, and the hunting out and punishment began of those who had collaborated with the Germans or had supported the wartime government of Pétain at Vichy. Amongst those who had supported Vichy had been a fair proportion of the French bishops, who had seen it as their duty to obey the *de facto* government of Pétain, and who now seemed likely to suffer a purge from Paris. The new government was asking for the removal of no less than thirty-three bishops, which presented Pius XII with a crisis which he hoped his new Nuncio could resolve. Roncalli, negotiating with the Foreign Minister, Georges Bidault, secured that there should be a full investigation into the behaviour of each of the accused; in the end the resignation of only three bishops was required. Clearly such a negotiation could not possibly have been conducted by the previous Nuncio, Mgr Valerio Valeri, who had represented Pius XII at Vichy during the German occupation, and who was therefore no longer *persona grata* with many of those who were now in power in Paris.

These new forces in France, it should be noticed, were largely Catholic; such were de Gaulle himself, Bidault, Robert Schumann, and those religious progressives of the Left who belonged to the group which expressed its views in Bidault's paper, *l'Aube*. Roncalli was now finding himself in the historic position of papal diplomats in France, trying to keep peace between liberals and traditionalists, within the bosom of the Church, only this time the liberals were in the ascendant. One of their enthusiasms was the worker-priest movement, which was carrying on its mission in the factories and causing concern both to some of the French hierarchy and to Pius XII. Roncalli, characteristically, went around to look at the movement for himself, and then persuaded leading members of the French hierarchy to go and talk the matter over with the Pope. He did not altogether avoid the charge of interference, or some of the unpopularity resulting from the restrictions later imposed on the movement by Pius, but he remained *persona grata* with all groups, tactful, courteous, and charming, always ready to see both sides of a question, and even to imply that Rome had not always been right: in June 1950 on the death of the veteran Christian democratic pioneer, Marc Sangnier, he wrote a letter to his widow of such charm as to sweeten, were that possible, the bitter memory of those dark days, in 1910, when Pius X, suspecting her husband of Modernism, checkmated his movement by suppressing his paper *le Sillon*.

On January 12th, 1953, Roncalli was created cardinal; on the 15th he received the red hat from his friend, the agnostic President of France, Vincent Auriol, acting for Pius XII. On the same day the Pope nominated him Patriarch of Venice.

His cup had thus been filled to overflowing with honours. We no longer meet, in his diary, references to a painful struggle to mortify within himself the desire for preferment; nor were they needed for, without his seeking preferment, he had been most notably preferred. There were no further honours for which an ecclesiastic who had attained the age of seventy-one could reasonably look. Henceforth his meditations express rather his gratitude for all that God had done for him, being filled with self-reminders that he is nothing, a sinner, wholly dependent upon God. They show, too, a preoccupation with his advanced age, and with the death of friends, borne in heavily upon him during the next two years, in which three of his sisters died, including the two to whom he was most devoted, Ancilla and Maria, who had kept house for him for most of his life. His own death, he believed, was approaching. He feared lest "the thought of the short time which remains for me to live slacken my ardour. With the help of the Lord this shall not happen. 'I neither fear to die, nor refuse to live.' The will of the Lord remains always *my peace*.

"The span of my life – too much honoured, far beyond my merits, by the Holy See – stretches from my native village to rest amongst the cupolas and pinnacles of San Marco.

"I want to put into my Will the prayer that there may be reserved for me a place in the crypt of the cathedral near the tomb of the Evangelist already become so dear and familiar to my spirit and to my prayers. Mark, son of St Peter, of St Peter the disciple and inter-preter."[1]

But God willed otherwise. More than five years after these words were written he would be called, at the age of seventy-seven, to begin a new work, transcending in importance all that he had done in his life hitherto. And even the next five years at Venice, would not prove easy, for what still lay ahead of him there was not the relaxation which his arduous career, and the reputation of the city as a beautiful backwater, led some to suppose. He had been hoping that, after so much diplomacy and paper work, he would now have the chance to become a real pastor of souls: "For the few years that remain to me to live *I want to be a real pastor*, in the full sense of the word, like blessed Pius X my predecessor (as Patriarch of Venice). . . . "[2] But there were difficulties: "The tasks arising out of my ministry, or out of matters more or less related to my ministry, occupy me too much, and nearly suffocate me. . . . "[3] His habitual temptation towards avoiding the controversial, or unpleasant grew upon him, so that he became more conscious of "the temptation to indulge somewhat my peace-loving temperament which is apt to make me prefer a quiet life rather than endanger myself by adopting a risky course".[4]

The position of Patriarch of Venice was not, in fact, the soft post that

[1] *Giornale*, p. 289.   [2] *Ibid*., p. 288.
[3] *Ibid*., p. 293.   [4] *Ibid*., p. 292.

the tourist might suppose. It was made more difficult than it had been by the influx of population into the large industrial growth on the mainland, around Mestre, by the closing of the naval arsenal at Venice, with consequent unemployment, and, as Roncalli observes, by the shortage of funds with which to deal with the incessant appeals for help.

Nor was he left alone, to do as he thought best, for the all-seeing vigilance of Pius XII, growing ever more active in the nineteen-fifties, extended into every corner of Italy, including the Veneto. Thus Roncalli found himself attending retreats, arranged by Rome for the bishops in his own patriarchate, at which the retreat-giver was provided by the Pope. In May, 1955, he sat, at one of these retreats, under the Jesuit, Father Riccardo Lombardi, Radio Priest and founder of the "Movement for a Better World", sponsored by Pius XII. Falconi tells us[1] that Roncalli was sceptical about the value of this movement; the Patriarch's own diary tells us, a little enigmatically, that it caused him to give more thought to religious education and that he proposed to refer the matter to his suffragan bishop.[2]

But it was on the political plane that the pressure from Pius XII was strongest, and the political action required of Roncalli cannot have been altogether congenial to him. What he was expected to do was to keep the civic committees of Catholic Action up to the mark and to make sure that they fully understood that it was not permitted to Catholics to vote for Communists, or to give them support of any kind, and that they also understood that Socialism and Communism were in essence the same, both being rooted in the same false philosophy, and that Catholic politicians must resist all temptation to make pacts or deals of any kind with the Socialists – which was something the more left-wing Christian Democrats were increasingly inclined to do.

It is hard to believe that Roncalli, who went out of his way to be friendly with people belonging to all sections of opinion at Venice, much cared for these directives, and after he became Pope he reversed Pius XII's policy. But whatever his personal opinions he carried out the

[1] Carlo Falconi, *Pope John and his Council* (London, 1964), p. 226, note.
[2] *Giornale*, p. 293.

Pope's orders to the letter,[1] evidently feeling that it was his duty, in obedience, to do so. It had been his duty, for so many years, as Delegate or Nuncio, to carry out faithfully the orders of Pius XII, that it could hardly have occurred to him to do otherwise now; besides, had he failed to do so he would have run counter to the first principle of his whole spiritual life, *obedientia*. He must, also, have been shocked by the personal attacks on *Papa Pacelli* in some parts of the Press. Though his own approach to problems was quite different from that of the Pope; though he was much more inclined than Pacelli to work with, not against other people, he had a profound respect for the Pope whom he served for twenty-seven years and Pacelli, in his turn, both as Secretary of State and as Pope, appreciated the value of a servant who knew how to obey, how to make unpalatable policies agreeable abroad, and how to win good will for the Papacy. There existed between these two men the mutual respect of two contrasted characters. On the occasion of the twenty-fifth anniversary, on March 9th, 1950, of Roncalli's consecration as a bishop, Pacelli wrote him a cordial letter,[2] enumerating his services to the Church. And when, at last, in October 1958, Pacelli was dead, and Roncalli stood beside him in St Peter's, gazing at the wax-like face which he had always seen so animated, what he saw distressed him, but his heart "followed that great and glowing spirit on into the land of the living."[3]

Three days after the opening of the conclave which followed Pacelli's death his fellow cardinals elected Roncalli. They were electing the member of the Sacred College most experienced in diplomacy, who was universally liked, and whose personal piety was beyond question. They may have been influenced by the fact that he was not closely associated with the late Pope (as, for instance, Montini was); conclaves tend to vote for a change. They can hardly have expected that, at his age, he could accomplish much; but after so much had been done for

[1] Cf his address to the civic committees at Venice of June 9th, 1956, published in his *Scritti e Discorsi*, Vol. III, p. 159. Fuller consideration of Roncalli's political policy, as Patriarch of Venice, is given on pp. 181–185 below, with quotations from this speech.

[2] Pub. in *Souvenirs d'un Nonce*, p. 182.   [3] *Scritti e discorsi*, Vol. III, p. 712.

so long by one man they may have thought that a change of régime in this respect, too, would be no bad thing. If, however, like much of the Press, they expected Roncalli to be a *papa di passaggio*, they were to be deceived. For he would not prove to be a transition pope. He would prove, rather, to be the pope under whose guidance the Church would undergo transition, transition such as she had not known since the days of the Counter-Reformation.

PART II

What he taught

1 · A NEW KIND OF PAPAL TEACHING

Popes always show a great respect for their predecessors' teaching, frequently quoting the words of previous occupants of St Peter's chair. They don't want to seem original; they prefer not even to appear to innovate. When discussing matters of faith they like to give chapter and verse from the Bible.[1] And in their political and social teaching, too, they look for the precedent, as do British judges, or civil servants.

In particular, they quote their immediate predecessors. But since the tendency, in papal elections, is for the pendulum to swing, so that a 'liberal' pope follows a 'reactionary', some rather surprising results sometimes follow from this reverence for "Our predecessor, of undying memory." Thus Leo XIII, whose attitude towards the Europe of his day was more than a little different from that of his predecessor Pius IX, went out of his way, in his *Immortale Dei* (1885), to endorse the *Syllabus of Errors*, in which Pio Nono had denounced every liberal tendency of his times; indeed he even went so far as to praise, explicitly, Gregory XVI's *Mirari Vos*, in which that Pope condemned the political freedoms demanded by the liberal Catholics.[2]

John XXIII does not separate himself from this papal tradition. He quotes Pius XII frequently. He does, however, sometimes imply that he is not anxious that the Church, in his day, should be too directly linked with Pius IX, telling us, for instance, that she has maintained this or urged that "especially during the last hundred years". He does not claim continuity with the politico-social teaching of Pius IX (greatly devoted as he was to that Pope) but only with that of Leo XIII. True, Leo XIII endorses Pius IX; but Roncalli only recognizes a development of social teaching extending from the time of Leo XIII to his own time.

[1] Even where this seems superfluous. Pope John, in a letter to Cardinal Agagianian, begins: "We feel we owe a special debt of thanks to the benign Providence of Our Father *who is in heaven* (Mt. 5:6) ... "(AAS, LIV, p. 429.)

[2] Leonis XIII *Acta*, Vol. V, pp. 139, 140. English text in *The Church Speaks to the Modern World: the Social Teachings of Leo XIII*, New York, 1954, pp. 176, 177.

And he stresses that he has in mind, particularly, as his own social starting-point, Leo's *Rerum novarum* (1891), which is the foundation of the Church's modern social teaching.

John was as anxious as any previous pope to reaffirm some continuity in papal teaching; but in fact, in his brief reign, he changed both its spirit and its content. Still more surprising, he introduced a quite new note of hesitancy. He even hinted that he could be wrong, that he was only expressing his own view. Though he speaks as Supreme Pontiff he does not always pontificate, and the dew of doubt, refreshing readers grown accustomed to expect from popes only uncompromising certainty – even on political matters – makes their minds receptive and the readier to respond to what the Holy Father wants to suggest to them. It was something new, indeed, when a pope, in an encyclical letter, was prepared to say that this or that was only his personal opinion, using such phrases as "We consider" or "We maintain" or "certain factors would seem to have contributed".

Of course all popes have shown spiritual humility, calling themselves unworthy successors of St Peter, or "dust and ashes, though Vicars of Christ"; but they have only meant that they were morally unworthy of their position, not that they were in doubt when they were teaching. Yet doubt where doubt is due, as it is in all questions of politics and economics, is both intellectually proper and persuasively effective, and part of the charm of Pope John was his refusal to pontificate on public affairs; one feels he is only giving advice; with Leo XIII and with Pius XI one is not allowed to forget that they are laying down the law. Roncalli's hint that previous popes have not always been right, politically speaking, is strangely effective: when he implies that he is in agreement with the social teachings of the popes only over the last hundred years we note, with gratitude, that he is aware of differences between his own teaching and that of Pius IX, or of Gregory XVI. It is no more than a hint, but it is infinitely valuable; and it is one which has not been forgotten by Pope John's successor. It is hard to find, amongst Pope John's predecessors, admissions that there were political errors in the papal past; we have to go back to the days of the sensitive Pius VII, who was prepared to disavow the warlike policies of the Renaissance popes.

It is, of course, unreasonable to expect papal teaching on political and social matters to remain unchanged, since the world is always changing. Popes speak to their own generations in terms which they will understand; it is no use expecting Rome to be *ahead* of her generation in the advice she gives. Did not Our Lord Himself refrain from telling His disciples many things which were beyond their understanding, promising that the Holy Spirit would guide the Church later into all truth? Not, for instance, until the nineteenth century are we given by Rome an explicit condemnation of slavery – and in view of the hard things that have been said of him it is pleasant to recall that it was Gregory XVI who gave it. Before Gregory's day the institution was too widely prevalent in the world for such a ruling to win acceptance. Previous popes were content to warn masters to treat their slaves humanely. In the same way it is no use expecting Renaissance popes to have nineteenth-century notions about democracy or nineteenth-century popes to have twentieth-century ideas about the unity of the world or about social security. Popes are not prophets; in their teaching office they have been concerned rather to warn the world where and how it has gone astray and to remind it of the eternal verities which it is ignoring. The novelty of Pope John consisted in his embracing, with enthusiasm, novel ideas about world unity, colonialism, aid to underdeveloped countries, social security, and the rest, which belonged mainly to such recent times as the period since the Second World War; it consisted in his accepting these new ideas, saying they were good, and urging the world to pursue them.

Popes have seldom before been as up to date as that. And John XXIII's achievement was the more remarkable because of his advanced age. Already, by the end of the Second World War, he had reached the age at which most men's ideas have become fixed. Yet he threw himself, with enthusiasm, into the new political and social notions which had only come into general circulation after 1946.

He was, in fact, uniquely up to date and, in social matters, an innovator. In both respects he was original, and it is unreasonable to reproach his predecessors because they were less contemporary-minded. Criticism is only proper where a pope is well behind the best social and political thought of his day, which is something that should be acknowledged in respect of Gregory XVI and of the later years of

Pius IX. The legitimate complaint against the political encyclicals of Gregory XVI (*Mirari Vos* and *Singulari Nos*) and of Pius IX (*Quanta Cura*, to which was attached the famous Syllabus of Errors) is that they were behind *their own* times. The various freedoms advocated by liberals generally, and also by the liberal Catholics (freedom of speech, of the Press, of religion, and so on) had already become common form in France, England, and America. They were not really rash novelties. It was the papal political attitude that (because of the special circumstances of the Papal States) had fallen behind the times.

Since Pope John endorsed the political principles of the liberal Catholics they have at last become a part of the official attitude of the Church. It is a changed attitude, for Roncalli (implicitly) repudiated Gregory XVI and Pius IX when he asserted, in *Pacem in Terris*, the *right* of a man "to worship God in accordance with the right dictates of his own conscience, (*ad rectam conscientiae suae normam*) and to profess his religion both in private and in public", and "to be accurately informed about public events"[1] which involves some measure of freedom of speech, and of the Press. It was also a changed attitude when he faced about and *welcomed* the progress which had been achieved in so many branches of human endeavour and when he expressed the view that (where the circumstances were propitious) democracy was the best form of government, whereas Pius IX had refused to be reconciled with "progress, democracy, and modern civilization", and had discouraged the establishment of democratic governments.

Perhaps, if some earlier pope, in the epoch since 1870, had felt able or inclined to dissociate himself from Pius IX's famous condemnation, or from the bitter words with which Gregory relegated to eternal reprobation the ideals of the liberal Catholics, it might have helped to clear the air and have prevented decades of subsequent suspicion. But papal solidarity was too strong; no pope felt inclined to state that, politically speaking, Pius IX had been wrong. Besides, while liberal ideas might seem tolerable abroad, the Vatican still regarded them with deep suspicion in Italy. So resource was had to the notion of the *thesis* (that toleration and democracy were in principle bad, or at best dangerous) and the *hypothesis* (that they should be accepted where they

[1] CTS, p. 10. AAS, LV, p. 260.

were established). Later on, when Catholics generally had too widely come to accept the liberal ideas, it was explained that Gregory and Pius had only really been condemning religious *indifferentism* (the idea that all religions were equally valid) not toleration as we understand it, namely respect for the conscientious conviction of the individual. But, if this is so, it becomes increasingly evident that men like Montalembert, in the last century, were misunderstood, for they were not religiously indifferent. They wanted to safeguard the freedom of the individual conscience, but they were not allowed to do so because any informed conscience which did not accept the Roman position was regarded as a bad conscience, and because "error has no rights". Pope John's position on the right dictates of a man's conscience represents a clear advance on the teaching of his nineteenth-century predecessors, even involving a repudiation of much that they taught, and it is best that this simple fact should be openly acknowledged. Candid acknowledgement can only embarrass those who fail to realize that the real tradition of the Church is "a tradition of growth in fuller understanding of the truth".[1]

It may, on the other hand, be unreasonable to expect the Roman government, even in temporal matters, to admit that she has changed her policy; it is not the habit of any kind of government to make such admissions. When, in 1929, Pius XI signed the Lateran Treaty which ended the papal claim to sovereignty over central Italy, nothing was said about the fact that articles 75 and 76 of the 'Syllabus of Errors' condemned those who advocated such a course of action. And although Pope John was perfectly happy to admit, on several occasions, that papal policy *vis à vis* the eastern Churches had not always, in earlier centuries, been wise, during the developing quarrel with Constantinople, and while his successor has shown himself equally ready to say the same thing, neither pope felt it necessary to allude to the fact that

[1] Cf the article by John Courtney Murray, S.J., 'On Religious Liberty', in *America*, November 30th, 1963, p. 704. An article of exceptional interest by Douglas Woodruff in the *Tablet* (October 3rd, 1964) entitled 'The Council and the Rights of Consciences' shows that it is still the custom to explain the religious intolerance of Gregory XVI and Pius IX by saying that they had to combat the indifferentism of the liberal Catholics. Yet Montalembert and his friends, who were far from indifferentist, were pleading for toleration on the same grounds as those expounded by Pope John and pleaded at the Council.

Article 38 of the 'Syllabus of Errors' states that it is an error to say that "the Roman pontiffs, by their too arbitrary conduct, have contributed to the division of the Church into Eastern and Western".

It is arguable, indeed I think it can be argued with some force,[1] that at the time when Pius IX was refusing to be reconciled with progress, democracy and modern civilization, some of the things which men were doing, especially in Italy, in the name of that secular trinity, were worthy of his reprobation. By the time John XXIII was extending a welcome to those same vague concepts men were, perhaps, behaving rather differently. Yet the current idea of what was meant by the words was still, in the twentieth century, not widely different from the ideas of Gladstone or Cavour about them, and it ought to be noticed that the most important difference between the years 1861 and 1961 was not a different meaning attaching to those words but a different kind of pope. Where the one condemned the other welcomed the world in which he found himself. The real analogy lay between John XXIII and that critic of Pius IX, the Archbishop of Paris, Mgr Darboy, who wrote to the Pope, after he had issued his Syllabus, and told him: "You have distinguished and condemned the principal errors of our epoch. Turn your eyes now towards what she may hold that is honourable and good and sustain her in her generous efforts." That is exactly what John XXIII did. He turned his eyes to what was good and sustained his epoch in its generous efforts.

Pius IX did not take the Archbishop's advice. And after he was dead his successors maintained the tradition of reproach which he had done so much to strengthen and confirm until, with Pius XII, this pessimism reached a perfection of philosophical expression and a sad and beautiful dignity which raised it to the sublime atmosphere of great tragedy.

Pius XII believed that the world had gone desperately astray since the time of the Reformation and that the source of such evil lay in that great act of infidelity, that breaking away from the allegiance to Rome, which had led on, in due course, to secularism, to liberalism (in the continental

[1] I attempted the task in the chapter on the 'Syllabus of Errors' in my *Pio Nono*.

sense of laicism, politics without reference to God and His law) and to atheistic socialism on the one hand and monopoly capitalism on the other. And he expressed his view with unequalled eloquence, and desperate sincerity, in his first encyclical letter, *Summi Pontificatus*, of October 20th, 1939, soon after the outbreak of the Second World War. It was the good fortune of English readers that this remarkable document was translated, under the title *Darkness over the Earth*, by the late Mgr Ronald Knox,[1] from whose rendering of it the following quotations are taken:

"The beginning of all the troubles which are driving this age of ours by a headlong course into spiritual bankruptcy and impotence for virtue, is the impious attempt to dethrone Christ. . . .

"As you know, Worshipful Brethren, the reason why the principles of morality in general have long since been set aside in Europe is the defection of so many minds from Christian doctrine, of which Blessed Peter's See is the appointed guardian and teacher. As the centuries rolled over Europe, its nations were welded together by that doctrine, and it was the Christian spirit which formed them. Ennobled by the Cross, humanized and civilized by its influence, they reached such a level of statesmanship and of citizenship that they could pass on the lesson they had learned, in its various forms, to the other nations and countries of the world. Then a time came when many of the Christian family separated themselves from the infallible teaching of the Church; and it was after that that they went, alas, even farther, and rejected the very doctrine of our Saviour's divinity, which is the fountain and the focus of all Christian teaching. In doing this, they were hastening on a general deterioration and decline of the religious idea. . . .

"They did not guess what would follow, when the truth which sets us free had been exchanged for the lie that makes slaves of us. In repudiating God's law, so fatherly, so infinitely wise, and Christ's commandments, breathing of charity, uniting men together and drawing their minds to things above, they did not reflect that it would mean handing themselves over to a capricious ruler, the feeble and grovelling wisdom of man. They boasted of progress, when they were in fact relapsing into decadence; they conceived that they were reaching

[1] See *Selected letters of Pius XII*, CTS, 1949, p. 3.   AAS, XXXI, p. 413.

33

heights of achievement when they were miserably forfeiting their human dignity; they claimed that this century of ours was bringing maturity and completion with it, when they were being reduced to a pitiable form of slavery. . . .

"It is beyond question, that when the nations of Europe were still bound together by that common tie which observance of the same Christian law and tradition engenders, there were quarrels, there were revolutions, there were wars which brought havoc with them. But it is doubtful whether there has ever been an age like the present, an age in which men's spirits were so broken by despair, so busily alive to the difficulty of providing any remedy for their disorders. In earlier times, men had a clear consciousness of what was right and what was wrong, what was allowable and what was forbidden. Such a consciousness made agreement easier, curbed the fierce appetites that had been aroused, opened and paved the way for an honourable settlement. In our day, discords arise not merely from the violent impulses of an ungoverned temperament, but more commonly from a confusion and a revolt in the depths of the human conscience. It is this which allows all the canons of private and public honesty and decency to be overthrown in our light-hearted modern fashion. . . . "

Pius was writing these words at the time when Hitler and Stalin were coolly partitioning Poland and digesting the spoils. But in the the west, though war had been declared, fighting had not started, the bombs had not begun to fall. Moreover Italy was still neutral. As so often with papal encyclicals, this one has, unmistakably, one eye fastened on Italy, just as Pius IX had Italy in mind when he drew his own melancholy picture of the fruits of progress, democracy, and modern civilization. Though so much more profound than Pius IX, in his thinking and his learning, Pius XII showed, in this first encyclical of his pontificate, that he belonged in the same tradition of protest against the outlook of his times which had inspired the earlier Pope's protests. Born in 1876, two years before the death of Pius IX, he had grown up in Rome in the eighteen-nineties, at the height of the Italian anti-clerical movement, when secularist and materialist teaching was dominant at the University of Rome, and repeated in the schools, and the past history of the papacy was being bitterly denounced because of the current quarrel with "the prisoner in the Vatican". The young seminarian, Eugenio Pacelli, naturally revolted against his environment and, following the line which Leo XIII was encouraging as the proper corrective to the errors of the age, he drank deeply from Thomist philosophy, and from its classical sources. In the isolated atmosphere of the 'black aristocracy', to which he belonged, and which supported the 'prisoner Pope', Pacelli took it for granted that the angry repudiation of his age, with which Pius IX had closed his long pontificate, had been necessary and right. And his studies only confirmed the belief which he shared with the reigning pontiff Leo XIII, that all the tragedies of the age, indeed those of the last three centuries, stemmed from the revolt against Rome and the Church in the sixteenth century – a revolt which had at last reached Italy herself.

And now, at the age of sixty-three, mature, experienced by long diplomatic service in the political realities of the world, well acquainted with Hitler, with Mussolini, and with the Communists, he surveyed from the Chair of St Peter, as Supreme Pastor, a world which seemed to be going down to ruin at the beginning of the Second World War. How right he had been! How right Pio Nono had been! This "darkness over the earth" (the *motif* of his encyclical) was the terrible fate to which the pleasant paths of materialist progress, the attempt to run the world without the Church, without God, had brought mankind! – to Stalin – to Hitler – to the Second World War. Not only the tragic conflict then breaking out in Europe, not only the darkness which had come over the world (as at the time of the crucifixion) but all the stupid materialist error and optimism which he had suffered around him in his impressionable youth, which he had despised in the Rome of the nineties, urged him forward in his attempt at last to recall mankind, even after four centuries of error, to the follies of their apostasy:

"Christ, who has made Us His Vicar, in an hour of great decision, when He stood before the man who represented what was then the highest authority on earth, uttered those noble words, 'It was for this that I was born, it was for this that I came into the world, to bear witness of the truth; every one that is of the truth, hears my voice.' To bear witness of the truth is the highest debt We owe to the office

We hold and the times We live in. We are bound to fulfil that duty with all the firmness of an Apostle. And this involves exposing and rebuking men's errors and faults in a way which will make it possible to prescribe for the evils We have diagnosed: 'You shall know the truth, and the truth will make you free.' In the fulfilment of this task, We shall not be swayed by human or earthly considerations. We shall not allow diffidence, or disagreements, or rebuffs to interfere with Our undertaking; We shall not be deterred by the fear that others will fail to recognize or will distort Our motives. Only, in doing Our part with all diligence, We shall be governed by a motive of fatherly love. . . . "[1]

The solemn tone of these words, with which he introduced the main message of *Summi Pontificatus*, was maintained by Pius XII in his many writings, throughout his pontificate. He was warning the world, over and over again, pointing out the error, exposing the philosophical mistakes, showing the historical consequences. And as he grew older, and less inclined to listen to those around him, so his admonitions became loftier and loftier, more certain, more insistent.

What we may call the admonitory tone of Pius XII has been the characteristic note struck by the papal encyclicals in the modern age. No doubt, with Pius XII, they attain to a philosophical assurance and a felicity of phrase only excelled by that supreme master, Leo XIII, who was Pacelli's own model; no doubt, too, with Pius XII, they display an even greater cogency of argument and urgency of appeal, such as befitted the times in which he lived, times even more cataclysmic than those of Leo. But the temper is the same, with Leo as with Pius, and the pupil was not greater than his master. To Leo the times were out of joint, humanity had taken the wrong road (Pio Nono's root idea), the error was philosophical and historical – open your eyes, he tells mankind, cease to be blind, return to the right way, restore her proper position to the Church, recognize the divine disposition revealed in the natural law. Nor did the pontificates of St Pius X (1903–14) or Pius XI (1922–39) vary the pattern very much. If St Pius, in his celebrated condemnation of Modernism (*Pascendi Dominici gregis*, 1907), introduced a note of invective which the courtly manners of Leo XIII

---

[1] *Selected letters of Pius XII*, p. 10.   AAS, XXXI, p. 420.

and Pius XII would not have allowed them to use, and which even the high-tempered Pius IX used only occasionally, in speech, not on paper, St Pius X's message was yet the same: mankind was being led astray because led away from Rome. And when Pius XI denounced the philosophical errors of Communism (especially) and Nazism (forcefully) and Fascism (more gently) in his *Divini Redemptoris* (1937), *Mit brennender Sorge* (1937) and *Non abbiamo bisogno* (1931) respectively, he maintained the argument on the same plane, telling mankind it had gone astray politically and socially because it had ceased to look to the Church for guidance. For their logical precision and their attention to actual political fact the writings of Pius XI may perhaps be preferred to those of his predecessors and of his successor; but the point we need to notice here is that they take their place in the long sequence of censure which had been codified by Pius IX in the Syllabus, given a philosophical basis by Leo XIII, supplied with teeth by St Pius X, and would be sublimated by Pius XII.

What place have the encyclicals of John XXIII in this tradition?

Clearly, they do not belong to it.

The note of alarm and admonition is scarcely audible. Instead, Roncalli turns to those movements which are deserving of praise and commends them; he picks out those bodies which need encouragement – the United Nations, relief organizations, colleges of further education – and encourages them. The reader is made to feel that, although the Pope is only too well aware of the shadow of the bomb, he just cannot bring himself to believe it is actually going to be dropped. He is, by his own admission, an optimist; he is glad to point to what is good; he thinks in many ways the world is a better place than it was; he thinks there have been enough admonitions, and that they have not been very effective. He is shocked only by the prophets of doom. Most emphatically he does not agree with Pius XII that "it is doubtful whether there has ever been an age like the present, an age in which men's spirits were so broken by despair, so busily alive to the difficulty of providing any remedy for their disorders".

It was not Roncalli's experience that men's spirits were broken, in that sense, by despair; he had seen men struggling, in the Balkans, in Africa, in Italy, in France, towards a better way of life. Deliberately turning his back upon the tradition of reproach and censure, he appealed in his encyclicals to "all men of good will" to go forward, in confidence, building afresh, and building better; to all Christians, united by virtue of their common baptism, all men of good will, united by their common recognition of the natural law, given by God, Whose sons they were, whether they recognized Him or no. Picking up the liberal Catholic tradition, with its acceptance of the new liberties, and its confidence in a better future, founded on freedom, he deliberately turned his eyes (as Archbishop Darboy had urged Pio Nono to turn his) towards what his epoch held that was honourable and good and he "sustained her in her generous efforts".

Should this reversal of attitude – for it was no less – be accounted for by the changed circumstances of Europe and the world in the year 1958 when Roncalli was elected?

Circumstances certainly matter. Papal pronouncements on political and social questions are necessarily determined by the requirements of their age. Thus the pronouncements of Gregory XVI, which stressed the blessings of order, the need for censorship, and the duty of obedience to hereditary monarchs, reflected a state of affairs, in the eighteen-thirties, when revolution was endemic in Europe, and was nowhere more menacing than in the papal states. In these circumstances Gregory's duty seemed to him clear: to preach unqualified obedience, civil as well as religious. Similarly the development of the Italian revolution in the days of Pius IX and Leo XIII engendered the hostility of both popes towards the current liberalism of their day, just as Modernism (social as well as religious) shocked St Pius X, Communism angered Pius XI, and the menace of Soviet aggression, under Stalin, preoccupied Pius XII.

But were the dangers and difficulties faced by Roncalli, after 1958, any less real?

In some ways, certainly. Kruschev had succeeded Stalin; the Church behind the iron curtain, especially in Poland, was beginning to live under more tolerable conditions; and the Communist challenge was less pressing in Italy. But Kruschev had not, in 1958, given evidence of a change of Soviet policy; in Poland a respite had been gained for the Church only by concessions of which Pius XII had not approved; in Italy the Christian Democrats had lost ground and were much weaker than they had been in 1949, the year when Pius XII had yet felt it necessary to threaten with excommunication those who voted for the Communists or their supporters. And, as always, there were new causes for papal alarm. The Chinese onslaught on the Church had only just begun, and the opening of the new pontificate coincided with the grave crisis in the Congo, where the ill-prepared withdrawal of a Catholic European government was leading to disorders and dangers which, invited Communist intervention. Above all, the fear that the hydrogen bomb might actually be dropped had grown even more acute; the Cuban crisis was yet to come.

It is evidently only fanciful to suppose that a better world situation, when Pope John was elected, freed him from the anxieties that had led his predecessors to multiply their warnings and their prohibitions. The dangers continued; and the apostasy was equally evident. Papal protests vary according to circumstances, but there is always plenty to protest about. Gregory XVI and Pius IX may have done much to set a fashion, but papal protests against the revolutionary tradition go back far behind Gregory XVI to the days of Pius VI (1775–99) to whom had fallen the duty of denouncing the great French revolution itself. Not until we get back as far as the reign of Pius VI's predecessor, Clement XIV, do we find a pope who was by way of sending cheerful letters out to the world; Clement reserved his melancholy censures not for the world, but for the Jesuits, as a result of his being persuaded into the odd diagnosis that they were a prime cause of the human distress.

Pope John, in short, in the optimism of his encyclicals, was *sui generis*. He was not unaware of the evils, or the errors, or the apostasy, or the deadly danger. But he was more impressed by the opportunities, by the improvements, and by the many causes for encouragement, and he preferred to give his attention to these. This does not mean that he disagreed with what Pius XII or any of his predecessors had said – anyhow what they had said during the last hundred years. Indeed, his constant quotations from his predecessors, and especially from Pius XII, and his many public expressions of admiration for that Pope, suggest something more than the customary papal solidarity. He was well aware that Pius was a scholar of exceptional distinction and he was under little temptation to disagree with him about any of the many topics on which he wrote. He just wanted to draw attention to something else, to the other side of the coin. He felt no obligation to write philosophically, or historically, about the sources of men's sorrow merely because his predecessor had done so. He felt free to be silent on such themes, believing – with some reason – that they had already been amply developed, and wanting to devote his attention to what he did know about, namely the actual life of the world of his day, the life of the people he sprang from at the foot of the Alps, life in the Balkans, outside the Catholic fold, or the life he had seen in France, too often estranged from Christian belief, but not estranged from pursuing what was good. On this experience he drew; an experience gained from the world. And it was thus that he caught the ear of the world.

2 · ABOUT PERSONAL RIGHTS AND SOCIAL SECURITY

A tradition of rebuke – the tradition of papal teaching in modern times – need not be merely negative. The element of censure may predominate, as it did in the encyclicals of Gregory XVI, of Pius IX, and of St Pius X, who were more concerned to eradicate certain new growths than to plant something fresh in their place. But censure may sometimes be matched and balanced by positive and new teaching, adapted to the times, as occurred in the encyclicals of Leo XIII and Pius XI, where they were concerned with the social problem, and in those of Pius XII, where he was concerned with world affairs.

The biggest positive contribution to social advancement achieved by the papacy between the days of the French Revolution and those of the Second World War was, as all agree, the assertion of the right of the labourer to a just wage, which Leo XIII put forward in *Rerum novarum* in the year 1891. Rightly, this encyclical is now regarded as providing the Great Charter (as Pope John called it) of Catholic social teaching, so that later papal reformers have taken its principles as their starting-point and have issued their encyclicals on convenient anniversaries – on the fortieth Pius XI's *Quadragesimo anno*, on the seventieth Pope John's *Mater et Magistra*.

When however Pope John spoke, in *Mater et Magistra*, of "Our responsibility to take up this torch which Our great Predecessors lighted ... a Torch to lighten the pathways of all who would seek appropriate solutions ... " we may be in some danger of supposing that what had happened, in 1891, was that an enlightened pope, far ahead of his times, had detected the danger to human society arising from the degradation of the masses of the proletariat in the factories, under a régime of unbridled capitalism, and had lit a torch to show the way out into the paths of social justice and peace.

Such a view would be less than just to the lay organizers of Catholic Workers' Unions, or 'mixed' associations of employers and workers, especially in Germany, France, and the United States, and also to enlightened Catholic employers in those countries who had been struggling ever since the eighteen-fifties to soften the rigours of rugged individualism. It would also put into a false perspective what was the nature of *Rerum novarum*. So far from being the torch of the pioneer, Leo's encyclical was, in fact, like most encyclicals, the result of mature reflection after a long period of watching the social scene and the efforts with which Catholics and non-Catholics were trying to improve matters for the workers. Leo was deciding what was legitimate and what was not legitimate in these social endeavours; what was in accordance with Natural and Divine Law and what was in opposition to it, both on the side of the employers and on the side of the workers. It is indeed arguable that his intervention was much overdue. What is now called the social question had become only too apparent to many secular reformers by the year of revolutions, 1848, and it played a part in those revolutions, particularly at Paris. By the 'sixties, when the First International was organized, the 'socialist menace' or 'the plight of the workers' (according to the point of view) had become a matter of urgency even in Italy, where the followers of Marx and Bakunin were contending, in the *Romagna*, with the adherents of their opponent, the prophetic idealist Mazzini, who was trying to organize the workers into associations much more like those adumbrated later in *Rerum novarum*. But none of this attracted much attention at Rome (though a condemnation of Socialism was included in the 'Syllabus of Errors' in 1864) because what seemed more important matters, and notably the attempt to save the papal states, preoccupied Roman minds as the Italian Risorgimento ran its political course.

In truth, Rome did take cognisance of the social question rather late in the day, and by the time she did so the workers in the growing industrial cities of Germany and France had largely been lost to the Church. That she was thus tardy was due mainly to her political pre-occupations; but we have also to remember that the industrial revolution developed later, on her own doorstep, in Italy, than it did in northern Europe. What decided Leo, thirteen years after he had been elected, to issue *Rerum novarum* was the success of the Catholic Congress movement in Italy, in assisting and co-ordinating the efforts of Catholic social workers, the reports he was receiving abroad from socially minded bishops like Ketteler of Mainz, Manning of Westminster, or Gibbons of Baltimore, and most of all the arrival in Rome of hordes of peaceful and earnest workers, brought by the idealist Léon Harmel, who asked for his blessing. Unless he were to repudiate the Catholic social movement and lose all surviving contacts with the workers Leo had to say something.

What he said was nevertheless of the first importance. Modest as his claim for a 'just wage' for the worker may have been, and unshakeable his conviction that the class structure was ordained by God, Who had made men high or lowly, he yet made clear something of vital importance which had been forgotten, namely that the worker had the right to his livelihood, that it was an *injustice* to pay him starvation wages or to leave him to the mercy of the so-called laws of supply and demand. It was in extending the realm of human rights into the economic field that Leo was original, and he did this in accordance with the principles of that Thomist philosophy which he did so much to revive. For he was really saying that the economic order, like all other aspects of the human order, ecclesiastical or governmental, existed for the sake of man, that the ultimate purpose was to enable man, in freedom, to live his own life and to save his soul. What was necessary to him, to enable him to do this, was his *by right*, and no government, or employer, might take it from him; their duty was to see that he had it.

This is why *Rerum novarum* is so important, and why Pius XI's encyclical, and even John XXIII's *Mater et Magistra* can be seen only as extensions of it, being extensions of the conception of human right, of what is necessary to the development of human personality. In the case of Pope John's encyclical, however, these extensions are so startling, and the sociology implied so 'socialistic', that not only Leo, but Pius XI or Pius XII would have been astonished by the claims that he was making. For Pope John was inviting the State to provide for man in a way which to earlier popes would have seemed an infringement of his personal liberty, an interference with his human rights, whereas to John these extensions seemed necessary to meet every man's right to develop his personality to the full.

It will be convenient to summarize, however briefly, the Leo XIII–Pius XI line on the social question, in order that we may appreciate the extent of Pope John's originality:

(1) Workers have a right to the *Just Wage*, which means a wage that will keep themselves and their families "in decency" (Leo was much concerned that the menfolk and the womenfolk should not have to sleep in one bedroom). If the employers will not pay a just wage the State should support the workers in their struggle to get it. But the workers must try to secure this wage by negotiation or arbitration; only when all else has failed have they the right to strike. And in no circumstances at all have they the right to use violence, or to raise a revolution.

(2) *Socialism*. 'Pure Socialism' (meaning Marxist Socialism, and especially the First International) is not compatible with Catholic teaching because it looks upon the material organization of human life, in this world, as the final objective of government. It therefore ignores or denies the Catholic view that the ultimate purpose of government is to safeguard personal rights, so that a man may freely achieve his supernatural end. It is a danger to the freedom of the Church, to religious education, to the freedom of the family. However, with Pius XI, "Moderate Socialism" (especially the Second International) is distinguished from "Pure Socialism", or Communism, because it has lost much of its doctrinaire Marxist basis, and is prepared to allow freedom to the Church, to acknowledge some parental rights, some right to private property, etc, and its aims have become scarcely distinguishable

from those of some Christian democrats. Pius XI is prepared to concede that some forms of property are best reserved to the State – "goods which carry with them a power too great to be left to private individuals without injury to the community at large".

(3) In the structure of *Trade Unions* Leo XIII hoped to see a revival of the medieval guild organization, in which employer and employee were combined in a "vertical union". But he came to accept the "horizontal union" (or normal trade union structure) while hoping that the workers could achieve most of their purposes through co-operatives or mutual assistance associations, provided they were not run by anti-Catholic organizations, such as the Freemasons.

(4) *Unrestricted Capitalism*, which takes no consideration of employees' welfare, thinking only of profit and power, and treating human beings inhumanly, as though they were merely machines, is illicit. Employers must consider the human rights of their employees (and especially their need to fulfil their religious duties on Sundays). Pius XI speaks of capitalism (meaning unrestricted capitalism) in almost Marxist terms, as though it had killed itself by becoming monopoly capitalism, thereby eliminating the very freedom which had brought it to birth and given it vitality. "Free competition has destroyed itself; economic domination has taken the place of the open market. Unbridled ambition for domination has succeeded the desire for gain; the whole economic régime has become hard, cruel, and relentless, in a ghastly measure. . . . "

(5) Pius XI developed the concept of the *Subsidiary Function*. This means that a greater body should never be used to perform a function which can be equally well performed by a lesser body: thus the State should not try to run what can well be left to a regional council, or a regional council what can be left to a local council, or any public body what can be performed by the family. (Much in his encyclical was aimed at the Fascists as well as at the Communists.)

"As we pass all this in review," says John XXIII in *Mater et Magistra*, "We are aware of Our responsibility to take up this torch which Our great Predecessors lighted, and hand it on with undiminished flame. It is a torch to lighten the pathways of all who would seek appropriate solutions to the many social problems of our times. Our purpose, therefore, is not merely to commemorate in a fitting manner the Leonine Encyclical, but also to confirm and make more specific the teaching of Our Predecessors. . . . "[1]

This was an understatement. Even if we grant, as we must, the common philosophical ground shared by Pope John with his predecessors – the ground of personal right – we can only accept his statement that he was commemorating, confirming, and making more specific the teaching of his predecessors as another example of the papal habit of deferring to the past, of avoiding the appearance of innovation. Yet he was innovating. *Mater et Magistra* does not merely make more specific the teaching of Pius XI, it develops it out of recognition by giving to the State functions which Pius would never have dreamed of giving it and by recognizing personal claims of the individual upon the community which would not have occurred to him. This might be called 'developing'; it could hardly be called 'making more specific'.

With *Mater et Magistra* we are, in fact, brought right into the world of the Welfare State. Gone is not only the semi-feudal world in which Leo saw the simple workman, surrounded by his family, settling down to his frugal but sufficient meal, the just reward of his labour. But gone, too, is the world of Pius XII, who referred, with evident alarm, to communal kitchens, free health services, and free education.[2] Now it is not only free education that is being claimed; it is further education for all those suited by their ability to benefit from it.

The Pope is not merely accepting, he is embracing what many would call socialism, and he is acknowledging that a new concept of the duties of the State is involved. He calls it "an increase in social relationships" and "a development of the social life of man". " It is an effect" says *Mater et Magistra* "and a cause of the growing intervention of the State even in matters of such intimate concern to the individual as health and education, the choice of a career, and the care and rehabilitation of the physically or mentally handicapped."[3] No longer is the State seen as merely the ultimate protector of the basic right to a minimum wage or,

[1] CTS, p. 18.   AAS, LIII, p. 413.
[2] *Address to Womens' organizations*, October, 1945, *Selected letters*, p. 325. AAS, XXXVII, p. 288.
[3] CTS, p. 20.   AAS, LIII, p. 416.

as Pius XII put it, of "the right to the indispensable means of obtaining a livelihood", but it is recognized as the active agent in promoting human welfare in a manner undreamed of by Leo XIII and deprecated, when they saw it developing, by Pius XI and Pius XII.

Yet the political philosophy of the papacy is not basically changed by John XXIII because he is still thinking in personal, not collective terms. It is not in the name of any supposed superior rights of the community that John XXIII welcomes "an increase in social relationships" but because this increase "makes it possible for the individual to exercise many of his personal rights, especially those which we call economic and social, such as the right to . . . preserving good health, receiving further education, and a more thorough professional training; the right to housing, work, suitable leisure and recreation".[1] What is revolutionary, with *Mater et Magistra*, is first the welcoming of the much wider role played by the modern State and second an enormous enlargement of the traditional papal picture of the natural rights of the individual. If the Church as a whole comes not only to accept but to advocate the whole range of natural rights adumbrated by Roncalli, and to welcome the State as the natural agency for implementing them, she will, in effect, be abandoning her attitude of suspicion towards the claims of the liberal or socialist State and entering into partnership with it in promoting a new phase in the life of human society. Not since the early middle ages, when she helped to evolve the legal, economic, and educational structure of the west has she been enabled to play a role of this constructive kind. What is involved is nothing less than abandonment of the idea that she must resist those governing powers which she can no longer control.

Pope John was not unaware that there were dangers involved in allowing the State, or any other collective association, to do so much for the individual:

" . . . this multiplication and daily extension of forms of association necessarily entails a multiplicity of restrictive laws and regulations in every department of human life. As a consequence it narrows the sphere of a person's freedom of action. The means associations use, the methods they follow, the atmosphere they create, all conspire to make

[1] CTS, p. 21.   AAS, LIII, p. 416.

46

it difficult for a person to think independently of outside influences, to act on his own initiative, to exercise responsibility and express and fulfil his own personality."[1]

Perhaps this was the least the Pope could say, if only out of respect for his predecessor's fears concerning the dangers of allowing the "amorphous mass" to submerge the individual.[2] But it doesn't worry Pope John for long.

"Must we then conclude" he asks (following immediately on the passage just quoted) "that increased social action necessarily reduces men to the condition of being merely automatons? By no means."

What are his safeguards against the evils associated with state control and bureaucracy?

" . . . a sane view of the common good must be present and operative in men invested with public authority."

(We all hope for this; but we should be rash to expect it.)

"We consider it altogether vital that the numerous intermediary bodies and corporate enterprises – which are, so to say, the main vehicle of this social growth – be really autonomous, and loyally collaborate in pursuit of their own specific interests and those of the common good."

The implication of this appears to be that, for instance, institutions of further education, or health services, or broadcasting and television systems, should not be administered by civil servants but, while operating under a charter given to them by the State, should be free from State interference in their daily administration.

"So long as social action does in fact adhere to these principles, within the framework of the moral order, it is not of its nature dangerous or detrimental to the individual." He quotes Pius XI who, in *Quadragesimo anno*, urged the development of independent higher corporations and professional institutions. Both popes were, indeed, seeking to prevent the control of such institutions by political elements, whether Communist, Fascist, or those of any over-bureaucratic State. But the kind of social agencies of which Pope John was thinking were, of course, much

---

[1] CTS, p. 21. AAS, LIII, p. 417.
[2] Cf Pius XII's Christmas Message of 1944, *Selected Letters*, pp. 301–311. AAS, XXXVII, pp. 10–23.

more 'advanced' and much more pervasive of the life of the individual than those which Pius XI had in mind. Pius XI had only been talking about reconciliation and welfare within particular industries.

Pope John had never been to the United States. Had he done so he might have been more impressed by the power of 'admass' over the human spirit, through advertisement of every kind and the collective pressure of mass suggestion. Dangers of this kind are clearly not eliminated by ensuring that "the numerous intermediary bodies and corporate enterprises" are "really autonomous", indeed they may be increased if there is no public control over such pressures. State control can be an important guarantee against some of the evils which the Pope is anxious to avoid, as may be seen in the broadcasting systems of western Europe. Roncalli gives a warm welcome to "the Press, cinema, radio, and television", which have made it possible "for everyone to participate in human events the world over", and he treats these as one element in the desirable "growth in social relationships", which "enable the individual to exercise many of his personal rights". Some, however, will feel that he is optimistic when he says that they will not be "dangerous or detrimental to the individual", provided that they operate "within the framework of the moral order". If the role of the State is to be limited to 'encouraging' and 'co-ordinating' who is to ensure that these modern agencies of mass communication do operate "within the framework of the moral order" or that, as he requires, they "loyally collaborate in pursuit of their own specific interests and those of the common good"? We may assume that he expects the requirements of morality to be safeguarded, as they are today in Italy and elsewhere, by ecclesiastical censorship. But the need in some way to limit the seemingly limitless impact of admass, and thus to save the human spirit from being choked to death by the (artificial) cares of this world still remains to be met; the importance of meeting it was recognized more clearly by the fastidious and solitary spirit of Pius XII than by his more genial successor.

In the light of John XXIII's extension of the field of human rights, to include such matters as further education, health services, and 'suitable' leisure and recreation, Leo XIII's principle of the "just wage", to enable the Umbrian peasant whom he knew to bring up his family "in decency", acquires an almost patriarchal flavour. John XXIII, extending a broad hand of welcome to changes which have been introduced, mostly north of the Alps, and by governments quite alien to Catholic influence, ushers us into a world in which we find that the Italian peasant now has a God-given right to the enjoyment of the latest means of telecommunication, and a duty to send his brighter daughters to the local technical college, since there must be made "provision for all the citizens to share as far as they are able in their country's cultural advantages". (We may compare Pius XII's more modest "higher education for children of the working classes who are exceptionally intelligent and well disposed".)[1]

In this matter of education, opportunity and aid, Roncalli insists that the peasant is not to stand at any disadvantage when compared with the townsman. Pope John, as befitted a pontiff whose relatives were still working in the fields around Sotto il Monte, had a special care, in *Mater et Magistra*, for agriculture, and he gives a lot of advice on the subject. He does not altogether accept that the movement away from the countryside to the towns is a necessary part of economic evolution. He thinks it is also due to the desire to escape from uncomfortable living conditions to the "lure of novelty and adventure", and to "the attractive prospect of easy money, greater freedom, and the enjoyment of all the amenities of town and city life". The way to meet the problem, his encyclical tells us, is to improve conditions in the countryside. The position would be very different today if farming had not been allowed to become a depressed occupation. It is inadequate both in productive efficiency and in the standard of living it provides: "What can be done to reduce the disproportion in productive efficiency between agriculture, on the one hand, and industry and public services on the other, and to ensure that agricultural living standards approximate as closely as possible to those enjoyed by city-dwellers? . . . What can be done to persuade agricultural workers that, far from being inferior to other

[1] Christmas Message of 1942, *Selected letters*, p. 292. (*una formazione superiore per i figli delle classi operaie particolarmente dotati di intelligenza e di buon volere* AAS, XXXV, p. 20.)

people, they have every opportunity of developing their personality through their work? . . . "[1]

He has plenty of suggestions to make. Unlikely as it seemed that the world would be presented, in a papal encyclical, with a number of specific proposals for the improvement of agriculture, that is, nevertheless, what John XXIII proceeded to give, at some length, in *Mater et Magistra*. The words of his encyclical (whoever wrote them) are here responding to Roncalli's personal convictions, to his memories of Sotto il Monte, and his knowledge of the gross disproportion, in Italy as a whole – and especially in the south – between the lot of the industrial worker (and the government official) and the lot of the peasant. But what it is discussing is also a world problem, evident enough in most countries. Here are some of the recommendations:[2]

" . . . considerable thought must be given, especially by public authorities, to the suitable development of essential public services in country areas: roads, transport, means of communication, drinking water, housing, health services, elementary, technical and professional education, religious and recreational facilities, and the supply of modern installations and furnishings for the farm residence. . . . "

The development of agriculture must keep pace with the other elements in the economy; one advantage of this will be that it will contribute towards "the stability of the purchasing power of money". Development should be gradual and facilities provided for the retraining of those made redundant by the modernisation of agriculture.

The encyclical goes on to consider taxation, credit banks, social insurance, price protection, and the promotion of ancillary industries. *Tax assessments* should take account of the fact that farmers have to wait longer than most people for a return on their outlay; *credit banks* should be enabled, by the public authorities, to lend money at a moderate rate of interest to farmers, because they must have capital, yet have difficulty in getting it because the private investor finds it more rewarding to invest in industry. The agricultural worker must share fully in *schemes of social insurance and social security*, which are of great importance today "in removing the wide discrepancies in the standard of living

[1] CTS, p. 36.   AAS, LIII, p. 432.
[2] CTS, pp. 35-43.   AAS, LIII, pp. 431-39.

enjoyed by the different classes"; such schemes must not discriminate, as they often do, against the agricultural worker: " ... modern economists must devise a suitable means of *price regulation* ... supervision by the public authority cannot be avoided altogether"; the fact that food is a primary need, and must therefore be kept cheap, must not be allowed to depress the wages of those engaged in agriculture. And it is very desirable to set up *ancillary industries,* in the farming districts: " ... the time has come to promote in agricultural regions the establishment of those industries and services which are concerned with the preservation, processing, and transport of farm products ... "; the presence of such undertakings will provide alternative employment to those who become redundant on the land without requiring them to leave their homes.

And so on.

Farmers are reminded that theirs is a noble calling, undertaken "in close harmony with Nature, the majestic temple of Creation", work which carries with it "a dignity all its own. It brings into its service many branches of engineering, chemistry, and biology, and is itself a cause of the continued practical development of these sciences .... " The family farm is still the most socially desirable unit of production, but only where farmers learn to co-operate, forming professional associations and unions and thus acquiring "a voice in political circles and in public administration. The lone voice is not likely to command much of a hearing in times such as ours."

These pages of *Mater et Magistra* are unique in the whole corpus of papal social teaching. Never have the needs of a particular branch of the economy been so seriously the concern of a papal encyclical. After more than a thousand years of relative indifference to the agricultural backwardness of the papal states, and a hundred years of only small concern for the hideous problem of agricultural poverty in Naples and Sicily, the Holy See was now taking her place, with Pope John, in the van of the movement for agricultural reform. Agricultural economists may differ about the merits of his particular proposals; but never has the cause of agriculture been more powerfully championed. In his enthusiasm for specific remedies the Pope leaves the area of general principles, and the assertion of rights and duties, to enter specific demands for specific remedies. It is almost as though Pius XI had issued an encyclical in 1931 with concrete suggestions for the attention of President Hoover as to how best to deal with the great economic depression. Pius XII had been fond of asserting the right of the Church to pronounce upon the principles governing any 'mixed' matter in which morals were involved, and he spoke very often on a wide variety of such matters. But, although he was not averse to giving advice, he did not do so in such detail, on a secular subject, as did John XXIII in the field of agricultural economics.

By comparison, what Pope John has to say about industry is less interesting. Following Pius XII he prefers the small industrial or commercial firm just as he prefers the family farm. He wants to see the small concern strengthen its position by means of co-operative unions; he believes that such concerns, 'perfected' by co-operatives, should be encouraged for "the common good", as well as to secure "technical progress".[1] He wants to see the workers given a share in the profits of the firms for which they work, and some real interest in the policies adopted by their firms. They should not be mere "cogs in the machine" but part of a "true community of persons". And he is specially concerned for their "thoroughgoing technical and general education" and their "professional organization", while it is for the government to "take the proper steps regarding their training, taxation, credit and social security."[2] It is also for the public authorities to "bring the workers into their discussions, and those who represent the rights, demands and aspirations of the working classes, not to confine their consultations to those who merely represent the interests of management."[3]

Amongst the many duties of the government is that of supervising and controlling "training, taxation, credit, and social security".

What sort of government is to be invested with these immense powers envisaged by Pope John?

A government limited in its authority, a government operating under

[1] CTS, p. 26.   AAS, LIII, p. 422.   [2] CTS, p. 27.   AAS, LIII, p. 423.
[3] CTS, p. 29.   AAS, LIII, p. 425.

law, a government operating within a constitution which separates the executive, the legislature, and the judiciary – in short a government rather like the American, or perhaps that of the Republic of Italy. In spite of its many new responsibilities in running a welfare state it must never forget that its powers are strictly limited, that it exists to protect human rights, not to create them. Those rights are given directly to human beings, by virtue of the Natural Law, which means by God. "We must, however, reject the view" says *Pacem in Terris* "that the will of the individual or the group is the primary and only source of a citizen's rights and duties, and of the binding force of political constitutions and the government's authority".[1] The Will of the People is no more the ultimate sovereign than the medieval monarch was. Popular assemblies, like princes, hold their power from God, and have to exercise it with a proper regard for His Natural Law.

So do dictators.

It is evident that by sticking to the principle of the Natural Law, and by insisting that the whole field of human rights – which he had so greatly extended in *Mater et Magistra* – is protected by Natural Law (which is God's law), the Pope was trying to protect mankind from every sort of political totalitarianism whether Communist, Fascist, or "totalitarian democratic". He was, in fact, trying to control the power of government although he had already so widely extended its sphere of influence. Not only does he reassert the traditional papal teaching on the limited role of government but he reinforces it by favouring the 'checks and balances' principle of the separation of powers. Decentralized democracy, or 'limited' democracy, is his ideal though, in accordance with papal tradition, when speaking of forms of government he speaks very guardedly. "It is not possible to give a general ruling on the most suitable form of government, or the ways in which civil authorities can most effectively fulfil their legislative, administrative, and judicial functions . . . a major consideration will be the prevailing circumstances and the condition of the people. . . . We think, however, that it is in keeping with human nature for the State to be given a form which embodies the threefold division of magisterial powers properly corresponding to the three main functions of public authority."[2] Hence

[1] CTS, p. 32. AAS, LV, p. 279. [2] CTS, pp. 28, 29. AAS, LV, p. 276.

his preference for governments based on the separation of powers. He supposes, perhaps optimistically, that under such constitutions civil servants will be arbitrators rather than petty despots; yet they are the people who will have to regulate his multifarious insurance, education, and health schemes. He believes, with good reason, that "It must be clearly laid down that the principal function of public authorities is to recognize, respect, co-ordinate, safeguard and promote citizens' rights and duties."[1] Always inclined towards the cheerful view, he considers that men have become "increasingly aware nowadays of their personal dignity, have found the incentive to enter public life and demand constitutional recognition for their own inviolable rights. Not content with this, they are demanding, too, the observance of constitutional procedure in the appointment of public authorities, insisting that they exercise their office within this constitutional framework."[2]

Clearly such principles leave no place for absolute dictators, with their secret police, or for totalitarian democracies, pretending to embody an infallible Will of the People. His attitude is generally in line with the precepts of his more recent predecessors. Yet even his immediate predecessors had been ready enough to make agreements with dictators and had sometimes preferred them to the democracies they supplanted. The preference clearly expressed in *Pacem in Terris* for democracy was, in fact, something new in papal political teaching:

"A natural consequence of men's dignity is unquestionably their right to take an active part in public life, though their degree of participation will necessarily depend on the stage of development reached by the political community of which they are members.

"For the rest, this right to take part in public life opens out to men a new and extensive field of opportunity for service. A situation is created in which civic authorities can gain from the greater frequency of their contacts and discussions with the citizens a clearer idea of what policies are in fact effectual for the common good."[3] And he points to the added advantage that ministers, in a democracy, tend to hold power for a shorter time.

---

[1] CTS, p. 31.   AAS, LV, p. 278.   [2] CTS, p. 32.   AAS, LV, p. 279.

[3] CTS, p. 31.   AAS, LV, p. 278.

So democratic government, in one form or another, seems to John to be good, and probably the best government for intelligent and responsible people. This marks a big change since the days of Pius IX, who was only prepared, grudgingly, to "condone" the granting of a constitution by King Victor Emmanuel to Piedmont; it is an advance even on Leo XIII, who only urged Frenchmen to rally to their Third Republic because it was the government constituted by law, and because a return to the Bourbons, desired by most French bishops, would have meant civil war. It is likewise an advance on Pius XI who, without expressing himself on the respective merits of different forms of government, in fact, where he was most concerned – in Italy – pursued policies which tended towards the establishment of an authoritarian régime.[1] It is, in fact, the first time that a pope has formally committed himself to the view that, other things being equal, democracy is best. Pius XII, it is true, wrote much on the subject of democracy, and gave a guarded welcome, in his broadcast Christmas Message in 1944, to the evident reawakening in Europe (and especially in Italy) of democratic ambitions as the power of Hitler tottered to its ruin.[2] In this message he welcomes the fact that men are becoming "more and more resentful of the exclusive claims of a dictatorial authority which allows of no control or discussion and were demanding a system of government more consistent with the dignity and liberty of the citizen". But he remains very cautious. He assumes that his listeners will expect him to favour dictatorship when he reminds them that Leo XIII said it was "not forbidden to give preference to moderate forms of popular government" and that "the Church does not condemn any of the various forms of government" and when (wishing to give support to the Monarchists in Italy?) he reminds them several times that democratic forms of government are perfectly compatible with monarchy. In general, he is mostly concerned with insisting upon the exceptionally high qualities needed to make democratic institutions work, and with the grave dangers incurred when "the people" sink to the level of "the amorphous mass". Democratic legislatures, he says, should comprise "a select body of men of firm Christian convictions, endowed with correct and sure judgement and a practical sense of fairness, in all

[1] See below, p. 173.   [2] *Selected letters*, p. 301. AAS, XXXVII, p. 10.

circumstances consistent". How often have these conditions been fulfilled?

By contrast, Pope John's open preference for democracy marks, if not a new departure, at least a new emphasis. And it marks historically, too, an interesting change because the Pope, though remaining himself a monarch (and an absolute monarch at that) seems to imply that the age of monarchy is over. He is thus registering the disappearance of the age of Bossuet, who taught the whole Church to believe that alliance between throne and altar was 'natural', and of Gregory XVI (1831–46), who thought that the first point in ecclesiastical policy was to maintain that alliance, however heretic the prince might be. Of course John XXIII, in saying what he did about democracy, was undoubtedly thinking about the dangers of dictatorships, not about the dangers of absolute monarchy; the significance of what he said, in favour of democracy, lies in its implicit warning against dictatorships. Yet the historian will be pardoned for noting that, on the long view, what is most remarkable is that a Pope should write an encyclical about civil government without even referring to monarchy. For fifteen hundred years the Pope had lived in a world of fellow monarchs; himself the senior of them all. That was the world which Pius IX, only a century earlier, took for granted. Now, for John, monarchy is not even worth a mention. The omission is interesting, because monarchy may not yet be quite as dead as that. It is possible that John XXIII's lack of interest in the monarchical aspect of his own office, his personal reluctance to wear the tiara, had something to do with it.

John was, in a personal sense, 'democratic', in a way in which no other Pope has been – certainly not that other pontiff from a humble home in the plain of Lombardy, St Pius X. He hated speaking *de haut en bas* to anyone; he was happiest when he could leave his throne and sit on the same level as his visitors, an equal amongst equals. In the conventional sense, in the American sense, he was 'really democratic'; he was not just playing at going slumming with the rest of humanity. And yet one should remember that, when he writes about democracy as a form of government, he does so with complete detachment. He evidently prefers democratic forms of government, given the right conditions, but there is no hint of a 'religion of democracy', no suggestion that to call something 'undemocratic' is more damaging than to call it sinful.

This is because the form of government, to any pope, is something of limited importance. Even the importance of government itself is not to be exaggerated. It is important; but so are many other things, some of them – religion, the family – more important. There has to be government, certainly – temporal government as well as spiritual – since man is a social animal. And temporal government, like spiritual government, comes from God, and has to be obeyed for that reason. But as to the form it takes, time and circumstance have much to do with that. All forms of government have their dangers, but democratic forms may have fewer dangers than most. "It is in keeping with their dignity as persons that human beings should take an active part in government" says *Pacem in Terris*, and goes on to note that they are taking their duties seriously. Men are demanding "that a clear and precisely worded charter of principal human rights be formulated and incorporated into the State's Constitution".[1] One may wonder whether the Pope or the Curia were always impressed by the precisely worded charters of principal human rights which they read; after all Rome had been writing moral-political charters for more than a millenium. At all events there remained this wide difference between Pope John's approach to democracy and that of people to whom democracy was a religion, namely that to the Pope, most certainly, whatever democracy was, it could never be a religion. He was in no danger of confusing *vox populi* with *vox Dei*, of assenting to Rousseau's dogma of the General Will. There was nothing necessarily immoral to him about non-democratic forms of government. He just thought that, in our own era, with a politically mature people, the advantages of democratic forms of government outweighed the disadvantages.

Government then for John XXIII, as for his predecessors, remains chiefly a matter of protecting and harmonizing human rights, rights which are not endowed by society but come from God. His unique

[1] CTS, p. 31.   AAS, LV, p. 278.

contribution was to extend the recognition of the range of these rights, so that they were seen to include those we now speak of as belonging to the Welfare State.

What had he to say about the old-established rights, those so dear to his predecessors, the rights of religion and the rights of the family?

On the rights of religion, understood as the rights of the Church, every Pope has been eloquent since the days of Constantine – indeed European history has rung with the clash of claim and counter-claim. It has sometimes seemed as though the Holy See existed just in order to defend these rights.

And John?

Every human being has the right "to worship God in accordance with the right dictates of his own conscience, and to profess his religion both in private and in public" (*Pacem in Terris*).[1]

Now this, indeed, was something different. This was the Pope saying that every honest Protestant had the *right* to his freedom of worship. It is true that, in the same paragraph, John quoted Leo XIII: "This genuine, this honourable freedom of the sons of God ... has always been sought by the Church, and always been most dear to her. This was the freedom which the Apostles claimed ... which the Apologists defended. ..." But they had not defended the sort of freedom Pope John was talking about. They had not defended the rights of Moslems heretics, or Jews, who sought to worship in accordance with the right dictates of their own conscience. Leo XIII was writing about something different; he was writing about the rights of the Catholic religion. The right of Waldensian Protestants, whether of upright conscience or no, to worship God publicly in Turin, was not "sought by the Church", in Leo's time, nor had it "always been dear to her"; the juxtaposition of Leo's outburst with John's simple statement, in the same paragraph, and linked by the phrase "Hence, too, Pope Leo XIII declared" is a juxtaposition of two related but not identical matters.

As we saw in the last chapter, what Pope John was really doing was to endorse not only Leo XIII but also the demands of the liberal Catho-

[1] CTS, p. 10.   AAS, LV, p. 260.

lics.[1] When the French liberal Catholics in the nineteenth century urged the essential justice of allowing freedom of religion, they were accused by Gregory XVI and Pius IX of religious indifference; they were told they were putting truth and error on an equal footing. Yet all that most of them were claiming was the equal right of all men to follow their conscience; they were not saying that the different choices men might make were, in themselves, equally good, or equally true. Rome, however, was not prepared to concede that there could exist a right to bring up children in an erroneous idea of God, although she had for long agreed that, in practice, it was often necessary to accept such toleration.

Roncalli's statement, in *Pacem in Terris*, greatly clarified the position because a man's right to worship God in accordance with the right dictates of his own conscience, and to do so publicly, must certainly include his right to teach his children his own beliefs. For the first time the right to Protestant, or to any other worship, as distinct from toleration of it, was clearly recognized.

On the other fundamental rights, the rights of the family, it would hardly have been possible for John XXIII to add much to what Pius XII, or Pius XI, or Leo XIII had so frequently and fully said. *Pacem in Terris* only sums up earlier teaching when it says: "The family, founded upon a marriage which is freely contracted, one and indissoluble, must be regarded as the natural, primary cell of human society."[2] But on the position of women he does have something new to say, in the same encyclical: " . . . the part that women are now playing in political life is everywhere evident. This is a development that is perhaps of swifter growth among Christian nations. . . . Women are gaining an increasing awareness of their natural dignity. Far from being content with a purely passive role, or allowing themselves to be exploited; they are demanding both in domestic and in public life the rights and duties which belong to them as human persons."[3] And earlier the encyclical

[1] I would prefer to say "Catholic liberals", but Montalembert, Lacordaire and the rest are too well known as "liberal Catholics", although they were neither more nor less Catholic than other kinds of Catholic. And I am not referring to the theological principles of Lamennais, or of others who fell into heresy.

[2] CTS, p. 11.   AAS, LV, p. 261.   [3] CTS, p. 19.   AAS, LV, p. 267.

speaks of the founding of the family as a matter in which "both the man and woman enjoy equal rights and duties".[1] The support which Pope John here gives to the new position of women in public life is different, in emphasis, from the words of his predecessors, who were less impressed by the advantages of the emancipation of women and their appearance in public life. Thus Pius XII, in his address to women's associations, had shown that he did not believe the "emancipation of women" had been altogether to their real advantage: "That public life has now for some time been developing in a manner unfavourable to the true welfare of the family and the true welfare of woman, is beyond dispute. . . . Equality of rights with men has led her to abandon the home, in which she used to reign as queen, and subjected her to the same burden and the same hours of work. No heed is paid any longer to her true dignity, to that which is the firm foundation of all her rights: her distinctive quality of womanhood and the essentially complementary character of the sexes."[2]

The many pages which Pius XII devoted to the subject of women are amongst the most eloquent, the most sensitive, and the most penetrating which he penned, in particular he elevated the concept of spiritual motherhood – the *métier* of those not granted the grace of physical motherhood – on to as lofty a level as could well be contemplated. But, on the earthly level, he was impatient, as we saw earlier, of "communal kitchens and other public services relieving her of domestic burdens . . . education without fees, public assistance in the case of illness. . . . " "Has all this," he asks, "improved woman's condition?" Roncalli, on the other hand, who knew more of what a peasant mother's work really meant, evidently welcomed the changes which were making the lot of the poorer class of women – like his relatives at Sotto il Monte – less arduous.

The welcome it extended to the evident "increase in social relationship", to the "development of the social life of man", as both an "effect and a cause of the growing intervention of the State", was the heart of the message of *Mater et Magistra*, which appeared in May 1961. In Roncalli's

[1] CTS, p. 11.   AAS, LV, p. 261.
[2] *Selected letters*, p. 325.   AAS, XXXVII, p. 288.

other great encyclical, *Pacem in Terris*, of April 1963, some of this message was repeated, especially as it related to forms of government. But in the later missive it is the world community the Pope is mainly concerned with, and how to promote world peace. And his vision has widened in another way. Whereas the first encyclical is addressed to "the clergy and faithful of the entire Catholic world", the new one is addressed "to all men of good will". We may follow him now into the wider world order.

3 · ABOUT WORLD ORDER AND PEACE

That popes should be concerned to promote political harmony in the world would seem only natural. As Vicars of Christ, who came to redeem all men, they should not be expected to favour the modern cult of nationalism. As representatives, on earth, of the God of love, who created all men, they must surely always work for peace. Mankind is their ultimate concern, not Italians, or Frenchmen, or 'the West', or even 'Christendom'.

So it would seem. But so it has not always seemed. It was one of the achievements of Pope John's pontificate that he renewed men's awareness of this universal quality, which properly belongs to the papacy, but which has always been liable to become lost to sight amidst the exigencies of more limited duties, duties more immediate, and thus apparently more compelling. Addressing himself to "all men of good will", he went out of his way to make friendly contact not only with the separated brethren but also with those who professed a philosophy hostile to Christianity, but whom he none the less recognized as sons, for whose salvation he shared an ultimate responsibility.

In doing this John XXIII was not so much asserting a new claim as trying to redress a balance. Popes in the past had too often been pre-occupied with their duty to nourish and protect the visible Church entrusted to their care so that they had given first place in their thinking in their plans to thwart heretical, schismatic, or secularist movements of all kinds. Their same sense of their duty as shepherds and protectors had led them to keep a close eye on politics. Evidently the political situation, whether in Italy, or in Europe, or in the Middle East, or in the New World, or even in Africa, India, or China might have important repercussions on the Church of which they had charge, leading perhaps to a closure of monasteries, or secularization of education, or cutting off of bishops from their contact with Rome, or even expulsion or imprisonment of clergy, *en bloc*. Sometimes such political preoccupations led popes into politics, whether to preach a crusade to save Palestine, or to coerce a European ruler who was denying the rights of the Church, or to enlarge the temporal possessions of the papacy in central Italy with a view to safeguarding the independence of the Holy See. These were the more worthy motives. There were sometimes others, less worthy, since popes, as Pius VII remarked, have been subject, like other men, to "human frailty" in these matters. But whether the motives have been worthy or unworthy the price paid for political involvement has been a stiff one, because it has necessarily obscured the wider vision and disturbed the detached serenity of universal judgement.

An undue papal involvement in politics, and especially local Italian politics, was never more serious than at the time of the Renaissance, when the need for the reform of the Church was paramount, and acknowledged, yet the exigencies of Italian politics seemed to Rome more compelling. That the failure of the popes to maintain a proper order of priorities at this time was a prime cause of the division of Christendom is now accepted.[1] But a comparable failure also occurred in the middle of the nineteenth century, when immense revolutions were taking place in the political, social, and scientific thinking of Europe, which Rome largely ignored because her attention was focused upon less important events in Italy.

The papacy's deep involvement in her own day-to-day struggle for political survival, in the last 150 years, and her rather odd relations with Italy, are something to which we shall have to return later.[2] But it is a mistake to forget this involvement, when one is looking at the papacy in world affairs, since this can lead one to think of the Pope

---

[1] It has been demonstrated in the first volume of Hubert Jedin's *History of the Council of Trent* (London, 1957).

[2] In Part IV.

as occupying a more detached position than he does. As Bishop of
Rome, Primate of Italy, and Head of a government which depends upon
an entrenched Italian civil service, the Pope's normal environment is
less cosmopolitan than that, say, of the Secretary-General of the United
Nations. No doubt he is much less influenced by his surroundings than
he was in the days when he was temporal ruler over central Italy. But it
would be absurd to suppose, for instance, that Pius XI, who wrote so
vigorously on the subject of Communism, Fascism and the so-called
Corporate State, was not thinking about Mussolini, sitting only a few
hundred yards away in the *Palazzo Venezia*, or that Pius XII, who
banned collaboration with the Communists in 1949, was not much
preoccupied with saving the Italian peninsula from the dictatorship of
Togliatti.

Pope John, for all his sympathy with the Italian peasant, for all his
love for Sotto il Monte and Bergamo, for all his desire to be a pastoral
Patriarch of Venice and later a pastoral Bishop of Rome, was less
concerned with 'saving Italy' than were Pius XI and Pius XII. Even more
important, he was less concerned, in the political sense, with saving the
position of the Church, or saving Christendom. He was largely free
from the counter-reformation habit of using politics as a weapon of
defence against heresy, from the Renaissance habit of using politics to
strengthen the papal position in Italy, and from the medieval habit of
using politics to build a papal ascendency over Europe. Setting aside
Roman or Italian considerations, setting aside even the immediate
'interests' of Christendom, or the West, *Pacem in Terris* looks steadily
at the world as a whole, and in this it differs even from *Mater et Magistra*,
where Italian considerations are still evident – especially in the agricultural sections.

In this remarkable new document, published only two months before
he died, Roncalli succeeded in lifting himself right out of his political
and even out of his clerical environment on to the lofty plane of
Father-in-God of all men, irrespective of their creed, their colour, their
continent, irrespective even of their acceptance of his own fatherhood.
We are allowed, as we read it, to forget, for a time, Pius XII's root
assumption that the great apostasy, the withdrawal of so many from
allegiance to the Holy See, leading to secularism, and so on to

Communism, has shrouded much of mankind in impenetrable darkness and divided humanity in two. Nor are we any longer in Pius XI's world of sheep within the fold, Communist wolves outside, and the Papacy standing sentinel at the gate. Still less are we in St Pius X's world of multiplying censorship or Pius IX's of *non-possumus* amd *non-expedit*. We are looking at the *whole* world, at Africa, and Asia, and the United Nations, in particular, and we are trying to see what will help to make mankind everywhere have life, in peace, and have it more abundantly, so that men may develop their faculties to the full, in this world, and save their eternal souls in the world to come. Here are the words Pope John uses in *Pacem in Terris* to explain why he claims the right to address the whole world: "We therefore consider it Our duty as Christ's vicar on earth – Christ, the Saviour of the world, the Author of peace – and as the interpreter of the most ardent wishes of the whole human family, in the fatherly love We bear all mankind, to beg and beseech men, and particularly statesmen, to be unsparing of their labour and efforts to ensure that human affairs follow a rational and dignified course."[1]

In order to appreciate more clearly what was new in Pope John's appeal for peace it is necessary to consider Pius XII's constant appeals on the same subject. Throughout his pontificate Pius XII had more to say about peace than about anything else. He appealed for peace thirty times in his first sixteen months as Pope. In the period after 1948, and especially through Holy Year 1950 (and he recalled that Holy Years had been first introduced as years dedicated to peace), he returned constantly to the same theme.[2] But he always linked it with justice. There could be no true peace except on the foundation of justice. And he found himself, not only in the Second World War but in face of the Soviet expansion into Europe afterwards, confronted by what he saw as unjust spoliation. His appeals for peace were appeals for the restitution of the spoils of aggression. When he cried out against wars of aggression, when he appealed over and over again for a return to justice and peace, men were left wondering how many wars of libera-

[1] CTS, p. 43.   AAS, LV, p. 288.
[2] See especially his radio appeal at the opening of Holy Year (AAS, XLII, p. 121, and in particular pp. 128, 129).

tion would be needed to restore justice, and thus to re-establish peace. "Any war of aggression," he said in his Christmas Eve broadcast of 1948, "against anything that the divine ordinance of peace demands unconditionally shall be respected and guaranteed, and hence protected and defended, is sin, crime, an outrage against the majesty of God. . . . A nation which is threatened by, *or already the victim of* [my italics] unjust aggression, cannot remain passively indifferent if it wishes to behave in a Christian manner; and it is even more certain that the solidarity of the family of peoples forbids others to behave as mere spectators in an attitude of passive neutrality. Who can measure the damage already done in the past by indifference of this kind towards the war of aggression? – an indifference which is quite unchristian."[1]

What countries were "already the victim of unjust aggression" in 1948? Those of eastern Europe. Pius was trying to rally statesman against the new, the Communist aggression, by reminding them of the disastrous consequences of the appeasement practised earlier, between the two world wars, that breakdown of collective security which, he points out, drove the nations, especially the smaller nations, to go on piling up arms in a panic. Since peace, in his view, depends absolutely, in the long run, on justice, it involves the recognition of the rights of the small countries, and also the rights of the Church. There must be no compromise with the aggressor, no attempt to patch up peace by sacrificing the rights of others.

What particularly shocked Pius XII, so that he gave stronger and stronger utterance to it, in Christmas message after Christmas message, was the continued failure of the nations, after the end of the war, to make a peace settlement based upon a new order rooted in the principles of justice and liberty. The kind of order he demanded he had outlined in his first Christmas message, *In questo giorno*, in 1939: it must respect the independent rights of all nations and also of minorities; it must provide for progressive disarmament; it must provide a supreme world juridical authority with power to revise treaties. And even then it would fail unless the peoples and their governments learnt to submit to "the sacred and inviolable standards of the law of God". To these

[1] AAS, XLI, p. 13.

principles Pius XII always adhered,[1] and when international developments after the conclusion of hostilities failed to measure up to them
he continued to protest. Remembering that Britain had gone to war in
defence of Poland, and encouraged by the terms of the Atlantic Charter,
and by his contacts with President Roosevelt, through Mr Myron
Taylor, Pius XII could not bring himself to accept the new state of
affairs which arose from the advance of the Russian armies into Europe,
President Roosevelt's policy of "trusting Stalin", or the agreements
made at Yalta.[2] Clinging to his principle that a peaceful international
order must rest on "justice and liberty", and especially on justice and
liberty for the small nations, and for the Church, Pius was altogether
unimpressed by the way in which the United Nations took shape in the
hands of Roosevelt and Stalin. He did not believe that it could fulfil
the function he had in mind for a world authority because it allowed
a key position, with a permanent seat on its Security Council, and a
veto, to a great power which denied the principles of its charter, flouted
its Declaration of Human Rights, prevented the admission, as members,
of a number of Catholic countries, and did not even mention the name
of God – the source of human rights – either in the Charter or in the
Declaration. Instead of a world authority resting on a new order of
justice and liberty, what seemed to have emerged was merely a pact,
without principles – a pact carried over from a war-time alliance. If the
United Nations really meant business let it, he protested, "become the
full and pure expression of international solidarity in peace, cancelling
from its institutions and from its statutes all traces of its origin, which
was rooted in the solidarity of war".[3]

The implication was clear enough. Justice was incompatible with

---

[1] Cf his Christmas Broadcast, 1943 (AAS, XXXVI, p. 11), "True peace is not
the result, so to speak, of a calculation of the balance of power but, in its ultimate
and deepest significance, of moral and juridical action" (p. 23). Moreover it
must rest upon the Christian faith. "Only then will it be able to preserve
humanity, after this lamentable war, from the unspeakable disaster of a peace
built upon false foundations, and thus ephemeral and deceptive" (p. 24).

[2] His anxiety, in the summer of 1944, to impress Roosevelt with the gravity
of the Communist danger, and with the need to rehabilitate Germany, is
recorded in *Wartime Correspondence between President Roosevelt and Pope Pius
XII* (New York, 1947), pp. 104, 105.

[3] Christmas Message, 1948. AAS, XLI, p. 12.

Soviet predominance. A just world order demanded freedom for eastern Europe. A just world order could not give a position of privilege, within the world authority, to a power which denied God, religious liberty, and the rights of small nations. Meanwhile the repeated Communist demand[1] that the atomic bomb (still an American monopoly) be banned elicited from Rome the view that what was needed was general disarmament, following the establishment of a just order.

Yet justice and liberty, as Pius XII understood them, evidently could not be attained without war, a war for the liberation of eastern Europe. Was it 'doctrinaire' of him to insist on the impossible? Did he really want the western powers to undertake the emancipation of, say, the Baltic countries, on his principle that "the solidarity of the family of peoples forbids others to behave as mere spectators" when a nation is "already the victim of unjust aggression"? Were the western powers to risk war to rescue eastern Europe? Were atom bombs to be dropped on Moscow? – for there was no other way to fight the Russians.

We need not suppose that Pius XII contemplated anything so drastic either in 1948 or, later on, in 1956, when the Soviets overran Hungary. It might seem to him strange that American morality should halt the navies of Britain and France, in their tracks, on the way to Suez, while swallowing, with little fuss, the Soviet invasion of Hungary. But he was not suggesting atomic war over Hungary,[2] nor over any other eastern European country. What he was urging was non-recognition of the existing unjust situation, and refusal to base a new order at the United Nations on it. How justice was to be restored to those regions he does not make clear; one is left to assume he believed that, given firmness and resolution, a way would, in the end, be found. But one needs to notice that his principle that "any violator of international law ought to be placed in an infamous solitude outside civilized society",[3] which implied a system of sanctions, was not likely to change the policies of the Soviet Union but was liable, at the least, to prolong the cold war.

[1] E.g. at the Stockholm Conference of March 1950.
[2] He issued three successive encyclical appeals on behalf of Hungary, October 28th, November 1st, and November 5th, 1956. (AAS, XLVIII, pp. 741-49).
[3] Christmas Message, 1948. AAS, XLI, p. 12.

While the Communists considered that Pius was a warmonger more moderate critics considered that he was being unduly doctrinaire. Since when, they asked, had the papacy been so interested in the independence of small nations or in collective security? The freedom of nations was an idea born of that European liberalism which the popes had fought in the nineteenth century; the small nations of south-eastern Europe, which the Pope was now so anxious to protect, owed their very existence to their successful revolt against the Austrian Empire, an Empire Rome had done her best to defend. As for collective security, that had been invented by a most un-Catholic professor from Princeton, at a peace conference from which the Holy See had been excluded. Could it be that the Pope was championing the rights of small nations and collective security now because the aggressor which had overrun them was atheistic Communist Russia? Had he been equally concerned to invoke collective security when Italy and Germany had been the aggressors? Had he, as Papal Secretary of State, used his position in 1935 to restrain Mussolini in his act of aggression against Abyssinia? Was he really in a position to complain about "the damage done in the past by indifference towards the war of aggression"? In 1950 he made clear his approval of the United Nations' intervention against the Communist aggression in Korea;[1] could it be that it was not so much aggression as Communist aggression that moved him? That it was Catholic religious liberty he sought to protect?

The special concern of Pius XII for the defence of Catholic liberties was as indisputable as it was natural. How could he fail to respond to the cry of the oppressed Poles or Hungarians? But his appeal for a world order based on justice and liberty, and especially religious liberty, might have been more impressive to non-Catholics if he had been especially careful to insist that he was talking about religious liberty for all religions, everywhere, and for all peoples, in whatever part of the globe. True, only the Communists could take seriously the Moscow Conference of the Orthodox Churches of July 1948, held under the protection of the "God-sent leader" Stalin, at which those present

---

[1] The Papal Nuncio to Holland was present at the *Pax Romana* congress of August 1950, which endorsed the UN intervention. (Cf O. Halecki, *Pius XII*, pp. 308, 309.)

condemned Pius XII for "provoking fratricidal wars against democracy in defence of Fascism". But Pius XII did not make it as clear as Pope John made it that what he was concerned about was the religious freedom of "all men of upright conscience", and if he had done so his position, before the bar of world opinion, might have been stronger than it was. It is reasonable to doubt whether he really saw the need for freedom for the Coptic Church in Abyssinia or for the Protestants in Spain as equal, in principle, with the need for freedom for the Catholics in Hungary and Poland. He fought – magnificently – for Catholic freedom; but it was left to John XXIII to convince the world that what the Holy See wanted was the religious freedom of all men.

What Roncalli said about religious liberty probably did more than anything else to persuade mankind that he had the well-being of the whole world at heart, as well as the flock that acknowledged him as its shepherd. And the same impression was strengthened by his pragmatism. He was seldom doctrinaire either about Communists or about anybody else. He never pretended that he regarded Communist philosophy as other than false; but he did not see why this should prevent Catholics and Communists from collaborating fruitfully where they had the same objectives. Why should they not collaborate to maintain peace, since they both wanted peace? To Pius XII this had meant conniving at injustice and appeasing an aggressor who would only go on to demand more. But although the logic of Communist theory implied this (and Stalin's policies endorsed it) Pope John was less impressed by logic or by theory than had been his philosophically minded predecessor. Communist theory might imply liquidation of private property, eradication of religion, and ultimately world conquest, but what if, in practice, the Communists could be induced to adopt a less rigidly doctrinaire attitude? What if there were hints that the Catholic religion might be allowed greater freedom in eastern Europe? What if the present aim of the Communists were peaceful coexistence with the west? " . . . a false philosophy of the nature, origin and purpose of men and the world", says *Pacem in Terris*, should not be identified with an economic, social, cultural or political programme, "even when such a programme draws its origin and inspiration from that philosophy".[1]

[1] CTS, p. 57.   AAS, LV, p. 300.

In other words, Communists may profess and teach a false philosophy, but they may also have good practical objectives – especially the attempt to organize peace. It was pragmatic of the Pope to adopt this attitude, and it was surprising that he put it into an encyclical; for the popes have normally upheld strict principle in their encyclicals while allowing, in their application, pragmatic behaviour (hence the famous "thesis" – the truth – and the "hypothesis" – what may be done in a given situation).

And Roncalli goes farther. False teachings, he implies, have only a limited importance, because although "the philosophic formula does not change, once it has been set down in precise terms, the programme clearly cannot avoid being influenced to a certain extent by the changing conditions in which it has to operate".[1] Or, in crude parlance: there is no need to worry too much about Communist theory, it is what the Communists do that matters, and what they do (e.g. in welfare work or scientific education?) may contain "good and commendable elements".[2] Or again, Marxism may preach world revolution but, "in the changing conditions in which it has to operate" it may come to settle for peaceful coexistence.

Doctrinaire objection to Communist theory was not then to stand in the way of collaboration with the Communists for peace. Nor was it to stand in the way of making a start now with disarmament negotiations, even though mutual confidence between the parties was lacking. The danger of nuclear war, touched off by accident, and the dangers arising from nuclear tests in the atmosphere meant, for John, that the banning of nuclear weapons must first be tackled, and then a general agreement eventually reached about progressive disarmament. "Every aspect of the problem must be examined" says *Pacem in Terris* "so that eventually there may emerge some point of agreement from which to initiate treaties which are sincere, lasting, and beneficial in their effects."[3] Again it is the piecemeal, empirical approach. The world may not have time to wait for a restoration of 'justice' and 'liberty' before tackling the most immediate practical issues, those issues where a common interest in peace *does* exist. Such efforts may not achieve Pius's peace based on

---

[1] *Idem.*   [2] *Idem.*
[3] CTS, p. 43.   AAS, LV, p. 289.

justice; but they may stave off war and give time for, perhaps give rise to, a change of heart.

Essentially realistic too was his appreciation that both sides multiplied nuclear bombs because they were afraid: " . . . unhappily, we often find the law of fear reigning supreme among nations and causing them to spend enormous sums on armaments. Their object is not aggression, so they say – and there is no reason for disbelieving them – but to deter others from aggression."[1] He shows, too, that he does not believe that war, even for the rescue of eastern Europe, would be licit: " . . . in this age, which boasts of its atomic power, it no longer makes sense (*alienum est a ratione*) to maintain that war is a fit instrument with which to repair the violation of justice."[2] And finally negotiation, however slender the hope, should be undertaken because "by meeting and negotiating men may come to discover better the bonds that unite them together, deriving from the human nature which they have in common".[3]

For similar reasons Pope John refused to be doctrinaire about the United Nations. He devoted four paragraphs of *Pacem in Terris*[4] to a warm endorsement of its purposes and those of the international agencies set up by it, and he spoke of its Declaration of Human Rights as "a clear proof of the far-sightedness of this Organization" and "a step . . . towards the establishment of a juridical and political organization of the world community". No longer was the Soviet veto, or the power of the Soviet bloc, representing governments of which the Pope could not approve, treated as a stumbling block. The only qualification, in these paragraphs of praise, is a reference to earlier Catholic objections to the secularist framework of the Declaration of Human Rights, objections which the Pope accepts, in principle (they had been raised by the American bishops), but which he recalls only to brush them aside.

In the matter then of Communism and the cold war John XXIII made a new approach to the maintenance of peace.

He also had a new group of nations in mind when he spoke about the rights of all peoples to their independence. He said little to suggest

[1] CTS, p. 46. AAS, LV, p. 291   [2] *Idem.*   [3] *Idem.*
[4] CTS, pp. 51, 52.   AAS, LV, pp. 295, 296.

that he was preoccupied, as was his predecessor, with the problem of the nations controlled by Moscow – the "iron curtain" countries. But he said much to suggest that he was concerned about the newly emerging nations of Africa and Asia, and those receiving aid in Latin America. And he was particularly severe in his strictures on colonialism as well as particularly outspoken in his disapproval of economic or cultural imperialism. All this seemed to point a warning finger at the West, quite as much as at the East, if only because the involvement of the West, whether colonial, cultural, or financial, was so much greater, in the emergent countries, and the under-privileged countries, than was the involvement of the Soviet Union.

It is indeed hardly possible to interpret the words in which this matter is introduced in *Pacem in Terris* as other than an appeal to the West: "All men are united by their common origin and fellowship, their redemption by Christ, and their supernatural destiny. They are called to form one Christian family. In Our Encyclical *Mater et Magistra*, therefore, We appealed to the more wealthy nations to render every kind of assistance to those States which are still in the process of economic development.

"It is no small consolation to Us to be able to testify here to the wide acceptance of Our appeal. . . . " But " . . . We must insist on the need for helping these peoples in a way which guarantees to them the preservation of their own freedom. They must be conscious that they are themselves playing the major role in their social and economic development. . . . The wealthier States, therefore, while providing various forms of assistance to the poorer, must have the highest possible respect for their national characteristics and their time-honoured civil institutions. They must also repudiate any policy of domination."[1]

Pope John is concerned to avoid the formation of "power blocs" because they will interfere with that absolute liberty to which all peoples have a right. Pius XII had said the same thing, though with eastern Europe much in mind. That Roncalli was not thinking about eastern Europe is shown by the fact that his concern is with the poor, the underdeveloped, the "emerging" peoples. His eyes are upon Africa, and Asia, perhaps too on South America. He is thinking about the aid

[1] CTS, pp. 44, 45.   AAS, LV, pp. 289, 290.

which must be given to their peoples "without strings attached". He is warning not Russia but the West. He accepts[1] Pius XII's dictum that it is "inevitable that the powerful States, by reason of their greater potential and their power, should pave the way in the establishment of economic groups comprising not only themselves but also smaller and weaker states as well" (Christmas Message, 1941), but insists that there must be no compulsion involved. Nations, he argues, are always right to resist "an authority imposed by force or an authority in whose creation they had no part". By implication the European Community, the new pattern of the British Commonwealth, the Pan-American Union are acceptable, but the remnants of colonialism, or of economic and cultural imperialism, are not.

In saying all this Roncalli was still arguing in terms of human rights. Just as he had greatly extended the concept of these rights when he said they included the right to higher education, welfare services, and the rest, so he greatly extended it when he said that they included the right of every 'emerging' people to full national independence. Whereas Pius XII had been protesting against the sad spectacle of ancient Catholic states being brought under Communism, Pope John was claiming new rights, new liberties, on behalf of peoples whose claim to them was not self-evident, historically speaking. In other words he was *extending* the area of natural right, in the national and international field, as he had already extended it in the field of the individual and the family. For he fully accepted the philosophy of the "wind of change". He believed a new stage to have been reached in human affairs when the brotherhood of man demanded that both the political independence and the scientific and economic advancement achieved by the older and wealthier nations be extended to the 'new' peoples. Just as educational and technical progress meant that a *new natural right* to higher education had been created, for those who could benefit from it, so the political and economic progress of the world meant that a *new natural right* to national independence had emerged.

This new extension of the area of human right, while it attracted attention behind the iron curtain, where the Communists found themselves no longer the prime object of papal attack, and while it was

[1] *Ibid.*

73

warmly welcomed among the Afro/Asian countries, and at the United Nations, could not fail to raise eyebrows among some discerning critics in the West.

First, there was the surprising break with history. Throughout the nineteenth century the papacy had resisted the claims of the peoples to national independence, even the claims of the Catholic peoples, ruled by alien non-Catholic governments – even the claims of the Poles, the Belgians, or the Irish, who were supported by the liberal Catholics. Italians, in particular, had not forgotten Rome's resistance to their movement for national liberation. Yet what was wrong in the days of Mazzini was now declared to be a God-given natural right.

The new doctrine might, too, raise problems for peace. Would a 'Balkanization' of the world amongst small, weak, yet fully independent peoples provide the best guarantee for peace? And when did a people acquire the right to become a nation? Presumably when it achieved a successful revolution, since revolution had provided the cradle of most new nations. But then was not revolution still, as Leo XIII taught, always wrong, and did not Pope John himself teach, in *Pacem in Terris*, that nothing was ever gained by violence? Evidently the British policy of educating for independence and then granting it in advance of revolution would best meet Roncalli's purposes; evidently too, the kind of aid given by the American 'Peace Corps', disinterested aid "without strings attached", was in line with his thinking. But such words of commendation as he finds for the western powers are reserved in *Mater et Magistra* for the Catholics: "Catholics of the wealthier States are doing all they can to increase the effectiveness of the social and economic work that is being done for the poorer nations. We would give Our special approval to the increasing assistance they are giving, in all sorts of ways, to African and Asian students scattered throughout the universities of Europe and America; and to the care that is being devoted to the training of those persons who are prepared to go to the underdeveloped countries in order to engage in work of a technical and professional nature."[1]

Concern, amongst Americans, at the Pope's failure to mention the

[1] CTS, p. 48.   AAS, LIII, p. 445.

large part played in this education of Afro/Asians by the secular universities in America; concern, on the part of the British, at his ignoring of the relatively still larger part played by the British universities, or by the Commonwealth Education Plan, will be eased when it is remembered that this part of Roncalli's message comes from *Mater et Magistra* and was written around the end of 1960, when the question of the Congo and the question of Algeria were uppermost in his and in most people's minds. He had been to Algeria, and he had discussed its problems with the French during his term as Nuncio at Paris. And the circumstances in the Congo were still compelling. When he complimented the Catholics of the western powers for what they were doing by way of aid and education he was, in fact, balancing his criticisms of their colonialism, and his demand for local freedom, which were also aimed largely at the Catholic powers. If he said little to indicate his appreciation of enlightened policies in Washington or in London, he said nothing to show his appreciation of the fact that the Belgians in the Congo, or the Portuguese in Angola, or the French in North Africa had served for long as a political shield for Catholic missionaries and Catholic education and, in the past, had received recognition from Rome as bastions of Christian civilization at a time when popes still thought in terms of Christendom.

Pope John's ardent championship of the rights of the underdeveloped countries was in accordance with the generous and 'progressive' quality of his temperament but it was also realistic. Indeed the very survival of the Church in Africa and Asia was likely to depend on it. It did not require unusual political sensitivity, in 1961, to feel the "wind of change", or unusual political insight to perceive that the age of colonialism was over, that the peoples would emerge from the leading-strings of the British and the French, the Belgians and the Portuguese, and that when they did so it would be as well that they should look upon the Church as their natural friend and not as a western institution which had been left behind when the western overlords withdrew and which they were now free to destroy as an unwelcome reminder of the past. Pius XII had well understood the need to insist on the Church's universal mission of liberation and salvation and had been at pains to push ahead with ordaining native priests and investing native bishops. There must be no repetition of the error which had led to the misfortune of the Church in the far east, where she had been identified with the white man and his civilization. It was necessary to her survival, but it was also in accordance with her nature that she should become as fully the Church of the coloured man as of the white. By Pope John's time much progress had been made in achieving this in Africa; but most of the priests and teachers were still – perforce – white, and the point needed to be made explicitly and repeatedly, at the dangerous moment when the protective political shield was being removed. Some Europeans might feel that a word of papal recognition for the civilizing mission accomplished by the colonial powers in the past would not have come amiss. But in the ears of Africans, in 1961, it would have come deplorably amiss.

Not all the hard words of *Mater et Magistra* were aimed at the West. Sometimes, certainly, it looks as though it were Soviet economic imperialism that he was attacking:

"There is a further temptation which the economically developed nations must resist: that of giving technical and financial aid with a view to gaining control over the political situation in the underdeveloped countries, and furthering their own plans for world domination.

"Let us be quite clear on this point. A nation that acted from these motives would in fact be introducing a new form of colonialism – cleverly disguised, no doubt, but in no respect less blameworthy than that from which many nations have recently emerged. . . ."

These warnings must have been prompted, anyhow in part, by the policies of Moscow. But even here, the most striking feature is the implication that the colonialism "from which many nations have recently emerged" was blameworthy.[1] If the African reader was

---

[1] CTS, p. 46.   AAS, LIII, p. 442.   The English translation is admittedly here a free one, tending to strengthen the censure. The Latin text of this last paragraph is:

Ad quod si quando contendatur, in medio est apertissime ponendum, ad illud re vera tum contendi, ut genus quoddam colonicae dicionis instauretur, quae, licet honesto tecta nomine, superiorem illam exoletamque dicionem exprimat, quam civitates multae recens exuerunt; . . .

reassured, eyebrows were bound to be raised in London and Paris, in Holland, in Belgium, and in Portugal.

The Pope's warning was meant for the ears of the whole west, including America, not merely for the colonial powers. *Mater et Magistra* sought to save the newly emerging peoples from corruption at the hands of those who would help them:

"It pains Us to observe the complete indifference to the true hierarchy of values shown by so many people in the economically developed countries. Spiritual values are ignored, forgotten, or denied, while the progress of science, technology and economics is pursued for its own sake, as though material well-being were the be-all and end-all of life. This attitude is contagious, especially when it infects the work that is being done for the underdeveloped countries, which have often preserved in their ancient traditions an acute and vital awareness of the more important human values.

"To attempt to undermine this national integrity is essentially immoral. It must be respected and as far as possible strengthened and developed, so that it may remain what it is: a foundation of true civilization."[1]

Three things are necessary: first to give aid, second to give technical education, third to show a deep respect for the local culture.

First, the moral law compels those countries that can afford it to supply emergency aid, in the form of food, to those that need it. "Of itself, however, emergency aid will not go far in relieving want and famine when these are caused – as they so often are – by the primitive and underdeveloped state of a nation's economy. The only permanent remedy is to make use of every possible means of providing these citizens with the scientific, technical and professional training they need, and to put at their disposal the necessary capital for speeding up their economic development with the help of modern methods."[2]

But:

"The underdeveloped nations have distinctive characteristics of their own, resulting from the nature of the particular region and its inhabitants, with their time-honoured traditions and customs.

[1] CTS, p. 47.   AAS, LIII, p. 443.   [2] CTS, p. 45.   AAS, LIII, p. 441.

"In helping these backward nations, therefore, the more advanced communities must recognize and respect their individuality. They must beware of making the assistance they give an excuse for forcing these people into their own national mould."[1]

For Pope John all races and all peoples enjoy the same inalienable right to equal opportunity and equal respect as belongs to all human beings. His essential message, which he could hardly have made clearer, he summed up in *Pacem in Terris*: "Truth calls for the elimination of every trace of racial discrimination, and the consequent recognition of the inviolable principle that all States are by nature equal in dignity. . . . " "As we know from experience, men frequently differ widely in knowledge, virtue, intelligence and wealth, but that is no valid argument in favour of a system whereby those who are in a position of superiority impose their will arbitrarily on others. . . . The fact is that no one can be by nature superior to his fellows, since all men are equally noble in natural dignity. And consequently there are no differences at all between political communities from the point of view of national dignity. Each State is like a body, the members of which are human beings. And, as we know from experience, nations can be highly sensitive in matters in any way touching their dignity and honour; and with good reason."[2]

The principle is absolute. There are no inferior peoples, no inferior races. There is only a duty incumbent upon those who have to assist those who have not.

On the other hand, professional sociologists and economists, with no particular political axes to grind, may and do raise certain difficulties. What, for example, is to happen when economic and medical improvements, in the underdeveloped countries lead, as they do already, and must more strikingly in the future, to so rapid an increase in the population that food supplies, already deficient, become hopelessly outstripped so that thousands, even millions, starve?

To this familiar question *Mater et Magistra* replies in traditional terms. First, it denies that any immediate crisis is inevitable. Reliable figures, it

[1] CTS, p. 46. AAS, LIII, p. 442.
[2] CTS, pp. 34, 35. AAS, LV, pp. 281, 282.

argues, do not yet show an imminent problem arising from a disproportion between the increase of population and the supply of food.[1]
But further: " ... the resources which God in His goodness and wisdom has implanted in Nature are well-nigh inexhaustible, and He has
at the same time given man the intelligence to discover ways and means
of exploiting these resources for his own advantage and his own
livelihood. Hence, the real solution of the problem is not to be found
in expedients which attack human life at its very source [e.g. the
use of contraceptive devices] but in a renewed scientific and technical
effort on man's part to deepen and extend his dominion over Nature."[2]

Genesis tells us to "increase and multiply" and to "fill the earth and
subdue it" – not to destroy it. "We are sick at heart, therefore, when
We observe the contradiction which has beguiled so much modern
thinking. On the one hand we are shown the fearful spectre of want and
misery which threatens to extinguish human life, and on the other we
find that scientific discoveries, technical inventions and economic
resources are being used ... to provide terrible instruments of ruin and
death.

"A provident God grants sufficient means to the human race to find
a dignified solution to the problems attendant upon the transmission of
human life. But these problems can become difficult of solution, or
even insoluble, if man, led astray in mind and perverted in will, turns
to such means as are opposed to right reason, and seeks ends that are
contrary to his social nature and the intentions of Providence."[3]

Many social problems could be solved if the money now spent on
armaments were made available to solve them. But unfortunately
there has hitherto been little progress in disarmament. Must the tackling
of the problem of world hunger await an agreement on disarmament?
Pope John provided practical suggestions for meeting other problems,
without waiting for a general disarmament; but he provided none on
this. By providing what is really a religious answer to what most of the
sociological critics regard as a secular problem the encyclical is likely to
leave them dissatisfied. And on the question of fact, it is not practicable

[1] CTS, pp. 49, 50. AAS, LIII, p. 446.
[2] CTS, p. 50. AAS, *Idem.*
[3] CTS, pp. 51, 52. AAS, LIII, p. 448.

either to prove or to disprove the Pope's contention that, if the world made the provision and distribution of food, rather than armaments, her first priority, there would be no spectre of starvation. Meanwhile one can support his argument that this is what ought to happen while feeling sure that it will not happen and that, meanwhile, millions of people will starve.

Another question, of interest to economists, is posed by the Pope's desire to see every nation have an economy well balanced as between industry and agriculture. It is the duty of the Government, says *Mater et Magistra*, to promote the common good by bearing in mind the interests of the State as a whole; "which means that it must promote all three areas of production – agriculture, industry, and public services – simultaneously and evenly."[1] Economists, however, are liable to argue that it may be better that some nations should concentrate mainly upon appropriate branches of industry, others mainly upon certain crops or livestock. The prosperity of the world seems more likely to be achieved by specialization and free trade than by policies of national self-sufficiency. Considerations of national defence have led many governments into policies of self-sufficiency, but the Pope was far from anxious to see them impoverishing their countries from that motive. His principal motive for encouraging governments to promote "all three areas of production simultaneously and evenly" was doubtless his desire to improve the lot of the agriculturists. Yet even the perennial problem of southern Italy might be better met (as to some extent it has been) by emigration to northern Italy, or abroad.

With the Italian problem, no doubt, much in mind, Roncalli said much, as did his predecessors, on the need to allow free movement of population about the world. But he preferred that the workers be enabled to stay at home because emigration is a painful and inhuman business which breaks up the family, severs local loyalties, and weakens religion. He evidently wanted to see a world of small nations, each with a government trying to promote equally the different branches of the economy, although this is manifestly one against which objections can be raised, both economic and political.

[1] CTS, p. 42.   AAS, LIII, p. 438.

If the proliferation of a multitude of small governments pursuing economic self-sufficiency bothered Pope John less than the economic imperialism of great powers, he did not envisage a world in which such small governments were fully sovereign. Matters were to be adjusted, said *Pacem in Terris*, between all nations by the World Authority.

"The same principle of subsidiarity[1] which governs and regulates the relations between public authorities and individuals, families and intermediate societies in a single State, must also apply to the relations between the public authority of the world community and the public authorities of each political community. The special function of this universal authority must be to evaluate and find a solution to economic, social, political and cultural problems which affect the universal common good. These are problems which, because of their extreme gravity, vastness and urgency, must be considered too difficult for the rulers of individual States to solve with any degree of success."[2]

The language here is involved. What Roncalli is doing is to add to the hierarchical structure of Leo XIII's Individual, Family, Association, and "serenely regulating State" (each with its inalienable rights) a new apex, even more serene, even more remote, the "public authority of the world community". This World Authority possesses its own rights and duties, and is currently the United Nations, with its specialized agencies. "Its purpose is to create, on a world basis, an environment in which the public authorities of each political community, its citizens, and its intermediate associations . . ." can co-operate for the general good. In other words, it does not merely try to keep the peace, and provide security, but has cultural duties (Roncalli was a keen supporter of UNESCO, whose meetings Pius XII had encouraged him to attend, as an observer, in Paris) and enormous economic, social, and humanitarian duties, which are to be performed by its Food and Agricultural Organization, a body which is singled out for commendation in *Mater et Magistra*.

For his warm endorsement of the work of the United Nations, and his

[1] The principle that a higher power should not be used to perform a task which could suitably be performed by a lower power.
[2] CTS, p. 50. AAS, LV, p. 294.

confident and inspiring vision of its future, the Pope was rewarded with a special letter of thanks from its Secretary-General. His predecessor, as we have seen, had been critical of the structure of the new world organization, though he had collaborated with its specialized agencies. Roncalli welcomed it with characteristic warmth because he saw that the work it was trying to do was good and that it needed to be done. Empirical as ever, he would not allow its manifest limitations, nor the stultifying policies of the Soviet bloc, to cloud his confidence. Since it represented, politically, the world as it was, he would endorse it, and plead for it, and give it such support as he could, even though it did not represent the world as it ought to be – what Pius XII called a world order based upon justice. And in doing so he was faithful to his furthest aim, always to try to serve the well-being of mankind, not to limit his vision to that fifth of mankind which acknowledge him as its spiritual head, or to those nations which belonged within his fold, even though their wrongs might cry out for remedy.

4 · ABOUT THE VICAR OF CHRIST

When Cardinal Ottaviani said that the ultimate purpose of the Church was to preserve the faith it was objected against him that her purpose was to preach it and to practise it rather than to preserve it; indeed that she would only save her life by losing it. Evidently both functions – the inner safeguarding and the outward flowing – have always been inherent in the life of the Church, with her missionaries concerned to spread the faith and the papacy concerned to support them, but yet more obviously concerned to preserve true doctrine.

Pope John, however, was concerned with something further yet. The novelty of his pontificate consisted in his concern not so much to preserve the faith, or to present it afresh (*aggiornamento*), or even to spread it, as to provide for and to succour the whole of humanity; he seemed less preoccupied with the visible Church than with the world as a whole.

Here, indeed, was a revolution.

Yet there was nothing novel about the theology of Pope John's position. It may be stated quite simply in the proposition that, as representative of Christ on earth – representative, that is, of God, who created all men – he was necessarily concerned for the welfare, temporal and eternal, of all men. All men, all women, had been created by God with souls, all were of equal worth in His sight – Mr Kruschev, with his daughter, and his son-in-law; Anglican Archbishop Fisher; Mao Tse Tung; Fidel Castro; the Chief Rabbi; all his sons in God, alongside the holy nuns, the loyal Christian Democrats, or Generalissimo Francisco Franco. The world, and everybody in it, was his whether it accepted the fact or no; those outside his fold might, indeed, be even more his concern than those within, for he was representative of a Lord and God who had been willing to leave the fold in order to go out into the wilderness after the wandering sheep; who came not to call the righteous, but sinners; who had fed the multitude; and who, in the end, had died for all men.

Earlier popes, in differing degree, had shown an awareness of their special relationship with the whole of mankind. They had blessed, from their balcony, the city and the world, *urbi et orbe*. Pius XII had addressed his Christmas messages to all men; many of his addresses were delivered to audiences that were largely non-Catholic; and when he laid down the conditions of a just peace he was appealing to the political leaders of the world, of whatever faith. But there is this difference between Pope John's approach and that of his predecessors. Whereas they, in their major writings, couched their thoughts in terms of the need for a return to the fold, for recognition of the authority of the See of Peter, for an end to the great apostasy, Pope John did not. He may have longed, he may have prayed, he may have laboured as much as any of them for unity; and he knew quite as well as they that in that great structure of unity the Holy See must provide the corner-stone, that the special character of the papal authority must in the end be accepted. But he chose to say little about it. Where his predecessors lamented, appealed, or rebuked, he was silent. He was not directly trying to get the world 'back in'. He was going out into the world, to help the world, in whatever way the world was willing to be helped. And he did so because he was thinking of his role in different terms, he was thinking of all men as sons of God and therefore of himself as their spiritual father on earth, whether they chose to recognize him or no.

He was, of course, only changing the emphasis, not the theology. Rome has never doubted that God is equally concerned for the salvation of all men, or that Our Lord died to offer them all the means of salvation, but she has tended to emphasize the fact that He provided the specific means for their salvation when He founded His Church. If men rejected that Church they rejected Him. ("He that rejects you, rejects me.") If He went in search of the lost sheep, it was in order to bring that sheep back into the fold – i.e. into the Church. It has therefore seemed the first duty of a Pope, as Chief Shepherd of the flock, to safeguard the fold, and to bring into it all those willing to hear and to accept the message of salvation. For those who would not hear, who would not accept, there has seemed little to be done save to pray that God might enlighten them.

Pope John differed from his predecessors in taking a wider view of the possibility of his influencing the world at large for good. He was not inclined to go on repeating that his was the true fold and that the ills of the world were due to so many sheep preferring to wander in the wilderness. His desire to bring them in, *ut unum sint*, nobody could doubt. Yet while they remained outside he thought that he had a special message for them, a message that was not merely an invitation to them to enter.

In order that we may keep a due proportion in this matter we should again remember that Popes Pius XI and Pius XII also had much to say to those outside the Church. In talking to the world at large they would take their stand on the Natural Law because that law, which gives mankind a common basis of mutually acknowledged morality, provides common ground on which a pope may stand when speaking to those not of his faith. He knows that the Natural Law is given by God; to the world this may not be evident, but it recognizes the same law. So Pius XII would talk about the law which requires that the different nations should be politically free, or that the rights of religion should be respected, or that the political exiles should be restored to their own lands. But his words made a limited impression because the feeling existed that he was chiefly concerned on behalf of his own flock, or to safeguard the position of the Church. This was by no means always so; but such safeguarding did play a sufficiently large part in his thinking to have an adverse effect on the response with which he met from the world as a whole.

With John XXIII special considerations were not uppermost. His affection was all-embracing, so that he convinced the world that he had the interests of all humanity at heart, that he was concerned that mankind as a whole should live more fully the life given by God to be lived freely. Like his predecessor he invoked the Natural Law; indeed in his encyclicals, as we have seen, he considerably extended men's understanding of the range of its application. But in doing so he seemed less concerned to further any Catholic objectives, such as the recovery of the liberties of the Catholic peoples of eastern Europe or the safeguarding of the Church in Italy.

Popes move within the ambit of certain distinct circles of responsibility and of these it is possible to identify at least four. They are bishops of Rome, primates of Italy, heads of the universal visible Church, but also Vicars of Christ, which last makes them spiritual fathers of all men. Different popes have given special attention to one or to another of these responsibilities; the special attribute of John XXIII was that he was most concerned, in his public addresses and even in his policies, with the last of them, that outer circle which has generally been the most neglected.

It might have been quite otherwise. The warmth of his human nature might have led him to concentrate on the first of these functions, to give his attention even more fully than he did to Rome herself, to those on his own doorstep, to the needs of his own See. Assuredly he did not neglect Rome; he called and presided over the first synod of the Roman clergy that had been held since the year 1725. He visited the prisoners and the sick; he appeared, an unexpected guest, at the houses of religious communities. But Rome did not provide the centre of his thinking as it had provided the centre for some of his predecessors – for Pius VII, who excommunicated Napoleon because the Emperor had laid his sacriligious hands upon Rome, for Gregory XVI, who was especially hostile to liberals and revolutionaries everywhere because they threatened him with revolution at Rome, for Pius IX, whose conception of the relations between the Church and secular society arose out of his dramatic experiences at Rome. Even for Leo XIII, who tried to regain it, and Pius XI, who regained the part that mattered, the city lay near the centre of their political thinking, while Pius XII, for all the range of his thought and experience, was a Roman, nurtured and closely identified with that city which he later helped to save in the Second World War. Roncalli was much less preoccupied with Rome, nor were the roots of his private life deeply planted there.

He was also less concerned than were some of his predecessors with his position as Primate of Italy. Strictly speaking the popes were not primates of Italy before Italy was a political unity; but a special relationship had existed from time immemorial between the See of Rome and the various States of the Italian peninsula. What the popes, since Pius VI, had perforce to tolerate elsewhere (such as divorce laws, or other 'progressive' reforms stemming from the Napoleonic code) they would not tolerate in Italy. Later on, it was the desire to save Italy from Communism that led St Pius X into a political contact with the Italian nationalists, Pius XI into political contact with the Fascists, and Pius XII into excommunicating those who gave aid to the Communists. John XXIII was less concerned to 'save Italy'. He was, of course, a good Italian; his encyclicals show his concern with economic problems which were mostly Italian problems; he longed to see the Italian peasant better provided for and enjoying wider opportunities. But he was not preoccupied with the traditional politico-religious problems involved in the papal primacy over Italy, indeed it was held against him – with what justice we shall have to consider later, in Part IV – that in his search for a wider understanding and a wider co-operation between all men, everywhere, he endangered the special position of the Church in Italy.

And not only in Italy but in the world. For that same endeavour for wider understanding and wider co-operation, that concern of his for the world as a whole – the fourth, or outer circle – meant that he did not limit his sense of his mission to the care of the Catholic Church – the third circle – and some critics felt that he thereby imperilled the position of that Church everywhere. By embracing the fourth circle of activity, activity as Christ's Vicar, God's representative on earth, he was pursuing a policy which, if not new, was new in the scope that he gave to it.

It is not suggested that in furthering this aim he was in some way acting on his own, outside the Church. The Holy See only exists as part of the Church. The Holy See does not act outside the Church. Christ endowed His Vicar with special powers but they were powers belonging to him as Head of the Church, and it is not possible to imagine them in isolation, without relationship to the Church.

So when one speaks of Pope John as giving priority to a function of the papacy which lies outside the visible Church – the function of spiritual father to all men – one is not speaking of his acting on his own, but as seeking to lead the whole Church into this new and outward-looking position. It was as Head of the Church that he received Kruschev's son-in-law, Adjoubei, as Head of the Church that he encouraged Catholics to co-operate with all men of good will. He was setting a new example and giving new precepts to the Church as a whole.

The powers of the pope are usually exercised in safeguarding their flock against error (by definitions, condemnations and the like) or in ruling, encouraging and assisting the clergy in their efforts to keep the faithful within the Church's obedience and to nourish them with the sacramental life and with sound spiritual teaching. They are also used in support of those members of the Church who are drawn towards special religious vocations, or towards missionary work or other special endeavours which meet with papal approval. All these are internal functions. Externally, the popes have been concerned, for the most part, in modern times, with defending this varied life of the Church against interference, such interference as that of a Bismarck or a Hitler, a Cavour or a Mussolini; or again with protesting against the even more pervasive hostility of the various Communist governments. But Pope John was doing something else, something which lay outside the normal internal or external duties of the Holy See: he was trying to perform what he recognized as a duty of the Vicar of Christ towards all mankind. Hence his efforts to give guidance, in his encyclicals, on every sort of subject which might enlarge men's life and give them peace, hence his friendly contact with hostile governments, turning the other cheek towards persecutors, in an endeavour to lead the Church into active co-operation, for good, with all men, even when such men were teaching atheist and materialist philosophies, or holding bishops in gaol – remembering only that they, too, were sons of God, for whose redemption Christ died. The servant of the servants of God was becoming the servant also of mankind.

But he was trying, too to lead Catholics generally to act in a similar way, as brothers to all men; his could not be an isolated endeavour. Catholics were invited to collaborate for good with all men of goodwill and this would mean with men of very contrary beliefs, or of no belief, for it was certainly not to be supposed that goodwill was the monopoly of those of sound belief. Catholics were thus being led to collaborate with atheists, agnostics, or economic determinists. What was implied, indeed what was specifically said in *Pacem in Terris* was that movements (e.g. Communism) might start from false philosophies (Marxism) but they moved away from a literal acceptance of these philosophies, and developed practical programmes which could be very valuable. The clear implication of this was that philosophies, as such, were not really so paramountly or permanently important, historically speaking, as was supposed; what mattered equally was the practical programme pursued and the degree of goodwill. Here we touch the deepest difference between John XXIII and Pius XII, whose mind moved in terms of true and false philosophies, forever at war with each other; for whom false philosophies were the real root of evil so that their adherents (though often adherents in name alone) must be withstood in their public influence. One may compare the attitude of St Pius X who, guided by Cardinal Merry del Val, felt it a first duty to stamp out, by an elaborate system of censorship, a wide range of philosophical thinking, by no means all of it bearing directly on theology, which he lumped together under the generic name Modernism. Or that of Leo XIII who, because of the (uncertain) appearance of some errors within the movement known as Americanism was willing to cause the suppression of many apostolic activities and some rudimentary ecumenical endeavours in the American Church of the kind that have since been so encouraged. Or that of Pius IX who, with the eighty "false propositions" denounced in his Syllabus, checkmated social or political change.

To Pius XII it seemed evident that, because the official teachings accepted by the Communist leadership were atheistic, and remained unchanged, Christians must always oppose Communists. To John XXIII, as we saw in the last chapter, " ... a false philosophy of the nature, origin and purpose of men and the world" should not be identified with a party programme "even when such a programme draws its origin and inspiration from that philosophy".

The comparison is sometimes made, and may have value, between the attitude of Pius XI and Pius XII towards the Russian revolution (with the world-wide movement it initiated) and that of the nineteenth-century popes towards the French revolution (with the liberal movements that followed). For Rousseau and Voltaire we have to read Marx and Engels, for Robespierre Lenin, for the liberals the Communists. All that Pius XI or Pius XII said about Communism, in the twentieth century, can indeed be matched, with equal or greater force, by Gregory XVI's strictures, in the nineteenth, on the liberties demanded by the liberals – "stinking, poisonous source of error". But gradually – very gradually – the distinction was drawn in the nineteenth century between philosophical error and beneficial practice, between the thesis and the hypothesis, until at last some even of the philosophical principles of liberalism, as interpreted by the liberal Catholics, became acceptable. So, it may be, beginning with Pope John's invitation to Catholics to collaborate in good undertakings with Communists, and his implication that too much attention can be paid to philosophical labels, that the thaw will start. It is too soon to say. And the analogy, like most historical analogies, is inexact. French revolutionary liberalism did not stem from one philosophical source in the way that Communism did nor, though it persecuted the Church, was it always rooted in atheism, or in secularism. Reconciliation may prove more difficult. Yet, as Roncalli reminds us, *all* movements are in "constant evolution", and cannot avoid being subject to changes, "even of a profound nature". Even the enemies of religion may serve religion, without knowing it. "You made the Revolution," cried the liberal Catholic Montalembert to the French, "without us, and against us, yet for us, God willing it so in spite of you!" Even the wrath of man is turned to God's praise.

Papal denunciation of liberalism lasted till 1878; after that less was said about it, Leo XIII urging Catholics (outside Italy) to work loyally with the liberals. Papal denunciation of Socialism lasted till 1931 when Pius XI, without withdrawing his condemnation of the philosophical basis of Socialism, admitted that many of the programmes of the moderate socialists were good, and invited Catholics (in *Quadragesimo Anno*) to co-operate in them. Papal denunciation of Communism lasted till 1963 when John XXIII, without any philosophical change of front, implied that the importance of the philosophical roots of movements could be exaggerated and said that the valuable thing was to co-operate with all other men of good will, in good works.

The shrewd realism of Roncalli, then, had led him, just before he died, to a new position, on a matter of the first importance, though without his saying too much about it. Having started with a determination to be father-in-God to all men, and to lead Catholics generally to recognize in all men their brothers, he had ended not, of course, by denying any article of the faith, but by denying that the dialectic of history must always consist in a philosophical clash, and that it must always be a first duty of Catholics to oppose in every possible way the works of those wearing philosophical labels differently coloured from their own, and especially the works of those with labels coloured red. In this way he helped to open up a new hope for the world, and especially a new hope for Italy.

It has been said that what Pope John did was more important than what he taught; and further, that what he *was* held greater significance still. It may be so. All who met him were moved by the extraordinary power of the spirit of Christian charity which seemed to flow from him. And the importance of his action, in summoning a General Council and heading it into new, uncharted oceans, speaks for itself; it will be considered in the next part of this study. Does his teaching, as embodied in his encyclicals, bear comparison in importance with what he did, which may well have changed the course of the Catholic Church in history?

The answer should, I believe, be yes, although one needs to recognize in all frankness that, by comparison with the great encyclicals of his predecessor, those of Pope John are, intellectually speaking, often superficial. They are not, intellectually, to be compared with *Humani generis* or with *Mystici corporis* or even with that remarkable Christmas broadcast of the year 1942, in which Pius XII was treating of world peace and social order,[1] questions with which Pope John was also so concerned. Nor have they the classical qualities of *Rerum novarum*. Pope John was neither a philosopher, nor a student of modern history, nor a linguist, nor even a theologian in the sense that Pius XII or Leo XIII were. It is possible, too, that later generations will lose interest in many of the practical suggestions that loom large in the Johannine encyclicals: in their detailed suggestions for improving the status of agriculture and for raising the standard of living of those who work on the land; in their analogous suggestions bearing upon life in industry; in their specific demands for an extension of various services provided by the 'welfare state'; in their recommendations in the sphere of social insurance; and so on.

What matters, however, is not the detailed advice but the fact that the Pope is entering at all into these areas of human and social endeavour, bringing with him a blessing rather than a warning, and greatly extending the range of the "natural rights" recognized by his predecessors. Historians, social philosophers and economists are unlikely to regard the Pope's opinions on the balance in a nation's economy, or his perfunctory dismissal of the population problem, or even his uncritical championing of the 'natural rights' of any and every 'emergent' people as powerful contributions towards the analysis of the social question in Africa or Asia. They may also feel that his encyclicals do insufficient justice both to the recent record of the colonial powers and to the legitimate demands of those countries which he calls upon for cash, but allows no degree of control. Looked at in detail, the Johannine encyclicals are sometimes arbitrary in their recommendations and superficial in their judgements.

But when all this has been said, and the limitations of the encyclicals acknowledged, it is still true that they are not only important but quite literally epoch-making. For encyclicals do not need to be philosophical or literary masterpieces in order to change the course of

[1] *Selected letters*, p. 275. AAS, XXXV, p. 9.

history; indeed it is only too likely that some of the loftiest thinking of Pius XII was lost in the rarified reaches of the atmosphere, without visible influence, whereas other papal pronouncements, intellectually of inferior calibre (one thinks of Pius IX's *Quanta cura*, on Liberalism, or St Pius X's *Pascendi dominici*, on Modernism) had consequences of incalculable magnitude. It is for their shift in attitude, for the break they represent in the encyclical tradition, and for the new warmth of their fervour that they are likely always to be regarded as marking a new development in the teaching office of the papacy. It matters comparatively little whether their sociology, their economics, their historical ideas were – academically speaking – always argued at the highest level, but it does matter that they so extended the whole concept of human right. And it matters still more that, in these encyclicals, the Pope walked boldly into the field of world affairs, economic and political, and showed the depth of his concern that men should order them in accordance with right principle, and especially in peace, as befitted children of God, who had all been given the guidance of the Natural Law.

Roncalli's encyclicals are the lasting evidence of his characteristic, peculiar, and novel conception of the role of the papacy; of its concern with *all* men, and with the *whole* of human welfare, in its widest sense. Their warmth, their universality, the new areas of life with which they deal, their lack of exclusive concern with the claims of the Church, and their care for everybody at once distinguished them. We do not know the extent to which the Pope personally phrased them,[1] but we do know that he pondered long and earnestly upon *Mater et Magistra* and *Pacem in Terris* and that the beliefs they expressed were his own. To the former he referred, over and over again, in his subsequent public utterances. In the latter he enjoined, most emphatically, that its principles should become the subject of serious study in the seminaries. They provide the written record of his public purposes.

But can encyclicals of themselves engender a rebirth?

Encyclicals can kill – *Pascendi Dominici gregis* condemning Modernism, in 1907, and a host of earlier pronouncements show how effectively

[1] Mgr Pietro Pavan is credited with a large share in the drafting.

they can kill, or at least how many mouths they can keep shut – but whether they can also engender positive action depends upon how far anybody responds to them, and especially on how many bishops absorb their teaching with a will to do something about it. It is hard for the Pope to compel. The best example, in modern history, of an encyclical with a positive message remains *Rerum novarum*, in which Leo XIII asked for action, and ordered that his precepts should be studied in Catholic educational institutions. In this way he tried to make it an instrument of positive policy; but how successful was he? How much influence did he have on the hierarchy as a whole, or on the Catholic employer in the Mediterranean, for example, or in Latin America? Leaving aside those priests who were so outraged by *Rerum novarum* they refused to read it to their congregations, and ignoring, equally, those idealists who were already paying a just wage, it would be fair to say that the encyclical was mainly effective in so far as it gave encouragement to small idealistic groups which were struggling for wider recognition, and especially for recognition from the local Ordinary. It was difficult for the local bishop to be actively obstructive after the Pope had spoken. Thus Marc Sangnier's movement, in France, *Le Sillon*, derived aid and comfort from Leo's encyclical, until it became tarred with the brush of Modernism, and was consequently condemned.

In the same way the Johannine encyclicals were likely to give comfort and support to individuals or groups already working for the independence of emerging peoples, or on behalf of the United Nations. They might even reassure some African leaders that the Church was officially on their side. But they were not calculated to compel changes of policy within the hierarchy, especially as they were very careful to safeguard episcopal authority. And since they were pastoral rather than dogmatic there was no particular reason why they should have any important surviving influence after Roncalli's death. Those who were not much impressed by his advice (and it is clear that a number of the Curia came within this category) could always say that circumstances had changed. Pastoral encyclicals are more easily ignored than theological encyclicals because theology does not depend on circumstances. Whereas theologians of the future would have to reckon very seriously with Pius XII's great encyclicals, *Mystici Corporis* and *Humani Generis*, and biblical scholars would need to ponder his *Divino afflante Spiritu*, long after they had forgotten what he said about the Communists, John XXIII's major encyclicals were not dogmatic but pastoral. They could easily be ignored after his death unless the new spirit from which they sprang – *the aggiornamento* – became something more than a flame in the heart of an aging pontiff, unless it kindled the whole Church so that the fire became inextinguishable.

That could happen at a Council.

PART III

What he did

1·IN THE FIRST TWO YEARS

Few stories have been told more often, from varying angles, than the story of how the idea of a Council was born in the mind of Pope John, and what sort of Council it was that he envisaged. Yet there remains some mystery. The first official notice of the Pope's intention was fantastic – a short statement in the *Osservatore Romano* for January 26th–27th, 1959, to the effect that, to meet the errors of the time, and its excessive materialism, the Pope proposed to take three steps, namely to hold a Diocesan Synod of the clergy of Rome, to summon an Ecumenical Council of the Universal Church, and to bring the Code of Canon Law up to date. In a further paragraph it was explained that the purpose of the Council would be "not only the spiritual good of Christian people but equally an invitation to the separated communities to search for that Unity towards which so many souls aspire".

Two questions immediately presented themselves. First, how could the announcement of an event of such magnitude as the summons of a General Council be sandwiched between the announcement of two other events of a routine character? And second, was this an invitation to the separated communities to join in round-table talks with the Catholics about reunion? Not only did many Protestant groups suppose that this was the intention, but so did the Orthodox: the Patriarch of Antioch, in an interview on the day of the *Osservatore's* announcement, made it quite clear that he interpreted it in this sense.[1]

In short, the announcement was both buried and confused, nor did confident Catholic explanations that a General Council of the Church always and necessarily meant a meeting of bishops in communion with Rome carry full conviction because, in fact, a 'reunion Council', attended by Catholic and Orthodox bishops, had been held at Florence in the fifteenth century. On that occasion 117 Latins and 31 Greeks (the

---

[1] *La Croix* for 30.1.59, reported in *Documentation Catholique* (see Bibliography, p. 211) No. 1297, Col. 204.

latter not in communion with Rome) had sat down together, at sessions which the Catholic Church recognizes as part of a true General Council, and had agreed about controversial doctrinal matters concerning the nature of the Trinity, of Purgatory, and even the primacy of the Pope. If that could be done in the year 1438 it could be done again in the year 1962, and it would be rash to assume that this was not the sort of Council Pope John was at first hoping for. The most convincing explanation of the enigmatic and muffled manner in which his Council was first announced is that he wanted to test the reaction of the Orthodox, and perhaps of others, before he committed himself to the kind of Council he would summon. If the Orthodox had all been as warmly on his side as was the Ecumenical Patriarch of Constantinople he might have been encouraged to give his Council something of the mixed character of the Council of Florence. But they were not.

When, a month later, the text of Pope John's first statement about the Council was made available, it did not clear up the mystery. For the Pope's text showed that the *Osservatore* had not been guilty of obfuscating his remarks. He had, indeed, associated the Council with the Roman Synod, coupling them together as "happily contributing to the expected and desired Code of Canon Law which would accompany and crown these two examples of a practical application of ecclesiastical discipline suggested to Us by the Spirit of the Lord".[1] Nor had he made it clear what part, if any, the separated brethren would play. From heaven he had implored "a good beginning, a good continuation, and a happy success for these plans for courageous work, a light for the edification and joy of all Christian people, a renewed invitation to the faithful of the separated communities likewise to follow Us, in good will, in this search for unity and grace, towards which so many souls aspire from every corner of the earth".

What was the world to make of this? Did the Pope envisage a Council like that of Florence? Or did he (as later proved to be the case) envisage a Council of those bishops already in communion with Rome which would somehow provide an inspiration to those outside to reconsider their position and to work with Rome for an ultimate unity – a Catholic Council with, perhaps, some non-Catholic observers?

[1] DC 1300, Col. 388.

On April 4th he made his intentions a little clearer, when speaking to representatives of the Catholic universities: "As you know, We have decided, for numerous most important reasons, to summon an Ecumenical Council. By giving an admirable view of the cohesion, unity, and concord of the holy Church of God, a city set upon a mountain, [the Council] will, of itself, constitute an invitation to our separated brothers, who bear the honourable name of Christians, to return to the universal flock whose direction it was the changeless wish of Christ to confide to St Peter."[1]

There was evidently, then, to be no dialogue, at the Council, with those outside the fold; so far as this was to be a "Council for Unity" it would be one only indirectly; its ecumenical consequences were to flow only from its example and from its reforms. We may conjecture that the hopes of the indomitable Pope, whose own life in Bulgaria and at Istanbul had convinced him that the gulf between Catholic and Orthodox could be bridged (because it had been dug by political rivalry, more than by religious disagreement) had been disappointed during the previous few weeks. His first announcement of a Council, in terms which he must have deliberately left vague, had not produced that ready response from the world of Orthodoxy for which he had hoped. The Patriarchs had not chosen to take the hint. But Roncalli's confidence and his natural optimism were not to be repressed. When he returned to his theme at Pentecost (May 17th) there was no hint of disappointment in his voice:

"Here, for Us, is a subject of serene joy. Towards the end of January, on the Feast of the Conversion of St Paul, We announced the plan for holding an Ecumenical Council at which should be gathered together, as at a new Pentecost, first and foremost all the bishops of the Church in communion with the Apostolic See. This will be an Assembly demanding immense and deep preparation and from which may be expected, with the help of the Lord, a great sanctification of the clergy and a great edification of the Christian people while at the same time it will provide an encouraging spectacle for all those who nourish high hopes for the future of faith and of peace. . . .

[1] DC 1302, Col. 515.

99

"We shall have occasion to return to this subject, which is one to shake the heavens and the earth."[1]

For the first time the plan is beginning to be defined; the bishops to be invited, anyhow in the first instance, are those in communion with Rome. But there is no limit to the possible developments; they will be earth – and heaven – shaking. And somehow the Council will have an important bearing on the subject most in the minds of all men in the year 1959, namely the peace of the world. Already unity and peace, those deepest aspirations of Pope John, have become part of his vision of the Council, a Council which had been "suggested to Us by the Spirit of the Lord". (His Secretary of State, Cardinal Tardini, in conversation with whom the idea of the Council had come to him, was, by all accounts, less than enthusiastic; according to one account he thought the Pope "temporarily mad".[2] Antoine Wenger, editor of *La Croix*, tells us that Pope John told him, at an interview on February 27th, that the idea of the Council came to him suddenly, as an inspiration, only shortly before he was due to speak at St Paul's without the Walls.[3] It was the answer to his agonised prayer. At St Paul's he was to conclude the week of prayer for unity; what could he, the Head of the Church, *do* for unity? Surely he should do something? And the inspiration had come – a Council.)

Christian Unity, then, and World Peace. By Pentecost, 1959, if not earlier, these had become Pope John's preoccupations, and somehow

[1] DC 1306, Col. 769 (quoting *Osservatore Romano*).
[2] A point developed by "Lo Svizzero" in his *La Chiesa dopo Giovanni* (Ed. del. Borghese, 1963), p. 15.
[3] A. Wenger *Vatican II première session*, (Ed. du Centurion, 1963), p. 17. Roncalli was very fond of talking informally to people about how this inspiration came to him to summon a Council and he alluded to it publicly in *Superno Dei Mutu*, of Whitsun, 1959 (DC 1330). In his *Giornale Dell' Anima* he says (p. 330) that it was the first grace granted to him "to accept, with simplicity, the honour and the burden of the papacy", the second "to make seem simple and capable of immediate execution certain ideas, by no means complex, even quite simple, but of huge bearing and responsibility in the face of the future . . . without having thought of it before, to put forward for the first time, in a talk with my Secretary of State, on January 20th, 1959, the suggestions: Ecumenical Council, Diocesan Synod, codification of the Canon Law, without having previously given any thought to the matter.

"The first to be surprised by this proposal of mine was myself. . . ."

the Council was to serve both ends. If it did that it would, indeed, "shake the heavens and the earth" – but how could it fulfil so great a destiny? It could hardly do so if it were only intended to pave the way, along with the Roman Synod, for a new codification of the Canon Law. Undoubtedly the Pope had something much loftier in mind; but what sort of programme did he visualize? If he had his ideas about this he kept them to himself, or discussed them only with a few kindred spirits (of whom there were not many at the Vatican) and most notably with the Jesuit Cardinal Bea. Meanwhile he placed his faith in the guidance which the Holy Spirit would give to the Council, once it had assembled. Somehow (and he was not unaware of the new currents of thought which were flowing in other countries, and especially in France) the Council, by bringing fresh blood to Rome, would bring about an *aggiornamento* of the Church, revivifying her and bringing her into closer relationship with the actual contemporary world. Meanwhile there must be prayer, a continual stream of prayer, for the good success of the Council, and this he repeatedly asked for from the groups he addressed, as they visited Rome, prayer which should harmonize itself with that prayer which Our Lord prayed "that they may be one, even as thou, Father, and I are one". "*Ut unum sint*" became the text he repeated most often.

But in spite of the ardour of the Holy Father matters moved at a moderate rate. There was a tendency not to take the rather vague dreams of an old man – a *papa di passaggio* (a transition pope) – too seriously. In France there was some scepticism – and in France they knew the new pope; *pas sérieux* was an early French verdict on his proposal. Nor were the observations of those cardinals who bothered to reply to the Pope's request for their observations particularly helpful ... the Council, said one, should promote better knowledge of the Catechism ... it should launch, said another, a new campaign against Masonic Liberalism. ... Very significantly however (at least in retrospect) the first reply came from Cardinal Montini, Archbishop of Milan, the future Pope Paul VI, and he had at once grasped what was intended: "The Council will make Rome the spiritual capital of the world from whence the light will spread upon those places and institutions where men are working for the union of the peoples, for social peace, for the welfare of the poor, for progress, for justice, and for liberty."[1]

But Cardinal Montini was not a member of the ante-preparatory commission, set up on that same Feast of Pentecost, 1959, to begin preparing for the Council. Its president was the Secretary of State, Cardinal Tardini, and the other members were curial cardinals in charge of the various departments of the papal government. Their business was to do the work of collecting suggestions for the Council's agenda from the bishops, the Curia, the universities, and the seminaries, and at a measured pace they did so. Not till a year later, on the following Pentecost (1960), had they brought their task to the point where the Pope could set up the preparatory commissions which would sift the material collected and draft the Council's agenda (its *schemas*).

Meanwhile the Pope himself, in the first encyclical of his pontificate (*Ad Petri Cathedram* of June 29th, 1959),[2] had seemed to grow cautious, going far to persuade anxious cardinals that, after all, he would pursue traditional policies. He repeated Leo XIII's teaching that it is a law of nature that there should be disparity between the social classes; he endorsed Pius XII's injunctions to avoid contact with Communist teaching; he exhorted his readers to "that constant obedience demanded from all by the discipline of the Christian Church". The traditional arguments of the centuries of apologetic in defence of the Roman position were faithfully reproduced and those outside were invited to admire "this wonderful manifestation of unity" and were told that "We cherish the hope for your return". The appeal, to those outside, to pray with those inside for unity, is eloquent and moving, and the language is much warmer than that generally used by his predecessors; but it is cautious. The external aim of the Council is shown to be only to attract other Christians by providing an example of unity and concord. All hint that there might be 'reunion sessions' with representatives of other churches, some sort of dialogue between equals, is quite absent. Any reunion resulting from the Council will clearly only be a return of lost sheep to the fold.

However when, after the year spent collecting evidence, Pope John

[1] See Wenger, *Op. cit.*, p. 28.
[2] AAS, LI, p. 497. It is available in CTS translation, S. 254.

was able, at the second Pentecost of his pontificate (May, 1960), to nominate the preparatory commissions to draw up the Council's agenda he breathed new life into the project. (Pentecost was the right occasion on which to do that; he used successive Pentecosts for advancing the Second Vatican Council in the way Pius IX used the Feasts of the Immaculate Conception for advancing the First). "It is from the spirit and the doctrine of Pentecost that the great event of the Ecumenical Council takes its substance and its life."[1] He now made it clear that the Council was not going to be under the control of the Curia. "The government of the Church, which is the occupation of the Roman Curia, is one thing, and the Council is another."[2] (It was rather necessary that he should say this because, although the preparatory commissions, which he was now nominating, contained members from all over the world, with some well known 'liberal' names amongst them, each of these commissions was nevertheless put under the presidency of the cardinal who headed the corresponding department of the Curia; thus, for example, Cardinal Ottaviani, who (under the Pope) presided, as Secretary, over the Holy Office, became President of the Preparatory Theological Commission of the Council, the most important of these new commissions. In this way it was evident that the curial grip upon the work of the Council might easily become a tight one).

It was only on November 13th, 1960, just over two years after the Pope's election, and nearly twenty-two months since he had first proposed the Council, that these preparatory commissions at last met, at a ceremony in St Peter's, to begin their work. More than 2,000 replies had been received from the bishops, the universities, the heads of religious orders, and many others, to Cardinal Tardini's request for suggestions. Now the preparatory commissions (for theology; for bishops and government; for discipline; for the Religious; for the sacraments; for the liturgy; for studies and seminaries; for oriental churches; for missions; for the laity; for ceremonial) could begin work on the agenda, under the general guidance of a central commission, presided over by the Pope, and with the assistance (if they chose to use it) of a newly created Secretariat for Christian Unity under the

[1] DC 1331, Col. 804. (Allocation in AAS, LII, p. 517).
[2] DC 1331, Col. 803.

presidency of Cardinal Bea. And the Pope told them all, that day in St Peter's, that their task was not so much, as in past centuries, to concern themselves with "such and such a point of doctrine, or of discipline, which it was necessary to bring back to the pure sources of revelation and tradition", as "to show in its true light and restore to its real value the quality of human and Christian life, of which the Church is the custodian and mistress throughout the centuries".[1]

This, then, was what he meant by *aggiornamento* – the word he most favoured. It meant not merely a bringing-up-to-date of the Church's message, but an attempt to find the way to reawaken an awareness of the spiritual reality of life. Men had lost sight of this reality so that they had fallen a prey to "the seductions and the dangers of an almost exclusive preoccupation with material goods; forgetful of the principles of the spiritual and supernatural order, whose hold weakens. . . . "

For once, he seems to be bewailing his age. But his optimism soon returns. We have something more to do than "water with our tears our wretched road. On the contrary, we must recover our courage. No; Christ, the Son of God, and our Saviour, has not abandoned the world which He redeemed; and the Church, founded by Him, one, holy, catholic, and apostolic remains still, and for ever, His *mystical Body*."[2] What is needed is somehow to make much more effective the *rapprochement* between the visible Church and mankind as a whole and the Church must lead the way by first taking stock of herself, of her own life, and of the appearance she presents. If she can effectively do this then mankind as a whole will storm her doors, to be reunited with her.

But more than two years had gone by since the Pope's election. On the twenty-fifth of that same month (November 1960) in which he set the preparatory commissions to work he himself became seventy-nine years old. Would he live to see the Council summoned? His Secretary of State, Tardini, had said at a Press conference a year previously that at least three years of preparatory work would be needed before the Council could meet,[3] and in the first of those three not a lot of progress had been made. Had the leisurely pace of the proceedings even been deliberate? How many members of the Curia, who now presided over the different preparatory commissions, were in a hurry to see the

[1] DC 1341, Col. 1480.   [2] *Idem.*
[3] DC 1317, Col. 1494.

arrival of bishops from abroad who might take the opportunity to criticize their stewardship? What inducement, indeed, had the curial cardinals, whether 'traditionalist' or 'progressive', to hasten the arrival of hundreds of bishops whose very purpose must be to question the way they were running their departments? They had everything to lose and nothing to gain from the summoning of the Council. If, as was widely said, they were now "dragging their feet" in. preparing the *schemas*; if, as is likely enough, some of them still hoped that the Council might never assemble, because Pope John could not last very long and a successor (whom they would help to choose) might be differently minded, can one be surprised? The question whether they were 'traditionalists' or 'progressives' was not the only one involved; there was also the natural reluctance of professional officials to see their work interfered with by a host of more than two thousand amateurs.

But if their enthusiasm was likely to be limited why had the Pope made the curial cardinals presidents of the preparatory commissions? He had been careful to explain that the Curia was one thing and the Council another, but he had gone far to put the fate of the Council into the hands of the Curia. The assumption behind the summons of the Council was that the existing forms of expression of the Church's life were out of date; otherwise there could be no need for an *aggiornamento*. Why, then, did he put control of the agenda into the hands of the very people whose methods were implicitly under criticism? And, still more remarkable, why did he allow these preparatory commissions, despite their great size (between them they had some 800 members), to be composed so largely of those who had the favour of the curial establishment? The extent of their predominance was well brought out by those authors who concealed their identity under the pseudonym Xavier Rynne. These authors made various judgements, of varying value, but we are all in their debt for their analysis of the *Annuario Pontificio*, which drew attention to the "interlocking directorate of bishops and monsignors, all Italian", which controls the congregations of the Curia, so that certain names, for example those of Archbishops Parente and Felici, have a remarkable way of reappearing in key positions. But further, for showing that these same names reappeared amongst the lists of the members of the preparatory commissions which were drawing up the *schemas* for the Council. And finally for reminding us of the failure, often noted, to invite so many of the leading progressive theologians of the world to serve on these same commissions.[1]

On the face of it Pope John was allowing the Council to take shape in a way that seemed certain not to produce the *aggiornamento* of the Church which he wanted. One explanation of this paradox is that he was subtly allowing the Curia to think that it was going to be *their* Council, so as to ensure that they would not try to thwart it, while he himself knew very well that once it met it would cease to be theirs, that he (and it) would take over from the Curia. What eventually happened does lend some support to this interpretation, but it displays the Pope in an improbably Machiavellian light. A simpler explanation is that he hoped for a friendly Curia having himself, by March 1960, raised the number of Curial Cardinals to the unprecedented figure of thirty-three, and the Sacred College to no fewer than eighty-five. In any case, he can have had little choice in the matter. Nothing is more difficult for any government than to carry out a policy of which the heads of its own civil service disapprove; some concealment of his further visions must have imposed itself on the Pope. At the same time the merely mechanical difficulties would prevent him from trying to go ahead without the assistance of his civil service. Pius XII could achieve some independence of the Curia, but only in the field of theology, and of foreign policy, in both of which he was the master of them all. To guide the planning of the agenda of a modern General Council, of twenty-five hundred members, and then to assemble it, and set it to work, without using the existing machinery at the Vatican would not have been practicable, and even had it been practicable must have produced tensions which could have engendered a schismatic situation – hardly the best atmosphere for a Council of Unity. To let the Curia have the first word, but to try to prevent it from having the last, was the only course the Pope could pursue.

But might not the Curia have the last word, as well? Any pope less stouthearted than John could well have felt misgivings at the end of the year 1960. The preparatory commissions had settled down to work, but what sort of agenda were they preparing?

[1] See *Letters from Vatican City*, Faber and Faber, 1963, pp. 48–50.

And then again the reactions of the separated brethren continued to be a distinct disappointment. No conviction of the Pope's was deeper than that which had been born of his long years as Pius XII's representative in Bulgaria and Turkey – his conviction that Orthodox and Catholics *ought* to be reunited, there being no insuperable, theological differences to divide them, but rather differences belonging to the realm of Order, accentuated by centuries of political quarrel engendering a mutual distrust for which both sides were to blame. His own relations with the Orthodox in Bulgaria had been friendly, as they had likewise been in Istanbul. In the Orthodox world he had found the Holy Mass celebrated with the greatest possible reverence and dignity, by validly consecrated priests, in the presence of devout congregations; how should these Christians not be one with Catholics throughout the world, who shared the same faith, and who were consoled, like them, by invoking the intercession of the Holy Mother of God? This scandalous and essentially unnecessary betrayal of Our Lord's prayer to His Father, *ut omnes unum sint*, had taken hold upon his spirit, so that in his first Christmas broadcast as Pope, in 1958, he had gone out of his way to make a generous reference to certain Orthodox moves towards religious unity and political peace. There had been, he said, in the Balkans, proposals for common action which were "good and worthy of respect" and had only been frustrated by material interests and nationalist preoccupations that would not prevent him from making every effort to tackle "the agonizing problem of the broken unity of Christ's heritage" and to respond to "the invitation full of love of these separated brothers who likewise bear on their brows the name of Christ, read His holy gospel, and are not insensible to the inspirations of religious piety and the charity that blesses and does good". [1]

This was a very clearly marked overture, which was not ignored in the east. The Ecumenical Patriarch of Constantinople, Athenagoras I, gave it public welcome, in his own New Year's message, pointing out that it was particularly appropriate, at the time of the Feast of the Epiphany, when the thoughts of all Christians turned towards the east, that the Holy Church of Rome should do so; but that this was only to be expected from "the new Pope of Rome, John XXIII, who is so well

[1] DC 1294, Cols. 38 and 39.

known, loved, and respected in our ecclesiastical jurisdictions". But other branches of the Orthodox Church showed less enthusiasm, and some of the Protestants became alarmed. When the World Council of Churches met on the island of Rhodes in August 1959, some Catholic observers present mentioned the possibility of Catholic/Orthodox conversations to be held at Venice, and the Vatican Radio endorsed their remarks; but Protestant complaints that the Orthodox seemed to be going behind their backs, in conversing with Rome, led to denials from the Orthodox that any such conversations were planned, whether at Venice or anywhere else, and the Catholic/Protestant conversations, proposed for October at Assisi, were cancelled.

By the end of 1960, then, practical progress on the ecumenical front was hard to see, even though the Archbishop of Canterbury, Dr Fisher, had paid his courtesy call on the Pope and the Bishop of Southwark had done the same.

Meanwhile the Roman Synod, originally coupled by the Pope with the Council, had come and gone, during the week of January 24th, 1960, without attracting much attention outside Rome or making any marked impression inside. This is not to say that Rome, as depicted in the films of Fellini, was not as seriously in need of rededicated priests, to give her spiritual guidance, as any other great city of the world, or that the spectacle of the Pope endeavouring to set his own diocese in order was not a salutary one for other bishops. But the Pope's coupling of the Synod with the Council had suggested that there would be points of analogy between the two; indeed the saying had circulated that the Synod would be in some sort a "pilot project" for the larger assembly. If that were so it boded ill for the Council, for at the Synod a quantity of suggestions had been obtained from the Roman clergy, digested or discarded at the Vatican, written up in nearly eight hundred constitutions, incorporated into three large volumes, and submitted to the clergy of Rome for debate during the inside of one week. Scarcely any of the constitutions could in fact be debated because scarcely any of the clergy had the chance to speak. They did have the chance to send in their comments during a few weeks after the Synod had dissolved, but by June 28th the final constitutions were promulgated. If the Roman

Synod were really to be seen as a pilot project for the Council (as the Secretary of State, Cardinal Tardini, seems to have encouraged the Pope to see it, perhaps so as to relieve pressure on the preparing of the greater assembly) prospects for that greater assembly were dim indeed. For the constitutions of the Synod were a 'hand-out' from above, and largely of a disciplinary kind.

The Synod, however, was not really a pilot project for the Council. It was one of Roncalli's many enthusiasms, something he wanted to carry out, irrespective of the Council. His spirituality and experience made him rich in constructive ideas, but for so many of them (like his idea of a pilgrimage to the Holy Land and a meeting with the Patriarch of Constantinople) he was not granted the time before he died. This idea of a Roman Synod went back to roots in his early experience, to those impressionable years of his youth when he was secretary to Bishop Radini Tedeschi of Bergamo, who had moulded his outlook towards pastoral work. He had learnt from Radini Tedeschi what a really good bishop could expect from his diocesan clergy and how he could set the highest standards before them and draw the best out of them. But until he became Patriarch of Venice, at the age of seventy-one, Roncalli had never been in charge of a diocese, his life having been concerned with the missions and with diplomacy. As soon as he had been free to practise on his own account what his early training had taught him to see as the great vocation, he returned in spirit to Radini Tedeschi, holding a Synod of Venice (November 1957) at which he told his clergy why it mattered so much that they should be very careful of their daily spiritual duties, of saying their Mass prayerfully, of praying the Breviary, of meditating; telling them that in their preaching they should be gentle, avoiding harshness and controversy. His idea of holding a Synod of his Roman clergy, when he became Bishop of Rome, was entirely in accord with his deepest beliefs, and it is unnecessary to look further for his motives; that he should give an example to the bishops of the world, by taking his own episcopal duties seriously, seemed to him an evident part of his special duty as Bishop of Rome. But the paternalistic character of the occasion, of which the most important episodes were the Bishop's own homilies, differentiated it sharply from the freedom of a General Council.

By the end, then, of the year 1960 (which would prove to be nearly the half-way point of his pontificate) little had actually occurred of a revolutionary character, although a great deal had been said about *aggiornamento*, and about Christian unity, and although a new cordiality had been demonstrated on such occasions as the Pope's conversation with the Archbishop of Canterbury. Nor was it at all clear that anything revolutionary would happen. The decision to summon a General Council had been a big decision, certainly; but what sort of Council would it be? Perhaps it would content itself with codifying afresh the Canon Law, or with giving dogmatic definition to some of the teachings of Pius XII. A realistic appraisal of the membership of its preparatory commissions suggested that the *schemas* they would draw up would be far from revolutionary. Meanwhile Pope John was an old man. After an exuberant first two years as supreme pontiff he might be expected to relax.

Yet, in fact, in the next thirty months, what Karl Barth called "the event" (by which he meant an intervention of God) took place. First *Mater et Magistra* appeared (May 1961); then Cardinal Bea made of the new *Secretariat for Christian Unity* a platform from which the papal appeal for reunion reached every corner of the Christian world; and at last a dialogue began with Moscow, so that when the Council assembled, in October 1962, there were Russian Orthodox observers present. But further; in two dramatic battles, in October and November 1962, the Pope helped to take the leadership of the Council out of the hands of the Curia, and to put it into the hands of the bishops. And finally (April 1963) *Pacem in Terris* was issued, complementing *Mater et Magistra*, and literally reorientating the political outlook of the Church.

Thirty revolutionary months.

In view of the fraternal gestures which were to follow, which would induce some opponents to call him a tool of international Communism,[1] it is interesting to notice how closely, in the first two years of his reign, Roncalli followed the line of Pius XI and Pius XII in regard to the Communists.

[1] Cf the books of "*Lo Svizzero*".

True, his earliest declamations against the Communists were mostly against those of China; but this did not mean that he was "soft on Moscow", or anxious to take advantage of the rift between Moscow and Peking. That rift was not yet conspicuous in 1958; but very conspicuous in that year was an intensification of the Chinese Communist government's campaign against the Church which had led Pius XII, only four months before his death, to send his sympathy and advice to the Chinese hierarchy in his *Ad apostolorum principis* of June 29th. Pope John, addressing a secret consistory on December 15th, noted that, since his predecessor's letter, "a sombre silence, deeper each day, like dark clouds, covers those dioceses. We know that every means is used, every effort made to turn the faithful from the right road and from the unity of the Catholic Church.

"What a sad and afflicting sight! On the one hand the violence of the persecutors, trying to break the spirit of the Chinese Christians, already weakened by the harsh conditions of their life; on the other hand the torments, the anguish and the sufferings of the confessors of the faith who bewail and lament these sacrilegious acts!"[1]

This is in the style of Pius XII; it may, indeed, have been composed by the writer of the late Pope's encyclical to the Chinese hierarchy in the previous June. But it is not an isolated outburst. The new Pope was soon writing to console and fortify a victim of the Czech Communists, Mgr Beran, Archbishop of Prague, who had been suffering house arrest for ten years since being seized, in his cathedral, by agents of the government; already he had written letters of sympathy to Cardinals Mindzenty and Stepinac, under detention in Hungary and Yugoslavia, who had been unable to be present at the recent conclave or coronation. And within three months of his election he had written to console the clergy and faithful of North Vietnam.[2] His first Palm Sunday saw him likening those who oppressed the Church of Silence to those who cried out for the crucifixion of Our Lord and those whom St Paul called "enemies of the Cross of Christ".[3] In April 1959, he allowed the Holy Office to endorse the ban placed by Pius XII on Catholic electoral support for the Communists and to make it clearer

[1] DC 1294, Col. 3.   AAS, L, p. 984.
[2] DC 1298, Col. 283.   [3] DC 1328, Cols. 581, 582.

that the ban also covered support for those parties which were working with the Communists – i.e. the Socialists.[1] In his first encyclical, *Ad Petri Cathedram* (June 29th, 1959), he assured his readers, with what seems almost complacency, that "an impartial consideration of all the advantages that have accrued to the worker within recent years leads inevitably to the conclusion that they are the direct result of the zealous and effective social action taken by Catholics in accordance with the wise directives and oft-repeated exhortations of Our Predecessors ... those who wish to retain our Christian heritage must regard it as a most serious obligation in conscience to avoid those false teachings which Our Predecessors of happy memory, especially Pius XI and Pius XII, have already condemned".[2] And in his Easter message of 1960 his firmness on Communism was still made manifest and the world seemed wonderfully clearly divided between the sheep and the goats: "On the one side stand Christ and those who, within the Church, represent Him and who follow Him in holiness and charity and find in the Church wholesome doctrine, truth, justice, and peace. On the other side rages the anti-Christian spirit, which is error, a false conception both of private and of social life, an abuse of power which inflicts material damage, disorder, misery, and ruin. ... On this Easter morning, while around us everything engenders spiritual joy some of our brethren – and it is very painful to Us to be brought back to this matter – do not enjoy liberty, neither individual, nor civil, nor religious; year after year they have been subject to constraint and violence and have been the victims of a sacrifice at which a ceaseless oppression has met with nothing but their silence."[3]

Yet sometimes, even in this first phase of the pontificate, when the norms for so long laid down by Pius XII still set the pattern of papal utterance, some conciliatory notes were introduced by the new Pope which his predecessor would scarcely have allowed himself. There was an interesting example in the message he sent in February 1959 to the ceremony at Lourdes, when the centenary year of the apparitions ended. It contained an implication that the *motives* impelling the Communist revolt might be generous, when the Pope spoke of " ... these

[1] DC 1302, Col. 526.   [2] CTS p. 35. AAS, LI, p. 526.
[3] DC 1327, Col. 514.   AAS, LII, pp. 370, 371.

days in which millions of men have their conscience stirred – some-times, alas! are led to revolt – by the scandalous contrast between the well-being enjoyed by some and the lack of the very necessities of life suffered by others".[1] Nor did he neglect to pray for the persecutors: To Christ "rises an unceasing prayer, to gain, for Our persecuted bro-thers, constancy and strength, and for the miserable persecutors, 'who know not what they do' . . . enlightenment, pardon, and conversion".[2] And when Cardinal Stepinac, who had suffered for so long, in the custody of the Yugoslav government, died on February 10th, 1960, Roncalli went out of his way to recognize "a spark of human pity" in that government because it had emulated the government of Pilate by allowing its victim to be buried and mourned by his friends: "Amidst the immense grief which continues to penetrate Our spirit, We note the gesture of the authorities which, following the example of the ancient Roman governor, have allowed some expression of popular homage towards the venerated earthly remains of the illustrious pastor and father. . . . "[3]

The crumbs of consolation which reached Rome from behind the iron curtain were assuredly, as yet, not very sustaining, and Roncalli's references to the Communists seemed likely to continue to resemble those of Pius XII. But in the west, in France, he was expected to have something more positive to say. He had inherited from his predecessor a problem in France, presented by the movement launched by the 'worker-priests'. Some of these priests were trying to win the workers back to Christianity by sharing with them their toil, and the crudities of their life; and they had attracted much attention ever since their mission began in Paris, where Father Perrin had taken employment in a factory in 1944. In 1954 the French hierarchy, after conversations with Pius XII, had laid it down that such work must not occupy more than three hours of a priest's day, and that he must not enter into trade union activity. Pius had been anxious to preserve, for the priest, the necessary time for his spiritual duties – saying Mass, reading the breviary, prayer and pastoral work – and to ensure that he was not caught up in social

[1] DC 1298, Col. 276.
[2] DC 1306, Col. 771. (Pentecost, May 17th, 1959).
[3] DC 1324, Col. 344.   AAS, LII, p. 93.

controversy. From that time the amber light of caution was clearly shining for the worker-priests. But Roncalli, as Papal Nuncio in France, had shown appreciation of the generous motives of their movement, which had enjoyed the powerful support of his friend, Cardinal Feltin, the Archbishop of Paris. Though he had been careful not to give it any official approval, on behalf of Pius XII, the hopes of the movement's supporters naturally rose high when he became Pius's successor, and the disappointment when, in the first year of his pontificate, he banned it altogether was correspondingly great.

He did it quietly, on July 3rd, 1959, by means of a confidential letter from Cardinal Pizzardo, Secretary to the Holy Office, to Cardinal Feltin, Archbishop of Paris and President of the Workers' Mission. The reasons given were: " . . . On his days of work it would be almost impossible for the priest to fulfil all the duties of prayer which the Church requires from him on each day: the celebration of Holy Mass, faithful recitation of the breviary, mental prayer, visit to the Blessed Sacrament, and saying of the rosary.

"And even if some were to achieve this, they would still be devoting to manual work time which ought to be employed in priestly ministrations or in sacred study. . . .

"For the rest, work in a factory, or even in less important undertakings, gradually exposes the priest to being influenced by his surroundings. The 'worker-priest' not only finds himself plunged into a materialistic environment, harmful to his spiritual life and often even dangerous to his chastity, but he is also led, despite himself, to think like his brother workers on social or union matters and to take part in their quarrels: a frightening corruption which soon leads him to take part in the class struggle. But this is not permitted to a priest.

"Such are the reasons which have decided the most eminent cardinals of the Holy Office to decide upon the cessation of the work of priests as workers or employees in the factories and other such enterprises, or as sailors. . . .

"In the audience of June 11th, 1959, the Holy Father has deigned to approve these decisions and, when he received Your Eminence on the same day, he expressed to him his view on the matter. After having read the report which Your Eminence presented to him, His Holiness has judged it necessary to confirm the decrees of the Holy Office of the 10th and 24th June. . . . "[1]

Those who had supposed that Pope John, of worker origin himself, would favour the mission of the worker-priests had forgotten the depth of his attachment to the special character of the priestly office as hallowed by Catholic tradition. They had given too little thought to the strength of his own devotional life or to the training he had received from Bishop Radini Tedeschi of Bergamo, from whom he had gained so active a belief in the vital importance of strict attention to the full life of prayer, of spiritual exercises, and of piety. Whatever his sympathies with the workers, however great his desire to see them brought back into the fold, he was never likely to give his support to plans which involved any diminution of the time devoted by priests to their spiritual duties or which might tend to lead them into accepting the standards of this world. At his Roman Synod he not only exhorted the priests of his diocese to the most punctual fidelity in their devotions, but he tightened somewhat the regulations which kept their life apart from the life of the laity. Roncalli believed, in the fullest sense, in the special character and quality of the priesthood, and that it needed to be sustained by a special kind of life, and especially by the life of prayer and withdrawal.[2] Only from that soil could grow the priest's apostolate in the world.

Firm on the fullest traditional disciplines of the priesthood, he also showed himself firm, and conservative, from the beginning of his reign, on a subject of much smaller consequence – the use of Latin in the Church's liturgy. Just why he should have been so ardent for Latin has puzzled many who responded to his enthusiasm for an *aggiornamento* of the Church, but who thought that one way in which to bring her up to date would be to present her liturgy in terms intelligible to ordinary people in the twentieth century by using a language those

[1] DC 1313, Col. 1224.

[2] In the same month as he banned the worker-priests' movement he issued his encyclical *Sacerdoti Nostri primordia* on the centenary of the death of the Curé d'Ars, which gave him an opportunity to emphasize the priestly duty of prayer. DC 1310, Col. 1025. AAS, LI, p. 545.

people could understand. So unwilling have such critics been to believe that Pope John could really have intended to ensure that Latin should remain the language both of the sacred liturgy and of the higher sacred studies that they have invented all sorts of stories to suggest that he signed the Apostolic Constitution on the subject[1] without reading it, or even that he was so sure the Council would reverse his instruction that he was willing to appease the conservatives by issuing it. Such explanations do scant justice to his habit of giving the closest attention to the major documents sent out over his signature or to the fact that, on this occasion, he took the opportunity of the Feast of the Chair of St Peter (February 22nd) to commend his Constitution, in a special way, to a gathering which included forty cardinals, one hundred bishops, the whole of the Curia, the preconciliar commissions, and the professors and pupils of the colleges and seminaries of Rome. The point which he emphasized was that Latin, which had given unity both to the Church, and to the known world, in the days of the Roman Empire, and which had held the Church together after the rise of different nations, with their own vernacular languages, was more than ever needed today because of the multiplicity of new peoples, with different languages, which were achieving their independence. 'The language of Rome, used in the Church of the Latin rite, particularly between her priests from different territories, can once again give noble service to the work of pacification and unification.'[2] In other words, that very strangeness of Latin to the newly emergent nations which has seemed to many reformers the main argument against its continued use appeared to Pope John to be the chief reason why it should be retained; it would some-how "hold the Church together" in an increasingly particularist world.

But probably a stronger influence on Roncalli than the old arguments about the use of Latin in the past, or the new arguments about its potential role in emergent Africa in the present, was the simple fact that he loved Latin and believed it to be the "Church's own language." He also loved it because he was Italian enough to have a sentimental attachment to the parent of the Italian language and the expression of the

[1] *Veterum Sapientia*, February 22nd, 1962, CTS, No. Do. 334. AAS, LIV, p. 129.
[2] DC 1372, Col. 360.

Roman culture. Few Italians are keen vernacularists, and it would be surprising if they were. Roncalli loved Latin, too, with the love of the rather amateur scholar. It was a part of the panoply of learning which he personally shared. He might not be able to write or speak it in the manner of Leo XIII or of Pius XII, but he could take pleasure in it, and he was distressed when he delivered it badly in public. During his spiritual retreat before the opening of the Council he had Father Ciappi come and talk Latin with him every morning "in as much as I may need it during the general meetings over which I preside at the Council".[1] He took frequent opportunities to quote Cicero, or Lactantius, and in one of his earliest addresses he told the First International Congress of Ciceronian studies, assembled at Rome, that too many people were studying science and mathematics and technology and were becoming like the machines they made "cold, hard, and without love". Moreover "by a providential disposition of God, the wisdom of the ancient Greeks and Latins was often the dawn which heralded the gospel of Christ".[2] Had not St Augustine himself, in his *Confessions*, paid his tribute to Cicero's *Hortensius*? And so on. We have no reason to suppose that, when Cardinal Bacci told him that some of the reformers were calling in question the Church's continued use of Latin he was not properly shocked; and we know that, when the same Cardinal set forth the arguments for using Latin as the language of the General Council, he accepted them. Already Cardinal Tardini, the Secretary of State, had told the Press (October 31st, 1959) that Latin, "the language of the Church", would be the language of the Council, and that simultaneous translation, of the kind in general use today at international conferences, would not be provided "because in matters of faith, a word badly translated or at least not exactly translated could give rise to confusion"[3] – the confusion resulting from so many bishops being unable to speak or understand Latin readily seems to have been regarded as of less consequence. In the *Osservatore Romano* (July 3rd, 1960) Cardinal Bacci summed up by saying that " . . . this language which, at the beginning, cemented the union of so many peoples in the vast unity of the Roman

[1] *Il Giornale Dell' Anima*, p. 327.
[2] DC 1302, Col. 518. (Address of April 4th, 1959.)
[3] DC 1317, Col. 1494.

Empire and, later on, through the action of the Church, served to unite, in the brotherhood of a great family, that is to say in the *civitas christiana*, the barbarous peoples pouring in from all sides, can serve yet again as a powerful means of communication during the future Ecumenical Council and provide, not only a uniting link within the Church, but once again a uniting link between the peoples.

"Thanks also to this link of linguistic unity there will appear before the eyes of all the peoples divided by so many ideologies, so many conflicts, so many different idioms, the superiority of Rome. . . . "[1] Cardinal Bacci might perhaps have put the matter in a manner less calculated to pain American or German readers of the *Osservatore*; but at least he made his meaning clear. Somehow Ancient Rome, Latin, and Catholicism were one, and the aim was to re-establish the *Civitas Christiana*.

Besides the dubious history required to sustain such a concept (and ably exposed by Hans Küng in Part 3, Chapter 2, of his *The Living Church*) the kind of formal unity envisaged was strangely out of harmony with the kind of spiritual unity Pope John preached. Yet we are obliged to recognize that Cardinal Bacci's conception of the immense significance of Latin to Catholicism pleased the Pope. It is to be supposed that the Cardinal wrote the Pope's Apostolic Constitution on Latin; but the Pope endorsed it in the strongest terms. Nothing that any of his predecessors, even the Latinists among them, said on the subject of Latin went as far as *Veterum Sapientia*. After repeating all the familiar arguments about the value of a universal and immutable (because dead) language, about the need for a language which is "noble and majestic and non-vernacular", and after arguing that Latin makes for "highly intelligent thought and speech", this Constitution goes on to require that bishops and superiors-general shall be on guard "lest anyone under their jurisdiction . . . writes against the use of Latin in the teaching of the higher sacred studies or in the liturgy". Professors in universities and seminaries who are unable to teach the sacred sciences in Latin are to be replaced. The Sacred Congregation of Seminaries and Universities is to set up a Latin Academy which shall coin new Latin words to meet the new needs of today. And the same congrega-

[1] DC 1334, Col. 1008.

tion will draw up a syllabus for the teaching of Latin which shall be observed everywhere. Moreover all students for the priesthood are not only to study Latin diligently but also Greek.

One can only suppose that, having been taught in Latin, and having prayed in Latin, and being well versed in some rather simplified classical history, Roncalli had somehow come to identify the language with the Faith in a way which made him see an attack on the one as an attack on the other. Many (including Radini Tedeschi and Roncalli himself) had been worried by the witch-hunt set up in Italy as a result of the anti-Modernist campaign. But what are we to think about this implicit invitation to a witch-hunt against those questioning the use of Latin? We cannot escape from the difficulty by pretending that Roncalli intended that this Constitution, which he recommended and signed "on the occasion of this solemn assembly which is a prelude to the Council", should be revoked by that same Council. Nevertheless the Council did save the Church from the consequences of the position he had adopted. And, since he had always intended the Council to be free, he would doubtless have yielded with a good grace, and a broad smile, had he lived to see it debating, in bad Latin, the use of Latin, and deciding in favour of more limited use of that language in the liturgy.

This matter of Pope John's attitude towards the use of Latin has carried us out of the first half of his pontificate, since *Veterum Sapientia* was not published until February 22nd, 1962. But the decision to use Latin at the Council belongs to the earlier period and belongs, too, with the conservative and cautious preparations being made for the Council, which were modelled on those made by Pius IX for the First Vatican Council, and which left the real control in the hands of the Curia. Very little that Roncalli did before the opening of the year 1961 suggested that he had, in fact, radical intentions. He made friendly gestures towards other Churches. And he began the preparatory work for the Council. But it was still quite uncertain that the Council itself would prove to be a reforming Council. His favourite word for its task – *aggiornamento* – was very vague. It might yet end by codifying and defining the work of Pius XII.

One of the targets of the reformers was the Index of Prohibited

Books, drawn up by the Holy Office. But there is no indication that it was one of Pope John's targets. He himself appointed Cardinal Ottaviani to his post as Secretary to the Holy Office. In November 1959, an Italian congress of ecclesiastical censors met in Rome and was treated by the Cardinal to a passionate defence of the Index. "The red light which stops the reading of certain books," he explained, using rather an odd analogy, "is like a traffic signal. Nobody complains about traffic signals on the grounds that he is an intelligent and practical man who can judge for himself."[1] And the Pope, addressing the same congress two days later, left his audience in no doubt that their task, though it should be performed with charity and understanding, was of supreme importance, and that no compromises could be allowed which might be prejudicial "to the sacred deposit of doctrine or to the souls of the faithful".[2] In the following month he pleaded with the Union of Italian Catholic Jurists for a closer censorship of the sensational Press.[3]

The reformers were also asking for an extension of the role of the laity in the Church. Roncalli was eloquent on the value of the laity, especially in the field of education, and in the missions;[4] but he said nothing to suggest that they should cease to work only as auxiliaries of the clergy. Catholic Action to him, as to his predecessors, was an army directed by generals – the bishops – to whom obedience was obligatory.

In all these matters Pope John resembled somewhat that other pope of humble origin from the Lombard plain, St Pius X. An implicit faith, a simple piety, a strict devotion to Catholic traditions, and a complete indifference to worldly possessions were the glory of both.

Yet the strong, simple, implicit faith of the two men, their piety and their search for sanctification, led them, as occupants of the Holy See, in different directions. Whereas St Pius developed a deepening horror of divergence and 'insubordination', social and political as well as religious, Pope John, soon after his accession, was finding it necessary

[1] DC 1318, Col. 1571.   [2] DC 1318, Col. 1567.   [3] DC 1319, Cols. 1–6.
[4] c.f., especially, his encyclicals *Ad Petri Cathedram* (June 29th, 1959) and *Princeps Pastorum* (November 28th, 1959), CTS S. 254 and Do. 315;   AAS, LI, pp. 497 and 833.

to excuse himself for being so seemingly easy-going: " . . . let Us share with you a great secret, a fatherly confidence," he told a congregation at Santa Maria Maggiore: "The natural inclination of your new Pope to expound doctrine with calm and simplicity rather than to underline strongly points of disagreement or the negative aspects of thought and action does not obscure his appreciation of his formidable pastoral responsibilities, leading him to see the need, from time to time, to tackle this or that aspect of Catholic doctrine which is certainly not calculated to appeal to his listeners."[1] Perhaps he was sensitive on the point. *Vogliamoci bene* (let us wish each other well) had been a good signature-theme in Bulgaria; it may have impressed Italian audiences less.

But if he meant to try to be more severe he did not succeed. In the second phase of his pontificate, which may be said to have begun towards the end of the year 1960, his determination to move out into the world, with a new and positive message, and to avoid rebuke or censure, took increasing hold upon him. It was then that he became the "parish priest of the world". But this did not make him any less of a traditionalist so far as discipline or devotion were concerned. What he did want to see was a new relationship between the Church and the world. His *aggiornamento* was a bringing of the Church up to date, not by changing her discipline or her traditions, but by bringing her into a closer relationship with contemporary civilization.

2 · IN HIS LEAD TO THE COUNCIL

It was in the late autumn of 1960 that those who had become rather bored by the leisurely developments at Rome began to realize that something momentous was, after all, being prepared, and that those Frenchmen who had said that the Pope was *pas sérieux* were wrong.

November 1960 may be taken as the month when this new wind began to rise, not so much because that was when the preparatory commissions of the Council settled down to work (for the *schemas* they produced proved mostly dated and pedestrian), nor because this was the month when the Archbishop of Canterbury called on the Pope, but because it was the month when the Secretariat for Christian Unity

[1] February 15th, 1959, DC 1299, Col. 328.

began its labours. To those with an eye only for administrative machinery it might appear that this new Secretariat was of less consequence than were the preparatory commissions, its function being to feed those commissions with information and suggestions from the separated brethren. In a formal sense this was so; a Secretariat is subordinate to a Commission; but this would prove no ordinary Secretariat.

There was ground to be made up if the interest of the world were to revive. After the initial disillusionment in 'separated' circles during the year 1959, when it was seen that Rome did not envisage a Council of Unity but only a General Council of the Roman Church, there had been an understandable inclination to 'write off' the ecumenical potential of the Council, and the forming of the new Secretariat might have done little to reassure Christian opinion had not Pope John put it into the hands of a fellow septuagenarian, a year older than himself, with energy and vision almost equal to his own, the Jesuit Augustin Bea, whom he had created Cardinal six months earlier. To Bea, without doubt, he owed many of his own ideas about a new initiative to bridge the divisions between Christians; and to Bea he now gave a free hand. Even this powerful patronage did not enable the Cardinal to influence some of the preparatory commissions; by the powerful Theological Commission he was quietly ignored. But his Secretariat had a two-way function, to explain the separated brethren to Rome and Rome to the separated brethren. If it was blocked in its attempt to do the former it was free to do the latter because it was given a warm welcome by the world outside, and out into that world the Cardinal went, to Switzerland and Germany, to France and England, and to the United States, explaining what the Secretariat was for, inviting suggestions, opening up the 'dialogue', until the quip was running round the Roman cafés "See the world with BEA". With the help of his Secretary, Mgr Jan Willebrands, the Cardinal made contact with a wide range of Protestant groups, and they learnt how they could bring their beliefs and thinking to bear upon the work of the Council and where the Roman Church stood on the various matters affecting Christian Unity.

The Cardinal was not alone in this field. Taking their cue from the new Roman initiative many others, notably the theologian Hans Küng of Tubingen, were out on the lecture-platform, and their greater freedom from responsibility enabled them to say more startling things than passed the lips of the Cardinal. There were also five Catholic theologians present as observers at the Assembly of the World Council of Churches at New Delhi in November 1961, an innovation prepared by the presence of Mgr Willebrands at the meeting of the World Council's Central Committee at St Andrews in August 1960. But by the end of 1960 the normal avenue of approach for the separated brethren who wanted to make contact with the planning of the Council, as likewise for those at Rome who wanted information, became Bea's Secretariat, and it was the Cardinal and Willebrands who had most to do with laying down the lines along which better relations might be sought, at least with the Protestants.

The Cardinal's speeches were cautious, but they were also hopeful. There must be no "minimizing", he insisted, of any point of dogma. "When we talk of greater respect and understanding between Catholics and non-Catholics there is no question at all of adopting their outlook or their faith."[1] There could be no entry of the Catholic Church into the World Council of Churches because she herself *was* the Church. Those not in communion with Rome could only come as observers to the Council; they could not share in its work. On the other hand there was no doubt that all baptized Christians were members of Christ's mystical body, though they shared its life less fully if they were not in communion with Rome. It was wrong to regard their separation as the *fault* of Protestants; in the vast majority of cases they inherited a standpoint to which they adhered in good faith. And even their ancestors, who had made the separation, might not have been blameworthy; the blame might, in some instances (including that of England), be laid partly at the door of Rome, but only in the sense that even a loving mother may make mistakes, without ceasing, on that account, to be truly a mother. "This meeting" Cardinal Bea said of Dr Fisher's call upon the Pope "took place after four centuries of complete separation and while separation is still a sorrowful reality. For the Catholic Church ... it is a separation of the children from their mother the Church.

[1] Address of April, 1962, published in *The Unity of Christians* (Geoffrey Chapman, 1963). See p. 55.

We are, as it were, gazing in upon the private sorrow of a mother and her shame for a stigma which has brought disgrace and dishonour to her great Christian family."[1]

The Cardinal's speeches were realistic and moderate. He never disguised the fact that the obstacles in the way of unity were – humanly speaking – insuperable. Underlying a large number of them, he believed, was the difficulty Protestants had in grasping the idea of the Church, an idea so much fuller and more formidable for Catholics than for Protestants, and carrying with it a requirement of obedience which was both strange to Protestants and also out of harmony with the temper of the times, which set few limits to the moral freedom of the individual. But, as the Pope was always insisting, the matter would not be decided by human beings; Christ had prayed that his followers might be one, and in the end, because He willed it, one they would become.

Recognizing in the Cardinal and his Secretariat a genuine attempt on the part of Rome to enter into a dialogue on the problems of unity, the Protestant Churches responded generously. The World Council agreed to be represented at the Vatican Council, so did a number of its major constituent Churches, though notably not – as yet – the Orthodox Churches. Bea's Secretariat was not at first concerned with the Orthodox world, that being the province of the Preparatory Commission for the Eastern Church. The Secretariat's members were mostly drawn from leading Catholic clergy in Protestant countries, and in Germany and Holland, England and America, it was given a good welcome. Bea – a German – noted that the conditions for dialogue were especially favourable in that country where some dialogue, across the many deep divisions, was a practical necessity. In England the then Catholic Archbishop of Liverpool, John Heenan (well known to be a friend of the then Anglican Archbishop of York, Dr Ramsey), was a member, and Dr Fisher of Canterbury considered that the opening of this new channel of communication with Rome was "full of Godly promise".

Meanwhile the Pope was moving ahead. In an address on June 28th,

[1] *The Unity of Christians*, p. 69.

1961, he put into clear relation the two first functions of the Council: *aggiornamento* of the Catholic Church, and the opening of the way to Christian reunion: "God wills that to [the Council's] work on the condition of the Church herself, and her *aggiornamento*, after twenty centuries of life – which is the principal task – there should be added, as a result of the edification we may give, but especially by the grace of an all-powerful God, some progress towards the drawing together of Our Lord's mystical flock."[1] – i.e. the flock of all baptized Christians.

These objectives had now become firm, even crystallized, and the Pope never wavered in regard to them. All the world now knew in what sense this would be a "Reunion Council"; what was lacking in the organs of publicity at Rome was more than balanced by the zeal of Cardinal Bea.

Yet there was, in fact, a third objective gradually taking a stronger hold over the Pope's mind, though it was difficult of definition. Somehow the Council was to benefit no less a cause than the brotherhood and peace of mankind. Later on, in *Ecclesiam Suam*, Pope Paul would speak of three concentric circles: an inner circle, the Catholic Church, a middle circle, the separated brethren, and an outer circle, mankind as a whole. Pope John thought in the same terms; somehow the new light from the centre was to irradiate all three circles and bring new life to the world.

Cardinal Bea, however, was only permitted by his terms of reference to concern himself with the second circle, the unity of Christians; so it was perhaps natural that he should talk about what baptized Christians held in common rather than about what mankind held in common. In doing that he could hardly avoid drawing a sharp distinction between baptized Christians on the one hand and those who stood outside any Christian denomination on the other. "A baptized person" he said "whoever he may be, is not for us the same as a Moslem, a Buddhist, or a Brahmin. A baptized person is our brother in Christ, and we must strive to let him share, not only the graces the Lord gives him in virtue of baptism, but also all the other great graces which Jesus has placed in the hands of the Church, especially in the sacraments, and above all in the great sacrifice of the Holy Mass and of Holy

[1] DC 1358, Col. 1022.

Communion."[1] His view of mankind could be expressed in terms of their greater or their lesser sharing in the sacramental means of grace; indeed those are the terms in which he himself expressed it. The Moslem, the Buddhist, and the Brahmin are without the means of grace; the Protestant has some means, the Orthodox has more, the Catholic has most. "The Protestant inheritance from the Mother Church is not as rich as the Oriental, unfortunately, but they too have preserved precious elements of Catholic doctrine and worship, although the amount varies with the different forms of Protestantism. . . . "[2] What he believed to be most important was for Christians, as a whole, to present a strong front in the face of the non-Christian world. "The Church of Christ is faced with a secularized, technological and materialistic world. . . . The Church of Christ, today more than ever, needs to be strong, and its strength will depend on its unity."[3] If only Christians were united, in practical co-operation at least, what, he was fond of asking, might they not achieve? – for these Christians were almost a thousand million people, one third of the world!

But one cannot help noticing that he was far less inclined than Pope John to recognize *the brotherhood of mankind*, or to admit any relationship with the unbaptized, the non-Christians. Of the non-Catholic but baptized Christians – the separated brethren – he said that they belonged to the Church. "They are 'sons' of the Church and our 'brothers'; the Pope calls these 'separated brethren' also his 'sons'. This he does not say and could never say about those who are not baptized, who are not Christian."[4] Strictly speaking this was not so. The Pope did, on occasion, call all men his sons.[5] The theological truth which the Secretary for Christian Unity was expressing is clear enough; yet all men are brothers, in as much as the same God created them, and sent His son to redeem them, so that, potentially at least, His Vicar is their father, whether they recognize him or no. Already Roncalli had written in his journal: "All the world is my family. This sense of everybody belonging should colour my mind, my heart, and my actions, and give them life.

"This vision, this feeling of universality, shall enliven henceforth all

[1] *The Unity of Christians*, p. 81.   [2] *Ibid.*, p. 27.   [3] *Ibid.*, p. 34.
[4] *Ibid.*, p. 83.   [5] Cf below, p. 132

my constant and uninterrupted daily prayer. . . . "[1] And later, in the privacy of that same book, he affirmed that fatherhood of all men to which he could hardly give public expression: "After my first Mass, above the tomb of St Peter, there were the hands of the Holy Father, Pius X, placed on my head in first blessing of me in my new life as a priest; and after a further half century (fifty years exactly) here are my own hands extended over Catholics – and not over Catholics only – over the whole world in witness of my universal fatherhood. . . . "[2]

Those who called him the parish priest of the world, *Il Parroco del Monde*, were saying the same thing.

Cardinal Bea had been appointed to promote Christian unity. That was the extent of his mission – a sufficient one, in all conscience. But the way in which the mind of his master was already ranging more widely yet became clear for all to see when, in May 1961, he published *Mater et Magistra*. He was thinking not merely of reuniting Christians, or bringing those outside into the fold of the Church, but in terms of human rights and welfare, and of reconciling the nations with each other, whatever their religion, or lack of religion, or hostility to religion. In this lay the secret of the new hold he was now gaining over the imagination of the world; men sensed the fact that he sought disinterestedly, and on behalf of all men, unity, peace, and justice.

We scarcely get a hint, at this stage, in the speeches of Cardinal Bea, of this wider view, and it would have been inappropriate for him to have given one. His task was to help to bring the severed family of Christians together again. Nevertheless Moslems, Hindus, Marxists, scientific humanists and rationalists were all God's children, and the Pope was God's Vicar. If he could not bring them into the Christian family he could yet concern himself, and cause the Church to concern herself, on their behalf, and in doing that he and the Church would be helping to do God's work in the world. It was a world in desperate distress in the poorer countries and in desperate danger in all countries. Hence *Mater et Magistra*. And hence that peculiar aura of

[1] *Il Giornale Dell' Anima*, p. 304 (Notes of a spiritual retreat of November 29th to December 5th 1959).

[2] *Ibid.*, p. 307. (Notes on a spiritual retreat on 10th–15th August, 1961).

universal significance with which Roncalli was already beginning to surround the Council and his constant repetition of the words Unity and Peace, by which he meant nothing less than the unity of the world, and the peace of the world, peace between East and West, peace between new nations and old nations, and not merely unity and peace between baptized Christians – difficult as that would be to get.

We have, then, to notice, throughout the second half of the pontificate, not merely the important efforts of Cardinal Bea, and his Secretariat for Christian Unity, which helped to put the relations between Rome and the separated brethren on a new basis, but the growth of something wider, though more difficult to define, namely the efforts of Pope John to make the Council a light for all mankind and an occasion for the drawing together of humanity at large in her search for peace and justice. By the autumn of 1962, when the Council was on the point of assembling, this wider aspect of its significance had evidently come to dominate his thinking.

But it had always been in his mind. It appeared in an address he gave to the chaplains of Italian Catholic Action as far back as July 7th, 1959. He was talking about Saints Cyril and Methodius, whose feast day it was, and who were apostles to the Slavic world. "The admirable undertakings of Saints Cyril and Methodius bring before our eyes horizons which, indeed, we cannot yet clearly see, because a great curtain – the iron curtain – covers them.

"We like to think that, in answer to our prayers, and to our sacrifices, divine Providence is in the course of elucidating one of the greatest mysteries of history, the mystery of the mercy of the Lord for all peoples."[1]

We are told that the Pope spoke, on this occasion, with a very special seriousness and emotion; but it was not till the beginning of 1961 that he developed the theme of peace between East and West:

"It is the search after peace that we would commend to the whole world at the opening of this new year," he said in January. . . . "The brief and partial brightening of the international horizon only makes the general disillusionment more painful. We have even reached the point of abusing that sweet word 'peace', as though it were an instru-

[1] DC 1310, Col. 1052.

ment not for bringing men together in harmony but for fomenting rivalry and discord. [An allusion to the controversies surrounding the Communist sponsored Peace Congresses.]

"But We would like to hope – and in Our prayers We ask it continually of the Lord – that once the legitimate aspirations of the peoples towards liberty and independence have been satisfied, the richer will help the poorer, the stronger will sustain the weaker, the more advanced will guide the less developed, and all will in the end feel themselves to be brothers because all sons of the same very loving Father who is in Heaven."[1]

Here we have a preview of *Mater et Magistra*, which followed in May, with its concern for the underdeveloped and emergent nations. We also have a clear expression of the brotherhood of man under the fatherhood of God. And there is a seeming neutrality on the great quarrel between East and West: we are not given to understand that the eastern European nations – the Baltic states, Poland, Hungary, Czechoslovakia, and the rest – are the ones whose "legitimate aspirations towards liberty and independence" need first to be satisfied. What he says is that the "poorer" the "weaker", the "less developed" are the objects of his concern, and these would be the emergent nations of Africa and Asia. Had the Pope been *primarily* concerned for the rights of the Church he would have been *primarily* concerned, as Pius XII usually was, for the liberties of eastern Europe. But he was primarily concerned for the welfare and peace of mankind.

In May the great encyclical itself at last appeared.[2] The 'build-up' for *Mater et Magistra* was considerable; the Pope was concerned to hurry the various vernacular translations; he had given more than one hint that he was about to say something important. Later, during the remaining two years of his pontificate, he never ceased to hark back to it; its principles were to be studied in the seminaries, by Catholic Action, by sincere Catholics everywhere. We have already discussed its teaching. It is only necessary here to remind ourselves that its concern was with all men, in particular with their social welfare; their education;

[1] DC 1346, Cols. 226, 227.

[2] Text in AAS, LIII, p. 401 (Latin); DC 1357, Col. 945 (French); CTS pamphlet S. 259 (English).

their legitimate aspirations to national independence; their right, in poorer communities, to receive assistance from the rich; and their right, in international organization, to secure mutual aid, but above all peace. There is remarkably little in it about the Church, though the whole is naturally given a Christian, even a neo-Thomist theological basis, which brings it into some sort of relationship with the earlier social encyclicals, but does not persuade the reader that it takes its inspiration from them.

In the following summer (August and September 1961) came the Berlin crisis, arising from the East German decision to build the Berlin Wall. August was a month of constant anxiety about the danger of war, and on September 10th the Pope issued a powerful appeal for peace. Recalling the efforts of his predecessors to prevent, or to bring an end to the two world wars, he explained that the ways of peace were the ways of God and that "the Church, by her very nature, cannot remain indifferent to human suffering, even when it is only a matter of 'preoccupation, of an anguished anxiety. . . . ' "[1] He urged the world to remember that the Church was coming to the aid of World Peace by means of the General Council: "Consider that the Catholic Church, spread over the whole face of the globe – alas, today, disturbed and divided – is moving towards a world assemblage – the Ecumenical Council – directed towards the true brotherhood of the peoples."[2] And he made his appeal "to all Our sons, to all those whom We feel the right and the duty to call such, to those who believe in God and in His Christ, and also to the unbelievers, because all belong to God, and to Christ, by virtue of their origin and their redemption".[3]

It is interesting to notice that he makes clear, in this last quotation, the distinction he draws, in the manner of Cardinal Bea, between those he may openly call his "sons" (who believe in God and in His Christ) and those who do not believe but nevertheless are really his because they, too, belong to God, and thus to Christ, and so to Christ's Vicar.

We may also notice that his appeal was answered by Premier Kruschev:

"The concern for world peace shown by the Pope" said the Soviet dictator "shows that it is becoming better understood, abroad, that

[1] DC 1361, Col. 1202.   [2] DC 1361, Col. 1205.   [3] DC 1361, Col. 1203.

unreason and irresponsibility in world politics lead to no good. The Head of the Catholic Church is taking into account, to all appearances, the outlook of many millions of Catholics throughout the world, who are disturbed because of the military preparations of the imperialists. John XXIII pays his homage to sound reason when he warns those who govern of the danger of a general catastrophe and appeals to them to take into account the enormous responsibility which they bear towards history. Such an appeal is a good sign."[1]

"Good Catholics, like John Kennedy and Konrad Adenauer" are invited by Premier Kruschev to take note. They need not worry about the Pope's references to the judgement of God because, the Soviet leader explains, God does not exist. But they will do well to recall their responsibilities before their peoples, before humanity, and before history.

This was the opening of the so-called 'dialogue' between Pope John and Premier Kruschev, which would develop during 1962, and further still in 1963. The Russian leader found the new papal attitude useful, and was happy to treat John's words – illegitimately – as a warning directed against the West. All that the Premier and the Pope had in common was a desire to avoid war. But this was a very important link, and to preserve it the Soviet leader was prepared to be silent – or almost silent – about the Pope's concern for God, noting that the Pope was not saying much about his own concern for Atheism. It was a first practical demonstration of something which the Pope would later preach in *Pacem in Terris*, namely that it was not necessary to be in philosophical agreement with people in order to co-operate with them in matters which concerned the good of mankind. And we may note a further point, not lost upon the Russians: *Mater et Magistra*, taken in conjunction with Pope John's Allocution of January 1961, suggested that the Pope, in matters concerning the human welfare of the world, was more concerned – as we saw earlier – to correct the errors of the West than to blame the errors of the East. This may have been because of his concern for the emergent nations, which were mostly under western tutelage, or it may have been because only the West was likely to listen to him; but in either case his attitude was bound to be encouraging to Moscow,

[1] Interview of September 20th, reported by Tass. DC 1361, Col. 1201, Note.

where it was rightly concluded that a new wind was blowing in Rome.

So this third circle, the circle of world co-operation, of world peace, was growing steadily clearer and more compelling to the Pope. Somehow the light from the first circle – the circle of Catholic unity, as represented by the Council – had to spread out to clarify not only the second circle, Christian Unity, but the third circle, the Unity of Mankind. When, on February 2nd, 1962, the Feast of Candlemas, he signed the *Motu proprio* "Consilium", which fixed the date for the opening of the Council (October 11th 1962), he took the text of his allocution from the liturgy of the feast: "Jesus is the Redeemer of the whole human race; today He is saluted as 'a light to lighten the nations', the Saviour of all the nations. To Him therefore belong not only all those who are sons of the Catholic Church, but all those who are baptized in His holy name, and also all those who are equally His by right of creation and by the saving virtue of His Precious Blood, shed for the salvation of the whole human race. . . . May this redeeming blood fall upon all men, become no longer strangers or enemies but brothers; may it strengthen their will for peace, their longing after tranquillity and well-being . . . "[1]

Very striking was Roncalli's response to the ghastly event of New Year's Day, 1962, at Kongolo, in the Congo, where twenty-one Catholic missionaries were murdered by Gizenga's troops. He did not treat the event, in the usual manner, as one more opportunity to recall Christ's warning that His followers must expect to be brought before judges, and even killed; he reminded his listeners that the sacrifice and death of these missionaries, if accepted and suffered in His name, would bring a blessing on the victims and on all who understood the nature of their sacrifice, and would even obtain a pardon for the executioners themselves. And on this occasion, when he might have been expected to be most deeply concerned to proclaim a Catholic martyrdom, he broke away from the conception of himself as father only of Christians, and did what Cardinal Bea said he could not do, he called all men his sons: "In the face of such a tragedy, how could the Father of all souls,

[1] DC 1370, Col. 227.

the father of the whole human family, which God has entrusted to him, how could he be silent?"[1]

By June of 1962, with the opening of the Council in the autumn drawing near, we find the Pope adopting a mystical language in which it is hard to tell whether he is thinking more of the unity of the Church or of the unity of mankind so closely are the two ideas interwoven with each other, and both with the Council: "The horn has sounded for the Church to offer to that humanity which Jesus came to save the gift of unity and of peace, represented mystically by the sacrament of the Body and Blood of Christ.

"Unity and peace! A powerful cry, solemn, and giving courage. This is always the chief task of Holy Church, which rises above the personal interests of each man and of each nation."[2]

Two months earlier Cardinal Bea, addressing the foreign Press at Rome, had likewise widened the range of his own view to include not, indeed, the whole of humanity, but something more than baptized Christians: "The problems which humanity has to face today are, indeed, so enormous and so urgent that it is really indispensable to mobilize all those forces which are in agreement at least on the level of the religious idea, the idea of God, and the existence of a moral order. On that ground they can and they ought to seek to understand each other."[3] This would seem to include the Moslems, the Hindus, and the Jews, but not the Communists. The bond between men to which the Cardinal was here drawing attention was their acknowledgement of God, but the Pope was thinking more and more about something wider, the brotherhood of man, by virtue of that common fatherhood which many ignored, and many denied, but which was none the less a fact.

Though his mind dwelt so much in this outer circle of the Council's significance for the whole world, the Pope's feet remained firmly on the ground; indeed they were carrying him into the chambers of the various preparatory commissions. On several occasions he addressed the Central Preparatory Commission, of which he was President, though for its regular sessions he yielded the Chair to the Dean of the

[1] DC 1372, Col. 369.   [2] DC 1380, Col. 899. Speech of June 21st.
[3] DC 1376, Col. 666. Speech of April 25th.

Sacred College, Cardinal Tisserant, or to another senior cardinal. He read the various *schemas* which the commissions were producing. These included two somewhat divergent chapters on the problem of Christian reunion, one being part of the Theological Commission's *schema de Ecclesia*, and presented by Cardinal Ottaviani, the other being presented by Cardinal Bea on behalf of the Secretariat for Christian Unity. The somewhat stark historical and theological outline of the problem presented by Ottaviani stood in marked contrast to the positive and pastoral proposals of Bea, with their emphasis on mutual prayer and mutual study of scripture as the true bond between separated brethren.

"To create a certain unity between the two *schemas* on ecumenism (wrote the *Osservatore Romano*) the Theological Commission presented a *schema* on the Holy Virgin, Mother of God and Mother of men".[1] It was a favourite way with Ottaviani, and one he would follow again towards the end of the first session of the Council, to recreate harmony, at a time of tension, by uniting opponents in a tribute to Our Lady. Let them gather once more, as the medieval painters depicted them, under her all-embracing cloak. But this excellent act of devotion still left the gulfs to be bridged and the problems to be solved. The sessions of the Central Commission had brought the divisions out into the open and shown the Pope how wide was the difference in approach between 'conservatives' and 'progressives'. That his own view was close to Cardinal Bea's, that he wanted a positive advance towards Christian reunion and some message to the whole of mankind was well known. But he did not intervene, and in bidding farewell to the Central Commission on June 20th, 1962, he said nothing about the matters under dispute but asked its members only to make sure that they let the world know what a tremendous labour of preparation had been done there at Rome and to make themselves the heralds "not of a quiet rest there but of a resplendent dawn which will break in this coming month of October".[2]

Preoccupied, as he was, with the 'reunion' aim of the Council – the second circle – and with its message to humanity as a whole – the third or outer circle – the Pope might have been pardoned for feeling some

[1] DC 1380, Col. 924.   [2] DC 1380, Col. 903.

disillusionment as he rested, in the August heat, at Castel Gandolfo. The *schemas* – except for those submitted by Cardinal Bea – were mainly traditionalist and dull; if the Council accepted them it could hardly achieve the *aggiornamento* of the Church or pave the way for a renewal of her life or a wider sphere of influence. And the response from outside was still disappointing. Though the World Council of Churches would send observers, and a number of the Protestant Churches would send their own, the Orthodox, it seemed, would not; yet it was the Orthodox world which he had wooed so assiduously and with which his personal contacts were closest. It had seemed likely to be easier to establish a link with Athens, and with Istanbul, than with Geneva, with Augsburg, or with Canterbury; yet that link had escaped him. A conventional and conservative Council, well chaperoned by the prefects of the curial congregations, leaving the Protestant observers rather better informed, and the world as a whole a little more polite, but quite indifferent, seemed now the best to be hoped for. And, at eighty years of age, could he do much about it?

He could. On a torrid day in early September, exactly a month before the Council was due to open, he went to the microphone and put out a message over Radio Vatican to the world. His text came from St Luke, Chapter 21: " . . . lift up your heads . . . for the time draws near for your deliverance . . . look at any of the trees; when they put out their fruit, you know by your own experience that summer is near. Just so, when you see this happen, be sure that the kingdom of God is close at hand."[1] And thence he moved to the Easter liturgy: " '*Lumen Christi*'. The Church of Jesus, from every corner of the earth, replies '*Deo Gratias*': yes, it is the light of Christ, the light of the Church, the light of the nations.

"What else can a Council be if not the renewal of this meeting with the face of the risen Jesus, glorious and immortal King, radiant over the whole Church, to save, to give joy to, and to enlighten the nations of the world?"[2]

And what sort of enlightenment is this that the Council must give to the world?

[1] Knox translation.
[2] DC 1385, Cols. 1217 and 1218.   AAS, LIV, p. 678, etc.

After a mere sentence on the sort of enlightenment Catholics need, that they may understand better the "treasures of faith" and of "sanctifying grace", the whole of the rest of the speech is devoted to the enlightenment which the Council will give to the world, guidance to Christians "called to live as men among men, as Christians among Christians", who will bring "by force of example many other men, not yet Christians, to become such". This activity, "which is called exterior, but which is altogether apostolic", fulfils the commandment of Jesus to "teach men to observe all my commandments". The Church has to concern herself with the ordinary needs of all men, everywhere. And what is it that such men seek? "Man looks for family love beside his hearth, his daily bread for himself and those closest to him, his wife and his children. He feels within himself the desire and the duty to live in peace with his own national community and with the rest of the world. He feels the attraction of the things of the mind which urge him to educate and improve himself. Jealous of his liberty, he is ready to accept the necessary limitations to be placed upon it in order that his social obligations may be met."[1]

On these grave problems, he explains, the Council may be expected to propose solutions, because such solutions are demanded alike by the dignity of man and by his Christian vocation. But he betrays his anxiety lest the Council should fail to tackle them, or should do so inadequately, when he goes on to tell both it and the world what it is that the Christian faith demands: it demands recognition of the fundamental equality of all peoples in their international relations; and it demands, in the spirit of *Mater et Magistra*, that the Church be presented in her true role, as the Church of all men, and especially of the poor: "It is the duty of all men, and the imperative duty of a Christian, to take stock of what he has in excess of his needs, giving thought to the needs of others, and to strive most strenuously to ensure that the development and distribution of the resources of creation redound to the benefit of all men."[2] In short, only a month before the Council assembled, the Pope broadcast to the world what it was going to be about, and that proved to be nothing less than justice for all men, security, and peace. And to these he added freedom of religion, that is, freedom for men to teach

[1] DC 1385, Col. 1219.   [2] *Ibid.*, Col. 1220.

about God, and the supernatural, and to practise their faith. The whole message bears a striking resemblance to President Roosevelt's "four freedoms" – freedom from want, freedom from fear, freedom of speech, and freedom of worship. In fact the Pope, too, made four points, and three of them were the same as Roosevelt's. Freedom of speech, however, though implicit in all that Pope John taught, was not explicitly demanded by him on this occasion. His own fourth point was one which Roosevelt, or the world at large, would not have been likely to make. It was a demand for world recognition of the sacred character of marriage, carrying with it acceptance of the religious and moral purpose of marriage in the procreation of children.[1]

These, then, the Pope was saying, were amongst the things with which Christians must concern themselves and with which the Council would concern itself. Yet little that the Press had reported suggested that such matters would, in fact, be seriously discussed. The Pope was presenting a picture of the life of the Church in the world along the lines of *Mater et Magistra*, which was a sociological document. But the *schemas* were explaining the traditional rights of the Church in neo-Thomist terminology, and as though it were only necessary to remind the refractory few of their evident duties within the Christian Order of human society. The gulf was wide. It would seem that the broadcast was intended not only to alert the world but to alert the Fathers of the Church who would soon be assembling. Would they easily reconcile the kind of *schemas* they were now receiving from Rome with the kind of Council the Pope was talking about?

When the Council at last opened, the Pope, in his opening speech, drove his lesson home. True, coming at the end of a four-hour ceremony in St Peter's, and delivered in Latin, its impact was softened by the weariness and the incomprehension of its recipients. And when they came to study it in their own tongues, the Fathers of the Church were handicapped by the fact that the vernacular translations, given to the world Press, had been made from a bad Italian translation. But when the obstacles presented by a surfeit of ceremonial, an unfamiliar language, and the remarkable inefficiency – at this stage – of the Council's press service had been overcome it became evident that the Pope had given

[1] *Ibid.*, Cols. 1219 and 1220.

to the bishops the clearest and most positive guidance as to the way they should approach their task. They were to give the message of unity not only to the Catholic Church, not only to all Christians, but to all mankind: "Indeed, if one considers properly this unity, which Jesus Christ prayed for for His Church, one sees that it shines with a triple light, heavenly and health giving" – upon Catholics, upon Christians, and upon those of other belief. One way in which it will achieve this is by an *aggiornamento* of its presentation of the truth, which will have to be brought into harmony with the modes of life and thought of a new age, for only thus will souls become "more deeply penetrated and transformed by the faith". And then he told this audience of bishops, all of whom had been trained to believe that the most dangerous heresy was the idea that the faith "evolved", that it was not enough that they should go on explaining the old truths in the old way. "The deposit of faith, itself, that is to say the truths contained in our ancient doctrine, is one thing; but the form in which those truths are announced is another."[1]

However, the special quality of the Pope's opening address to the Council was its optimism. Pope John was an optimist by temperament, a quality that had helped to make him so popular during his twenty years in the Balkans and his eight in France. Like anybody else, a priest may be an optimist or he may be a pessimist. In his religion he may enjoy, as Roncalli did, the wonder of the working of the grace of God in the men and women he meets, whether inside or outside the Church: the sheer joy of family happiness, or of productive labour as Roncalli saw it at his own home or in the Bulgarian countryside. Or he may become gloomy at seeing so many who seem shut out, not merely from the Church's means of grace, but from those means that are scattered more widely in the world; whose lives are dulled by materialism, deadened against generosity, essentially sordid, and sometimes vicious. Or again, he may see the kingdom of heaven as fighting a defensive battle, in this world, and as reserved, at the last judgement, to a few; or he may believe that the Church will bring most men to see and to follow the light she offers. The general temper of the Church, since the seventeenth century, has inclined towards pessimism. She has evidently

[1] Speech printed in DC 1387, Cols. 1377–86. AAS, LIV, p. 786.

been more concerned to raise the barriers, to stave off further losses, than to risk collaborating with others, in the manner of those 'Americanists' whom Leo XIII discouraged. But there was no possibility of success for Pope John's programme for Catholics, by which they were to bring unity, justice, and peace to the world, unless they adopted the outgoing, which means the optimistic approach; his optimism was, in fact, an essential part of his revolutionary message without which that message could never have taken shape in his own mind or have been transmitted to the world.

So it is not really surprising that he chose, at the opening of the Council, to startle the assembled fathers by his famous "prophets of doom" remarks denouncing, in unambiguous language, those among his own advisers at Rome who could see no further than the mounting errors, the evils and the dangers of the times:

"It often happens that, in the daily exercise of Our apostolic ministry, We are shocked to discover what is being said by some people who, though they may be fired by religious zeal, are without justice, or good judgement, or consideration in their way of looking at matters. In the existing state of society they see nothing but ruin and calamity; they are in the habit of saying that our age is much worse than past centuries; they behave as though history, which teaches us about life, had nothing to teach them, and as though, at the times of past Councils, everything was perfect in the matter of Christian doctrine, public behaviour, and the proper freedom of the Church.

"It seems to Us necessary to express Our complete disagreement with these prophets of doom, who give news only of catastrophes, as though the world were nearing its end.

"In the present state of affairs, now that human society seems to have reached a turning-point, it is better to recognize the mysterious designs of divine Providence which, passing through the different ages of man, and his works, generally against all expectation, achieve their purposes and guide all events wisely for the good of the Church – even those events which seem to conflict with her purposes."[1]

Here we have an echo of the liberal Catholic thought of the nineteenth century. The Pope's protest is the same protest as was raised by

[1] DC 1387, Col. 1380.   AAS, LIV, pp. 788, 789.

Montalembert and his friends against the clerical pessimism that followed the French Revolution. To the clericalists that revolution meant that all human society was crumbling and the Church must shelter behind the tottering royal thrones. But Montalembert, as we have noticed earlier, warned them that that way lay death, that God could turn even the wrath of man to His praise. (The greatest of all the disasters, in the view of the Vatican of the later nineteenth century, had been the loss of the papal states, for whose return Catholics prayed, after Sunday Mass, for fifty years. But by the middle of the twentieth century Pius XII was speaking of that loss as a blessing in disguise, and a blessing in disguise is a disaster, wrought by the wrath of man, which God has turned to his praise).

The gloom which the Pope was so tired of seeing around him at the Vatican expressed itself in reiterated warnings about the Communist danger in Italy or about the drift of the newly emancipated peoples into the Communist camp; at least those were the warnings he must have heard most often. And he could understand them. For he felt as keenly distressed by what was happening in China, or by the oppression suffered by the Church of Silence in Russia, or by the hideous sporadic outrages in parts of Africa as did the prophets of gloom. But his way of meeting the danger was to try to persuade the Chinese and the Russian and the African revolutionaries that the Church was really on their side, in all their legitimate demands, only demanding, in addition, freedom and justice, and only seeking to bring to them, too, her message of good news – the means of grace and the hope of salvation. When he said that "against all expectation" "the mysterious designs of Providence" would guide "even those events which seem to conflict with her purpose" into the service of the Church he could well have meant that even the Communist revolution itself could serve her, although it so markedly conflicted with her purposes.

The events of the days immediately preceding and following the opening of the Council show just how preoccupied he was with the Communist world.

3 · IN HIS FINAL EFFORT FOR
UNITY AND PEACE

Much remains obscure about the strange circumstances in which, as matters turned out, the first session of the Council was attended by two observers from the Russian Orthodox Church but not by any observers from the other European Orthodox Churches, all of which recognize an historic primacy of precedence as belonging to Constantinople and are accustomed to allow her Patriarch to take the initiative, on behalf of Orthodoxy, in her dealings with outside bodies, though they expect to be consulted. But we are indebted to the Augustinian Father Antoine Wenger, indefatigable editor of *La Croix*, for discovering the essentials and publishing them in the second part of his *Vatican II, Première Session*.[1]

As a result of Roncalli's prolonged mission to Turkey, and of the strongly ecumenical outlook of Patriarch Athenagoras of Constantinople (since manifested in his relations with Pope Paul) hopes had been high, at Rome, that the Orthodox world would be shepherded by the Patriarch into full representation by observers at the Council. But that world would not be shepherded, and three days before the opening of the Council Cardinal Bea received from the Patriarch the sad news that "to preserve the unity of Orthodoxy" it would not be possible for Constantinople herself to be represented. It was with death, says Father Wenger, in his heart, that the Patriarch wrote this;[2] but he clearly felt compelled to do so by the fact that he was unable to obtain any positive reply from Moscow to his repeated inquiries as to whether she wished to send observers to Rome. Having also received little encouragement from Athens, he had finally felt obliged to turn the invitation down.

However, the Russian Patriarch Alexis and the Holy Synod of Moscow took the line that Rome had been at fault in issuing the invitation through Constantinople and insisted that the sending of observers was a matter for each of the autonomous Orthodox churches to decide for itself. As gradually it became clear, during the summer of 1962, that the Patriarch of Moscow might give a favourable reply to a separate invitation, if it were addressed directly to him, Mgr Willebrands

[1] *Éditions du Centurion*, 1963.   [2] *Op. cit.*, p. 239.

flew to the Soviet capital at the end of September, attended a Mass celebrated by Archbishop Nicodemus (Head of the Foreign Relations Department of the Moscow Patriarchate) and apparently gave assurances that the Council would not be made the opportunity for polemics about Communism, which might be offensive to sensitive Soviet ears. Even so, the Russians did not indicate that they would accept an invitation, contenting themselves with pointing out that they had not in fact received one. Willebrands returned to Rome on October 2nd, and on October 4th Cardinal Bea telegraphed to Moscow the official invitation. On October 7th the Patriarch Alexis of Moscow telegraphed the Patriarch Athenagoras of Constantinople saying that he had nothing to add on the matter of any representation of Moscow at Rome; but on October 10th he consulted with his Synod and the decision was taken to send two observers to Rome; Rome was informed by telegram on the 11th. The two observers arrived on the 12th, too late for the Pope's inaugural address but gratified to find themselves the object not only of much curiosity but also of much enthusiasm in a city where the news from Istanbul that the European Orthodox church would not be represented had arrived only three days before the news from Moscow that her largest branch in fact would be.[1]

These events were naturally grievous for the Patriarch Athenagoras. That he who had said of the Pope "there was a man sent from God whose name was John", and who was dedicated to the cause of ecumenical understanding with Rome, should end by being unrepresented at the Council was a severe fate. Nor could some bitterness and recrimination be avoided. Athens, hesitant in her own reply, had, like Constantinople, been by-passed by Moscow, so against the gain of seeing the forty or more millions of Russian Orthodoxy represented at Rome there had to be set renewed suspicions engendered in the smaller but ancient and influential patriarchates of the Balkans. Athenagoras, as we all now know, did not waver in his course, and would soon meet Pope John's successor at Jerusalem. But suspicion hardened at Athens, and in America the Orthodox Bishop Mgr Iakovos (whose jurisdiction comes under Constantinople) blamed the Vatican for trying to divide the Orthodox world by sending invitations to her Churches individu-

[1] Wenger, *op. cit.*, pp. 225–29 and 239–41.

ally. The initial aim of the Vatican, however, had been to see the Orthodox world represented as one whole, which was why her initial invitation had been sent only to Istanbul. When it became clear that Athens expected to receive a separate invitation one was also sent to her. Not till very late – October 4th – was a separate one sent to Moscow, a step to which Rome was driven by the evident fact that Moscow would not allow Constantinople to speak for her. Mutual suspicion between the Orthodox Churches thus played as large a part as their mutual suspicion of Rome in bringing about the sad situation by which the two Churches which were really nearest to Rome, religiously speaking, namely Constantinople and Athens, were not represented.

The decision of the Moscow Patriarchate was regarded in Athens as inspired by the Soviet government and no better than a shameful betrayal of Orthodox unity for merely political purposes, while there were those in the West who said that the two Russian observers were no better than Soviet agents. Politics clearly were involved; the observers could not have attended the Council except by permission of the Soviet government. But to pretend that the two who came, namely the Archpriest Vitalyi Borovoi and the Archimandrite Vladimir Kotliarov, were primarily Soviet agents was absurd. Both were dedicated, devoted, and honourable priests who made an excellent impression at Rome.

The Soviet government's decision to allow the Russian Orthodox Church to send observers to the Council was in harmony with the relaxation of tension between the Kremlin and the Vatican. Mention has already been made of Premier Kruschev's satisfaction at the Pope's endeavours for peace during the Berlin Wall crisis in August and September 1961. Even so, the Soviet Press was still, in 1962, treating the Council as a "western" affair which would be used as a platform for anathematizing Communism, or as a new form of "crusade" against the Communist east. Rome was pictured as trying to unite the Christian Churches, even the non-Christian religions of the world, in an all-embracing alliance to try to crush the Marxist world. But even if the Kremlin seriously believed this, the permission given to two observers from Moscow to attend the Council was a sensible move, as it must tend to 'soft-pedal' anti-Communist oratory at the Council, and to some extent discountenance the notion that the Soviet government was actively suppressing all Christianity. If two evidently devout and courteous Russian priests, who were nevertheless perfectly loyal to their government, attended the Council by their government's permission, and concerned themselves with its work on the same plane as the Anglicans or the Lutherans, with a view to promoting better relations between their Church and Rome, it would evidently make it much more difficult for the Council to 'line-up' the religious world against Moscow. In any case, there was much to be said, from the Soviet point of view, for having observers at so great a gathering, and one likely to influence the attitude of 500 million Catholics all over the world. Permission had already been given by the Kremlin in the previous year for the Moscow Patriarchate to join the World Council of Churches, and she had sent representatives to the Ecumenical Conference at New Delhi in November 1961. It was the representative of the Moscow Patriarchate on the Committee of the World Council, Archbishop Nicodemus, who held the conversations with Mgr Willebrands which led Moscow to accept the Roman invitation. The price which Moscow was willing to pay for these ecumenical moves was the sacrifice of the notion, so sedulously fostered by *Izvestia*, that Christianity was moribund – Roman Christianity in particular.

The opening of the Council, the welcome accorded at Rome to the Russian priests, and the satisfaction shown by the *Tass* agency, in its account of the Pope's opening speech (duly published in *Izvestia*) did not, of themselves, end the hostile reactions of the Soviet Press. But, as autumn progressed, the old hostility did yield to a polite curiosity. Certainly the Vatican went out of her way to procure this change. There had been almost nothing in the Pope's speech of which Moscow could complain. His only reference to the "Church of Silence" was brief; it expressed his grief that "a great number" of bishops were not present because they were imprisoned, or otherwise detained, for their faith in Christ.[1] But these were not, for the most part, Russian bishops; many were detained in China. Some, indeed, like the Hungarian Cardinal Mindzenty, or Archbishop Beran of Prague, belonged to

[1] DC 1387, Col. 1380.

client Soviet states; but there were also some bishops present from these client states, including Cardinal Wyszynski and sixteen others from Poland, four from East Germany, and three each from Czechoslovakia and Hungary. There were, however, none from Rumania. From Yugoslavia all the bishops attended; from Albania none.[1] The most important group of bishops belonging to the Soviet Union were the Ukrainians and these, being in exile, were present, though their leader, Archbishop Slipyi of Lwov, remained where he had been for seventeen years, namely in a prison camp in Siberia.

The few sentences in which the Pope referred, with such moderation, to the Church of Silence, were coupled with an expression of his lively satisfaction that the Council was free from any political controls ("profane obstacles"), by which it is assumed he was referring to the part played by secular governments at earlier General Councils, a part which some governments had attempted to play even as recently as at the First Vatican Council. By implication he was saying to the Communists: release our brother bishops, imprisoned unjustly for their faith, as we have freed ourselves from all political controls; the Council is not the ally of any government, or of any group of governments, against any other group.

The Pope's talk, on the day after the opening, to the members of the eighty-six diplomatic missions sent by the governments of the world was further calculated to mollify Moscow. Whereas Pius XII could hardly have confronted such a gathering without alluding to the plight of the Church of Silence, Pope John talked to them only of peace. Receiving them in the Sistine Chapel he directed their attention towards Michelangelo's huge painting of the Last Judgement, on the wall before them, and warned them that they would one day have to give their own account to the Supreme Judge: "Let all who bear the responsibility of government hear the anguished cry which, from every part of the world, from innocent children to old men, from individuals and from communities, rises to heaven: peace, peace. May the thought that they will have to render their own account prevent them from ever neglecting any opportunity to achieve that good which, for the human family, is the highest good of all."[2]

[1] DC 1387, Col. 1381. [2] DC 1387, Col. 1390. AAS, LIV, pp. 808, 809.

Eight days later, on October 20th, the Council issued its own "Message to the World". Inspired and drafted by the French, the idea of the message was approved by the Pope; like the Pope's addresses of September 11th and October 11th it was devoted, for the most part, to the themes of peace and social justice; God's love for man compelled man's care for his brother. No mention was made of the Church of Silence. Since only half an hour was allowed for discussion of the text amendment was difficult, but Mgr Fiordelli, Bishop of Prato, tried to secure that the plight of the Church behind the Iron Curtain was mentioned. After a Hungarian bishop and a Lithuanian (in exile) had recommended that it would be better not to include any such reference in a message of hope and brotherhood the text, as it stood, with the addition of a reference to the Blessed Virgin, was approved by an overwhelming majority. Amongst the very few who remained seated, as a sign of their disapproval, were the bishops in exile from the Ukraine.[1]

These Ukrainian bishops remained something of a thorn in the flesh of the Russian observers. Their special grievance was the continued imprisonment of their Metropolitan, Mgr Slipyi, Archbishop of Lwov, and eventually they drew up a document which said (to quote *La Croix* for November 22nd) that "to some it seemed that the arrival in Rome of Orthodox observers had been greeted with great acclaim whereas the absence of the Metropolitan Slipyi and his imprisonment had been left unmentioned. Mgr Slipyi has been 'illegally deported and has been in prison in Siberia for seventeen years'. He is the only survivor of eleven Ukrainian Catholic bishops sent into Siberia. The [Moscow] Patriarchate has 'assumed ecclesiastical jurisdiction over 4½ millions of Ukrainian Catholics, contrary to all right, divine, ecclesiastical, or human, by openly collaborating with the atheistic civil power, because that is the only way to suppress and liquidate the Catholic Church of the Ukraine '."[2]

The Russian observers were not pleased. A delicate situation developed which was only eased when Mgr Willebrands, on behalf of the Secretariat for Christian Unity, put out an official statement on

[1] Wenger, *op. cit.*, pp. 51–55. DC 1387, Cols. 1407–10.
[2] Wenger, *op. cit.*, pp. 235, 236.

November 23rd, saying that the Secretariat "deplores . . . everything which has appeared that is contrary to the spirit which has animated the loyal contacts made with the observer-delegates. It can only dissociate itself from them".[1] However, through the good offices it would seem of the Russian observers themselves, Archbishop Slipyi was, in fact, released by order of the Soviet government on February 10th, 1963, and the Pope was able to speak of a "touching consolation which, amidst the hidden things of God, can prepare for Holy Church and honest souls a new access of sincere faith and pacific and beneficial apostolate".[2] The Ukrainian Archbishop reached Moscow from Siberia on February 5th; Mgr Willebrands went there to meet him and brought him to Rome where the Pope greeted him with profound emotion.

This matter of the release of Archbishop Slipyi was the most striking manifestation of the real desire of the Russian observers, and behind them of the Patriarch Alexis and his Synod at Moscow, and behind them, again, of their government, to be accommodating, to remove obstacles to understanding, and to make of the Council an opportunity for some measure of *rapprochement*. In their various Press interviews the Russians were at pains to insist on the courtesy with which they were being treated, and they were invariably appreciative of the attitude both of the Pope and of the Secretariat for Christian Unity.

On the other hand the interpretation which they put on events was sometimes startling to Western ears. It was only a week after the opening of the Council that the second Cuban crisis developed, with the Russian despatch of ships bearing military materials to the island, and the American declaration that these ships would be searched and the landing of such materials prevented. At no time since the end of the Second World War had mankind seemed so near to total disaster, and on October 25th the Pope made yet another appeal over the Vatican Radio in which he repeated the solemn warning he had given to the diplomats, in the Sistine Chapel, only a few days before, and prayed that "all Our children, all who are signed with the seal of baptism and nourished by the Christian hope, all, indeed, who are united with us by faith in God may join their prayer with Ours to obtain from heaven

[1] *Ibid.*, p. 236.   [2] DC 1395, Col. 302.

147

the gift of peace; peace which cannot be true and lasting unless it is based on justice and equity".[1] This appeal, though scrupulously neutral in the matter under dispute, was particularly well received by Moscow, and in a Press conference at the end of the same month the Russian observers went out of their way to refer to it, though in singular terms. They were endeavouring to explain to a Soviet journalist the significance of the Pope's and the Council's work for peace: "Although the agenda of the Council does not include, as a separate item, the problems of the maintenance of peace, of peaceful coexistence, or of the strengthening of friendship between the peoples, this theme is mentioned in many of the Council's documents, and in Pope John XXIII's speech on the occasion of the opening of the Council, as well as in his speeches to the diplomats, the journalists, the observers, and in his broadcast message on the occasion of the American threat to Cuba, as well as in the solemn message of the Fathers of the Council to the peoples of the world."[2]

To most of those at Rome this reference to the "American threat to Cuba" would have seemed outrageous – had they known about it. But it was made by the Russian observers in an interview with a Russian journalist, and in Russia the Cuban crisis was known simply as the "American threat", a view of the matter which no doubt the two observers shared. All countries assume, in a crisis, that God is on their side; all countries pray for peace, hoping that their enemies may see reason. This habit of mankind may be odd, but it is usual, and it is therefore not reasonable to assume that these Russian observers were guilty, on this occasion, of any calculated 'double-think'. During the same crisis their master, the Patriarch Alexis of Moscow, sent a telegram to Mr U Thant, Secretary-General of the United Nations, and to the Patriarch Athenagoras of Constantinople, and to the heads of the other Orthodox Churches, asking them to protest against the American action, while Archbishop Nicodemus, in charge of the foreign relations of the Russian Orthodox Church, sent similar messages to the American Council of Christian Churches and to Dr Visser 't Hooft, Secretary-General of the World Council of Churches. Again, it is unreasonable to accuse the Russian Church leaders either of deliberate and sinister

[1] DC 1388, Col. 1444.   [2] Wenger, *op. cit.*, pp. 322, 323.

political misrepresentation or of exceptional political subservience. We are all alike in our national loyalties; even the Catholic Church leadership, in Germany and Italy in the Second World War, had little difficulty in accepting and sometimes endorsing the conviction of the faithful in those countries that they were engaged in resisting Allied warmongers and aggressors.

Having headed the Council in the direction he intended, the direction of Christian unity, world unity, and peace, Pope John withdrew, to watch the proceedings on his closed-circuit television set. What happened at the sessions in St Peter's after he had gone is not directly our concern here; in any case the story has been often told. But we need to notice that the group which is generally called conservative, the group which represented the prevailing view in the Curia, which followed the lead of Cardinal Ottaviani, and which had been prominent in the preparatory commissions that drew up the *schemas*, was also the group which was politically conservative, in the sense that it favoured firm resistance to the Communists and their supporters whether in Italy or in the world at large. Politically conservative bishops, admittedly, were not necessarily also religiously conservative; their political conservatism did not mean that they favoured retention of Latin in the liturgy or were adamant about according to tradition an equal status with Holy Scripture, as a source of Revelation. And even within the partly political sphere a bishop might, like many of the American bishops, be politically conservative on one point and liberal on another, be with Ottaviani about the Communists, but opposed to him and to the Curia in favouring the separation of Church and State.

All the same, there was a recognizable 'traditionalist' group, traditionalist both religiously and politically, which was in line, in its thinking, with Curialist attitudes, and which was strongly represented among the Italian bishops and among those who came from the Latin countries. And its natural leader was Cardinal Ottaviani, because his position as Secretary to the Holy Office, and President of the Theological Commission gave him, from the outset, a position of leadership, and because he showed hostility both towards religious and towards political change, and especially extreme hostility towards the Communists, for which he was well known at Moscow. When, therefore, the 'Ottaviani party' was worsted during the first session of the Council (first when the Council refused to accept the Curia's nominations to its commissions, and later when it rejected, with the Pope's help, the Theological Commission's *schema* on the Sources of Revelation – Ottaviani's own *schema*) those who were thinking about the political reconciliation of East and West, or about Christian Democratic collaboration with the parties of the Left in Italy, naturally felt encouraged. And although the Council was concerned with religion, not with politics, what was said by the Fathers of the Church, and still more what was not said, could not help having its bearing upon the political world outside. Thus if ordinary courtesy precluded a discussion of the religious conditions in Russia in front of the Russian observers there was also the consideration that such discussion might paralyse the efforts of the Vatican to help to achieve a political *détente*. Even the most unlikely subjects might have their political bearing. When the Council decided, on November 30th, not to alter its agenda (as Ottaviani wanted) to discuss the prerogatives of the Blessed Virgin Mary some Italians were saying that the Christian Democratic government in Italy needed a firm declaration by the Council about these prerogatives.

The Pope was ill at the end of November, but he rallied in the next month and was able to deliver his farewell address to the departing Fathers on December 8th. In doing so he took the opportunity to give them a broad hint that they were supposed to be giving their consideration to the whole world. Inviting them to enjoy, with him, a glimpse of the "health-giving fruits" which they must all hope the Council would produce in the future he added: "God would not wish that these fruits be gathered only by the children of the Catholic Church, but that they should be shared by our brothers who bear the name of Christian and also by those numberless men who boast a most ancient and glorious heritage of civilization, handed down by their ancestors, and who have not yet received the light of Christianity. . . .

"Our heart is waiting, Venerable Fathers, and We know well that your own hearts are filled with the same expectation."[1]

[1] DC 1391, Col. 10.

Most of them were seeing Pope John for the last time. He talked to them about their reunion in the following September and warned them of the work they would have to do at home during the recess. But he was not to be granted his deepest wish, to meet them again and to see them bring their work to its conclusion.

He had only six months left. But during those six months he took the boldest steps of his short reign in his endeavour to turn the Church on to a new course in world affairs. His farewell address to the Fathers of the Church had betrayed his concern that they should turn their eyes to the world at large. It might be necessary for him to give them an example as to how to do it. "When the time comes," he had warned them, "it will be necessary to extend to every domain of the Church's life, including the social domain, the decisions of the conciliar assembly."[1] But what would those decisions be? There were no conciliar decisions about the social domain because that domain had not been discussed. Yet the Pope had said, in his speech of September 11th, 1962, that the Council would be concerned with the external activity of the Church, with social justice, with liberty, with peace. It had not been concerned with these things yet.

If the Council were to fulfil Pope John's intentions it would clearly have ultimately to concern itself with the social and political life of the world. Who would give it a lead? – there was no lead in the *schemas*. There was *Mater et Magistra* to be sure; but that encyclical, having been ignored by the preparatory commissions, had been ignored hitherto by the Council; so, one might add, had *Rerum novarum* and *Quadragesimo anno*. The entire body of papal social teaching, since the time of the First Vatican Council, had been ignored both in the planning and at the first session of the Council. Yet that Council had been summoned to renew not only the Church but the world. It was intended to lead the Church to the aid of the world. Perhaps it had been right to start with Revelation and the Liturgy; indeed the Pope said as much in his speech concluding the first session. But he also said that it must move outwards in its thinking "to every domain of the Church's life, including the social domain". There was no clear sign that it would do so; the challenge he had issued in *Mater et Magistra* had not yet been taken up.

[1] *Idem.*

So he prepared a stronger challenge. *Pacem in Terris* would make good the deficiencies of the Council's *schemas*. If the Pope plunged Catholic thought, throughout the world, into the critical area of social justice and world peace, and the world responded, could the Council remain mute on these matters?

When they had all gone away he turned his eyes again towards the east. Athens, even Constantinople, had failed him; but Moscow had responded. This was strange, but perhaps providential; for it lay with Moscow to decide whether the world would move towards peace or towards war. And, thanks to the Russian observers, he was now in dialogue of a sort with Moscow, which was something no previous Pope had achieved with the capital of Communism.

What were his contacts? This, alas, is something about which we know all too little, as yet, and no doubt will know little for a long time. Carlo Falconi was assured that "journeys between the Vatican and the Kremlin have become much less rare . . . even a Cardinal went behind the Iron Curtain not long ago, under the guise of a harmless and impeccable scholar, the guest of a Moscow Academy."[1] We may be more confident of the influence at Moscow of the two observers, and may attribute to their favourable reports not only the release of Archbishop Slipyi but also the permission given by the Polish government, following the Kruschev–Gomulka conversations of November 1962, for a further ten Polish bishops to attend the Council.[2] And we know that Mgr Willebrands, of the Secretariat for Christian Unity, was *en rapport* with Archbishop Nicodemus, of the World Council of Churches and of Russian Orthodox foreign relations.

That the Soviet attitude was changing, at the end of 1962, is shown by the increasing attention given by the Russian Press to the Council and to its possibilities for peace. This change was discussed by Antoine Wenger in his essay *Le Concile et la press Soviétique*,[3] where he drew attention to the important article by P. Kolonitski, editor of *Science and Religion*, in its number for January 1st, 1963, and where he outlined

[1] *Pope John and His Council* (London, 1964) p. 120.
[2] See the *Tablet* for March 28th, 1964, p. 363.
[3] Wenger, *op. cit.*, p. 207.

the Russian's argument in this manner: "Pope John's addresses, at the time of the Council's assembling, Kolonitski told his readers, show a break with the traditional anti-Communist policies of the Vatican and especially those of Pius XII. But the past record of the Vatican, in respect of social progress, democracy, and peace, is so poor that words alone will not now suffice; there are, however, grounds for hope that they do mark a real change of heart and policy. Meanwhile peace is so much the most important goal for humanity that any event – even a religious one, like the Council – is to be welcomed if it can contribute towards removing the danger of war. If the Church is now turning away from the capitalist world this is because she wants to keep the workers with her, and the workers are turning to Socialism. The Council has been preoccupied with the liturgy, and this is natural because it is by making the liturgy more immediate, more meaningful, more beautiful, that the Church can keep the people with her. If they are being won over to materialism, it is necessary to the Church that they should now be brought more closely into participation in the spiritual mysteries of the faith. Meanwhile the reactionaries at Rome, led by Ottaviani, are trying to restore the Church's previous social and political 'line', and her anti-Communist fervour, and they may succeed. But the Pope and the majority of the Council appear to recognize the need to pursue the new line, and it is certain that "The authority and significance of the Council and of all the exterior activity of the Catholic Church depend upon the firmness and fidelity with which the course which has been chosen is carried out in practice."

This analysis is useful because it may well give us the thought, at that time, of the Kremlin. If so, then the Soviet government saw value in giving encouragement to the new policies, and in particular to Pope John, which would explain not merely the release of Archbishop Slipyi but also a more remarkable event, the interview with Pope John sought and obtained by Kruschev's son-in-law, Alexis Adjoubei, editor of *Izvestia*.

This interview took place when Adjoubei was at Rome, with other journalists, at the beginning of March 1963, on the occasion of the award to the Pope of the Balzan Peace Prize. The prize had been awarded by an international committee which included four Soviet representatives, all of whom had given their vote to Pope John. In his speech of congratulation, ex-President Gronchi of Italy (President of the awarding committee) underlined the range of the Pope's peaceful activity, extending outside the bounds of Christianity: " . . . by reason of his untiring efforts to contribute to the maintenance of peaceful relations between the States both by his peaceful appeals to the good will of mankind and by his recent diplomatic interventions. . . . " After referring especially to his efforts during the past year, to the Council, and to better relations between Christians, the President concluded by recalling how he had established contacts "extending far beyond the boundaries of the Christian community".[1] In his reply the Pope took the opportunity to underline, as was perhaps necessary, that he welcomed the award because it constituted a recognition of the "constant endeavours of the Church and of the Papacy for peace", "from Leo XIII to Pius XII", and the "perfect supranational neutrality of the Church and her visible chief".[2] Already the Communist Press was embarrassing him seriously, both in Italy and abroad, by treating him as though he were an ally of the Soviet and satellite governments, in whose eyes the movement for peace and the movement for Communism were one.

In what he said in his reply about Leo XIII and Pius XII Roncalli partially reassured the Curia and the parties of the Right in Italy and corrected those Communists who were saying wild things about the 'aggressive aims' of Pius XI and Pius XII. What Adjoubei, who was present as a journalist at these exchanges, thought about them we do now know; but he was not deterred from seeking his audience. After it, he answered his Press interviewers with great caution. There could be no coexistence, he said, between Communism and other ideologies in the realm of ideas; but the Pope was Head of a State. "Recently he has made statements in favour of peace and against war which have been appreciated by our public opinion. All this creates a certain easing in the international situation and confirms the sound basis of our policy

[1] Wenger, *op. cit.*, p. 291.
[2] DC 1397, Cols. 417–19.

of coexistence between States and social systems."[1] His rather absurd misinterpretation of the Pope's true position was made necessary by his own ideology. Nobody could suppose that what the Pope said was significant because he was Head of a State – a State less powerful than Monaco. His influence came from his headship of a Church. Yet Adjoubei could not say that his power came from a religious source because he was obliged to affirm that religion was powerless. Asked whether Kruschev would visit the Pope, he did not deny that his father-in-law might go to the Vatican, but he insisted that a formal invitation would be needed. Meanwhile the Pope had given Mrs Adjoubei a present for her father, the Soviet Premier.

The concern felt by the Curia at these events was expressed by Vatican Radio. On the day before the Adjoubei interview it warned listeners: "Stalin has gone. In the brief space of ten years Communism has liquidated even his memory. But not to lay aside his atheist and materialist principles, only to enable it to spread and apply them more effectively."[2] And a week later listeners were being reassured that the Pope was, after all, in line with his predecessor about the Communist danger. Quoting the (relatively mild) remarks of John XXIII of Christmas 1959, and his brief reference at the opening of the Council to "absent brethren", Vatican Radio drew the conclusion that "The words of John XXIII fully echo the encyclicals in which his predecessors condemned Marxist doctrine. True Catholics cannot be in doubt: their duties, confronted by Marxist atheism, are today, and tomorrow, what they were yesterday."[3]

But they were not quite. For in the following month appeared *Pacem in Terris*. Catholics were now (with proper safeguards) to co-operate with Marxists.

The teaching of this new encyclical has already been discussed, together with that of *Mater et Magistra*, to which it is complementary. The two encyclicals in fact cover much the same ground: economic, social, and educational problems; the emergent countries; food and population; colonialism; regional organizations; the United Nations; and the maintenance of peace. This similarity in itself is significant; since most

[1] DC 1397, Col. 420.   [2] DC 1397, Col. 421.   [3] *Ibid.*, Col. 422.

of the world problems discussed in *Pacem in Terris* had already been discussed in *Mater et Magistra* why was a new encyclical needed, and so soon after the previous one?

It was needed because *Mater et Magistra* had been ignored hitherto by the Council, which had no item as yet on its agenda about the Church in the Modern World. Unless the Pope himself were to take over the functions of the Cardinal Presidents of the Council by inducing them to introduce a suitable *schema* – a procedure which would have been at variance with his policy of leaving it free – he would have to sharpen the message of *Mater et Magistra* so that the Council would pay attention. If it did not, at least the world would.

There were differences of emphasis between the two encyclicals. Though they both spoke of justice, freedom, order, and peace as inter-dependent parts of one inseparable whole, *Mater et Magistra* was more concerned with economic and social justice, and especially with the agricultural community, with the emergent nations, and with colonial-ism, whereas *Pacem in Terris* was more concerned with political questions, and especially with the Communists, and with the work of the United Nations. And whereas *Mater et Magistra* moves slowly off the mark, with a wealth of repetition of the ground already covered by Leo XIII's and Pius XI's social encyclicals, *Pacem in Terris* moved briskly, and with greater self-confidence, though it is careful to keep quoting Pius XII. Perhaps its most permanently important paragraph was the one on religious toleration. But in the world context of the month when it was published – April 1963 – the points in it of widest interest, especially to the Communists, were two. One was its declara-tion that "in this age, which boasts of its atomic power, it no longer makes sense to maintain that war is a fit instrument with which to repair the violation of justice"; this seemed to carry the implication that injustice, such as the Soviet government had committed in Eastern Europe, could not rightly be remedied by war. The other was the permission which it extended to Catholics to collaborate with un-believers (Communists) to achieve "some external good". To any Italian this meant that Catholics were now free to vote for Com-munists, or for parties which supported them, such as the 'Nenni'

Socialists.[1] This was a reversal of the policy of Pius XII who, moved by the measures introduced against the Church behind the Iron Curtain, had published that decree of July 1st, 1949, which forbad Catholics – on pain of excommunication – to give political support to the Communists, a decree which Pope John himself, early in his reign (April 1959) had allowed the Holy Office to extend to cover support for the Socialists.

Since the Conference of Italian Bishops, confronted by the Italian General Election of April 1963, had put out, in March, a warning that Catholics should rally in defence of the Church,[2] the new line taken by the encyclical seemed the more startling. With the election less than three weeks off the Communist and Socialist press was enabled to point out that good Catholics were now free to vote for the men and measures they preferred (for instance, those most likely to alleviate poverty) irrespective of ideology. When, at the elections, the Christian Democratic party suffered serious losses (some four million votes) and the Communists made small and the moderate (Saragat) Socialists large gains the Pope, and his encyclical, were widely blamed, and the Pope himself seems to have been startled.

Roncalli was now bitterly attacked by the Italian Press of the Right, which had steadily supported the 'integralist' policies of his predecessor, in the interests of Italy, western civilization, and Christendom, three concepts which the *Tempo* and the *Giornale D'Italia* were inclined to treat as one. It was made very clear to him that he had sold the pass which his two predecessors had so stoutly held:

First, within less than two months of the Italian election, he had seriously prejudiced its outcome and confused the consciences of Catholics by receiving Kruschev's son-in-law. This could only have been a

---

[1] In an effort to reassure the Christian Democrats the *Osservatore Romano*, in its article 'Pacem in Terris', April 12th, 1963, insisted that the new encyclical said nothing more about political co-operation with the Left than had already been said in *Mater et Magistra*. It was necessary for the *Osservatore* to say something because the Italian General Election was due in less than three weeks.

[2] *Osservatore Romano*, March 14th. Catholics were reminded of their "grave obligation to vote and to make their choice with a vigilant Christian conscience knowing how, if necessary, to place their fidelity to essential Christian principles ... ahead of personal and particular interests."

deliberate attempt on his part to give support to the Centre-Left coalition (which had been formed in February 1962, unopposed by the Pope, and largely unopposed – in consequence – by the Church in Italy). *Il Tempo* thought the interview had been "a shocking act" coming "at the beginning of a highly delicate electoral campaign", and *Il Giornale d'Italia* warned that "the Church and religion follow their own road, which is not that of politics, or of the State. . . . the foreign policy of the Italian State cannot coincide with the 'opening to the gospel'[1] of John XXIII".

Next, the interview had been followed, little more than two weeks before the election, by the encyclical which, by freeing Catholics to vote for Communists, surrendered the fortress to the enemy.

Critics on the extreme right now put forward the argument that the interview and the encyclical were both part of a plot to wrest Italy away from the western alliance and that the Pope was the well-intentioned but politically naïve tool of "International Communism".[2] In this view the Council itself was chiefly important as a seed-bed for political subversion. The Pope himself, even in these circles, was given credit for being "guided by an over-all religious aim". "Interested groups" had taken advantage of his good nature. Actually, while Roncalli had sympathy with the Centre-Left in Italy, and seems to have thought well of its promoter, Amintore Fanfani, his aims were never narrowly political at all, still less were they governed by Italian politics. It is possible, of course, that Moscow prompted the Adjoubei interview with a view to sowing confusion amongst Italian Catholics, and taking advantage of the good nature of the Pope. It is equally possible, even probable, that the Pope decided to see Adjoubei because he genuinely believed in opening a dialogue of some kind with Moscow, and because

---

[1] A parody of the *Aperta a Sinistra*, or 'Opening to the Left', the name given to the Centre-Left coalition. Italian Press reactions at this time are more fully considered below, on pp. 187–8.

[2] The periodical *Borghese*, and the books published by its editor, Mario Tedeschi, popularized these views. But some analogous thinking was going on in the Curia. Some of the things Cardinal Ottaviani said about "little Communists in the sacresty", or about Christians of no position who, for personal gain, accepted bribes to promote the Centre-Left coalition (cf. *Il Mondo* for March 26th, 1963) implied that the Church was being politically corrupted by the Left.

he did not wish to give offence. What is not possible is to believe that he was thinking about the immediate influence of the interview on Italian politics, or about the electoral fortunes of the Centre-Left.

The timing of *Pacem in Terris*, which appeared so soon before the elections, and out of which the Communists made so much capital, was even more provocative than that of the interview. Was it really possible to believe that so radical a departure from traditional teaching, on a subject of such vital political consequence to Italians, could have been put out at that date without any intention of influencing the Italian voter?

Undoubtedly the Pope must have been well aware that Italians would connect the encyclical with the elections; if he were not aware of it there were plenty who would remind him. But we need to remember that there were other, and to him more important con-considerations, of which he was also aware. And of these the most compelling may have been his need, already discussed, to drive the Council into giving its attention to the world predicament, to the task and mission of the Church *ad extra*, to promoting the unity and peace of mankind. A new, and more pointed encyclical was the obvious means for doing this.

Even so, it may be said, could he not have waited another month? Why give the Italian parties of the Left such a political bonus at such a moment?

But then, why give the conservatives of the Right a bonus by with-holding a message which the world needed? His message was about human understanding, about justice, and about peace, and the world was thirsty for it. Peace was still in the balance; the thaw in the east, though apparent, was only partial; a new freeze-up might be coming. Moreover the committees preparing the agenda for the next session of the Council were already at work; time was short if he were to influence that session, and the text of this new encyclical, which he had inspired, commissioned, and partly written himself, was now ready for issue. He was not likely to be deterred from issuing it by the fact that he might damage the electoral fortunes of the Italian Christian Democrats, whose political strength seemed to him less important than it had seemed to Pius XII. Moreover, if he were going to change the rules governing the Italian Catholic vote – and *Pacem in Terris* did no less – it was clearly more honest to do so just before rather than just after a General Election.

His eye focused on the widest horizon of all, the unity and peace of mankind, and on the Council which was to further so great a cause, the Pope, ignoring the "prophets of doom", gave *Pacem in Terris* to the world, and it proved to be his Last Will and Testament. The very next month he was stricken; within less than two he was dead. During nine decisive months, from the day in September 1962, when he broadcast to the world that the Council was convening to bring her succour, to the day of his death, he was dedicated to this widest of his three visions, his vision of the unity and peace of mankind. To that vision, he taught, the Church, rejuvenated by the Council, must give herself, and so must all Christians and all men of good will.

Had he delayed to publish *Pacem in Terris* (even for six weeks) it would never have appeared. In that case his message would have been incomplete, for essentially this encyclical is complementary to *Mater et Magistra* and it explains the direction into which he tried to turn the Council. It is too early, as yet, to say whether the Council will prove to be capable of giving birth to all that Pope John hoped from it. It is too early to say whether his practical example in making contact with the other Christian Churches will bear fruit. It is too early to say whether his attempt to build bridges, both religious and political, over the top of the Iron Curtain, will lead on to better understanding between East and West. Perhaps he died too soon for this last and boldest of his initiatives to achieve what he seems to have hoped. But at least, because he did publish *Pacem in Terris* at the eleventh hour, he has left behind a rounded picture of his view of a true Christian social and political order in the world. Whatever the outcome of events, that will remain. And because we have that encyclical we shall always know what his vision for mankind was.

PART IV

His Attitude to Italy

From what has been said it will be clear that Roncalli, in his attitude towards world affairs, was what the nineteenth century called a liberal Catholic. Politically speaking he was an heir of Montalembert. He felt about the African and Asian peoples, whom he saw one by one winning their freedom, as Montalembert felt about Poland, about Belgium, and about Ireland; even as Byron felt about Greece or Mazzini felt about Italy. He was welcoming the newly liberated world and saying that, if only the peoples would recognize their rights as given by God, eschewing both materialism and imperialism, they could move on to a braver world yet.

It is a curious fact, indeed one of the little ironies of history, that if one is looking, in the nineteenth century, for the prophet whose vision of the *political* future of the world came nearest to the *political* world which Roncalli later welcomed it would be Mazzini. For he was the leading prophet, a century earlier, of free, independent, democratic, nations. He was also the prophet of the association of nations in a wider international grouping. And he insisted on the voluntary principle against the rigours of excessive State Socialism. He was the unyielding enemy of materialist Communism. He insisted upon Progress. He insisted upon God. He insisted upon the Duties of Man, as the only justification of the Rights of Man. He insisted upon personal liberty. It is true that Mazzini was a relentless enemy to the Pope and to the Church, in Italy, in his day; but that was because, at that time, they were the enemies of the kind of political world which Pope John was later to accept.

Roncalli would not have been encouraged, at his seminary in Bergamo or at the *Apollinare* in Rome to read Mazzini, and since later in life he seems to have read little except ecclesiastical history it is unlikely that he ever became acquainted with the writings of the man he must so often have heard denounced, but whom so many Italians, and other peoples, seemed to love. But then one day, while browsing in the

Vatican Library, in the autumn of 1960, he came upon one of Mazzini's pamphlets. Unfortunately it was one of the most anti-clerical ones. He might have read many pages, say, from *Faith and the Future* or from the *Duties of Man* and only have found reflected back to him his own social vision. But the pamphlet which he came across was *From the Council to God* in which, at the time of the First Vatican Council, the aging and disappointed patriot expressed himself with bitter irony at the expense of a Church which still stood in the way of the freedom of Italy.

Roncalli thought the preparatory commissions of the Second Vatican Council would be interested to hear about this pamphlet, so he told them what he had found:

"During these last months, while re-reading various examples of the abundant literature devoted to the First Vatican Council, celebrated by Our Predecessor of venerable memory, Pius IX, in 1869 and 1870, We happened to light upon a public address to the Press, the work of one of the most excited minds, and one most in favour at that time of anti-Roman frenzy. It was dedicated, ironically, and in shocking taste, to the bishops of the whole world who were about to come to the Vatican; saluting them, the author compared them with the eastern bishops of old, assembled at Nicea for the first Council of the year AD 325: 'Today you are reunited for a new and last Council at Rome. The first, that of Nicea, was a solemn and venerable triumphal baptism celebrating the unity of the religion that the times demanded. Yours, the last, will witness, whatever you may do, the public agony of a dying religion and, by the same token, the coming dawn of another religion. . . .'

"Such are his actual words of defiance and prophecy.

"A century later we can take the true measure of their inanity and of the real worth of these prophets of Baal – for they exist always – 'whose visions are nothing but dreams and folly'. . . . Leave them to talk; let us apply ourselves to vigilance and to patience 'so that we may gain the fruit of the promise'. . . . "[1]

Having castigated Mazzini, for his apostasy, his heresy, and the insolence of his pamphlet, Roncalli went on to express, on several

[1] Address of November 14th, 1960, DC 1341, Col. 1483.

occasions, the depth of his devotion to Pius IX, the Pope of 1870, and his hope that he might canonize that Pope during the course of the Second Vatican Council. "I am always thinking," he wrote in his journal, "of Pius IX, of saintly and glorious memory; and, imitating him in his sacrifices, I would like to be worthy of celebrating his canonization."[1] How fitting if the fathers of the Church, assembled in a new General Council, successors of the fathers of 1869-70, could in this way find themselves present to pay their homage to that earlier Pope who had withstood the assault, who had kept the torch burning, who had made possible the glorious events of 1962!

On the religious plane, nothing could be more natural than Roncalli's exaltation of Pius IX or his castigation of Mazzini. Yet on the political plane the position is (or should be) reversed. For Pius IX was the most resolute opponent, in his own day, of just those freedoms (and especially Italian freedom) advocated by Pope John in *Mater et Magistra* and in *Pacem in Terris*. Nor had Mazzini's political prophecies been inane, or his visions "dreams and folly". His visions, and those of his fellow liberals, had made a new world, a world which Roncalli welcomed as better than the old one, insisting that men had a *right* to those freedoms which Mazzini had demanded and Pius IX had rejected. If the world had followed the political advice of Pius IX, instead of the political advice of Mazzini, there could have been no free peoples for Pope John to welcome or instruct. Roncalli could not realize it, because he had not been seriously educated in modern history, but in fact his world had been made by Mazzini and the other liberals. Without them the progress, the liberalism, and the modern civilization which he welcomed, and which Pius IX had castigated, were not imaginable. In the historical order Roncalli was the heir not of Pius IX but of Mazzini. So far from being "dreams and folly", Mazzini's political vision of the future had proved astonishingly accurate – Italy free, united, and republican; a world of independent peoples, built on the ruins of the old Empires, yet coming together to join a common international association; an insistence on the rights of the individual, of the family, of religion – in short on the rights of the Charter of the United Nations, or those adumbrated by Pope John. None of the

[1] *Giornale dell' Anima*, p. 304.

mid-nineteenth-century prophets, not even Montalembert (who supposed the papacy would always need the support of the papal states), was better justified by events in the twentieth century than was Mazzini.

Yet he had been quite wrong about the Church. He had supposed that the papacy and, indeed, Catholicism were moribund. In this respect he was the heir of the eighteenth-century enlightenment and of the French Revolution; he was always being astonished by the Catholic revival in his own day and he would have been still more astonished by Catholic resilience in the twentieth century, and by the summoning of the Second Vatican Council. Earnestly religious, with a Jansenistic sense of duty, he never suspected the perennial vitality of orthodox, Roman, Catholicism.

Roncalli's somewhat *simpliciste* views about both Pius IX and Mazzini are a latter-day reminder of the hundred years' tragedy of Italy's relations with the Vatican, relations which Roncalli himself would go far, in the end, to put on a better footing. For the violence of Pius IX's reaction against the Risorgimento, which had robbed him of his States and set up a secular Italy, gave rise to a tradition at the Vatican of hostility towards Italy, and even towards modern civilization as a whole, which persisted and is still not unknown. In spite of the Lateran Treaty of 1929, which settled the Roman question, the bitterness inherited from the great *dissidio* has not yet worked itself out; even the most recent popes received their own education at Rome under its shadow. Pius XII, a Roman, was still being educated in the Rome of the eighteen-nineties, when the anti-clerical hostility of the liberals towards the Church was at its height, and a fine scorn it gave him for their impieties and follies. Roncalli reached Rome in 1901, when the situation was much the same, and there he imbibed the clericalist interpretation of the Italian Risorgimento. When he indulged in his little outburst against Mazzini in front of the preparatory commissions in 1960 he was striking a note which he might not have struck if he had known more about Mazzini, but it was a note that would vibrate in the heart of every senior member of the Curia. They had all been educated to hold in proper horror the spoliations and impieties of the liberals of the Risorgimento. They would all smile, or applaud, when the Pope could prove that the prophet of the Risorgimento had been wrong.

Yet the real tragedy was that they themselves had been cut off, by that lamentable quarrel, from the social, political, and cultural development of modern Italy and thus of modern Europe. After the crisis of 1860–70 the Pope (and the Curia) had become a "Prisoner in the Vatican" in a deeper sense than the merely physical; he had become the prisoner of an out-of-date culture. The events of 1860–70 cut the Vatican off, almost physically, from the modern civilization on her own doorstep, namely that of Italy, and she was not fully restored to it till after the Second World War. For although Pius XI made a formal peace with Italy in the Lateran treaty of 1929 both he and Italy were then living under the shadow of Mussolini, and the situation was both artificial and explosive. Only after the Second World War, in Pius XII's time, did the papacy and Italy at last confront each other openly again, though naturally both were on the defensive and clung to such safeguards as they could find.

What Roncalli did was to accept Italy, freely and without reserve, as he accepted that modern civilization of which she was a part. Italy, democracy, the independent and lay State, social justice – all these things he accepted, openly and freely, and thus he took the papacy at one leap into the western civilization of his own age, into the civilization which had been built by the liberals during the long *dissidio* when the Vatican had been cut off. When he published his encyclicals on social and political matters he was embracing a world which had been built by other hands, and was welcoming most but not all of it as good. And that was how, without knowing it, he met Mazzini. He did not read his writings, except on that one unfortunate occasion. He died without realizing his importance as a prophet. But he met him when he met the world, and accepted the world – progress, democracy, and the rest – because he was meeting a world which Mazzini, together with thousands of other liberals and Socialists, had helped to make.

But, oddly enough, it never seems to have occurred to Roncalli that there were two sides to the hundred-year-old quarrel between Italy and the Church or that his own political principles and policies were quite at variance with those of his predecessors, and derived, in fact, rather from their opponents. He had accepted, in his youth, at its face value, the clericalist case against the Italian liberals which he had been taught at Bergamo and at Rome, had accepted it with a single-mindedness as simple as that of an old-time English liberal imbibing the case against the Vatican. And being unphilosophical, and little concerned with the study of recent history, he never seems to have reconsidered, later on, in the light of the wisdom which experience brought to him, those traditions he had absorbed as a student about the birth of modern Italy. He took it for granted that the Italians had treated his predecessors shamefully, that their sorry behaviour had been a sad lapse in their generally good record of loyalty to the Holy See, but that fortunately, in the reign of Pius XII, they had begun once again to see the light. Here is what he said in 1958:

"Illustrious and holy Pope of the past century was that Servant of God; Pius IX: of whom it was written that no Pope was ever more loved and more hated in this world: and I remember all the help and the edification which it gave to me in my adolescence and my youth to read the moving story of his life and his pontificate. And, by contrast, men still remember, with a blush for the promoters of the diabolical deed, and a shudder in the soul of every well disposed person, the attempt to throw his sacred bones into the Tiber, on the occasion of their transfer to Campo Verano, in the Church of San Lorenzo, where the Catholics of Europe had prepared for him a most noble tomb, visited even today with respect and veneration.

"In 1903 I had just entered into my major orders when, on July 20th, at the age of ninety-three, there was extinguished that star of the first magnitude Pope Leo XIII, after twenty-five years as pontiff. Admittedly there were most solemn funeral ceremonies; but they were all of an official and ecclesiastical character and hidden in the basilica of St Peter. Civil and political Rome remained silent and scornful!

"The popes who followed, St Pius X, Benedict XV and Pius XI, were undoubtedly honoured, at the time of their deaths, with a real respect and with religious solemnities in perfect liturgical and pontifical style. But there was no marked concern in the outer world.

"But in the case of our Holy Father Pius XII – and it is most grati-
fying to recognize the fact – we are witnessing the unmistakable opening of new horizons, and something mysterious bearing witness to a
gradual improvement in the relations between the civil order and the
religious and social order: a more marked tendency amongst us to
respect that which is sacred: a willingness on the part of those belonging
to various political, economic and social groups to look us in the face;
a desire on their part for a better understanding."[1]

Thus Roncalli, preaching in St Mark's, at Venice, on the occasion of
the death of Pius XII.

But who had ostracized whom? Who had shut the doors of the Vatican? Who had barred the way of Italian Catholics into politics, by the
non-expedit? Who had refused to recognize the new kingdom? And
which had been the chief sufferer, in this lamentable affair, the Italians,
who had been taught to ignore the Church, in developing their new
society, or the Church, which had been cut off from the political and
cultural development of Italy and the world?

The *dissidio* had indeed been a disaster, a disaster for Italy but a
disaster, too, for the Papacy and for the Church. And it would not be
cured by any return of a prodigal, penitent Italy, disavowing Mazzini
and Garibaldi, to the feet of the Pope, nor even by respect for the
personal qualities of Pius XII. If a cure were to be effected (a matter
still doubtful) the healer would prove to be Roncalli himself because, in
his encyclicals and policies, he had caught up with modern civilization,
and thus with Italy. The healing would be the result not of a mere
'return' but of a two-way process, the renewed Christianity of Italy
on the one hand, but the renewed political, social and cultural awareness of the Vatican on the other.

Let us take another look at this disastrous *dissidio*. It was rooted in the
events of 1849, and of 1860–70, when the papal states were lost to the
Pope, and much of Italian life was secularized. Had it not been for these
events the popes would no doubt, in due course, have found a *modus
vivendi* with the modern world of liberalism, and 'moderate Socialism',
stemming from the French Revolution, in spite of what Gregory XVI
had earlier said about it; indeed Pius IX himself made a brave attempt

[1] *Scritti e discorsi*, Vol. 3, pp. 706, 707.

to do so during the first two years of his pontificate. But the events of the decade 1860–70 were so cataclysmic that they seemed, in the papal view, to end all possibility of reconciliation; the political spoliation of central Italy, when taken in conjunction with the secularization of the whole peninsula, appeared to be the work of the devil. Italy was evidently wrong; and therefore not only Italy but that whole modern liberal world which Italy was seeking to emulate. Let the Italians return in sackcloth and ashes – nothing less would suffice.

That this was the aged Pius IX's view is not surprising. That it was also Leo XIII's was a disaster, for this meant that there would be no change till the twentieth century, since Leo reigned till 1903, and during his long reign the position hardened, on both sides. Leo enjoyed a reputation as a diplomat and he is remembered for his enlightened endeavours to reconcile the German Catholics with Bismarck and the French Catholics with the Third Republic. But he did nothing to reconcile Italian Catholics with Italy, nothing to relax that *non-expedit*, laid down by Pius IX, which prevented obedient Catholics from taking any part in the political affairs of their country. It was in his long reign (1878–1903) that the habit was developed, in modern Italy, that good Catholics must look to the Vatican for permission to vote. Pius IX, in the crisis of his day, had introduced the *non-expedit*. But under Leo XIII this striking instrument of clerical political control became established as a habit, a habit which St Pius X, and Pius XI, and Pius XII modified, when they allowed Italians to vote for approved candidates, or parties, but which Pope John broke.

Leo was aristocratic, paternalistic and authoritarian, and a little closer in his thinking to Pius IX than has often been allowed; as a younger man he had been the first to suggest to Pius that he should publish a "Syllabus of Errors". He was certainly not a liberal, and the Johannine encyclicals, which pay homage to Leo's *Rerum novarum*, would have astonished and pained the author of that encyclical as much as they would have gladdened the heart of Mazzini. But Leo was a diplomat, with a finely developed sense of political possibilities, so that he readily embraced the distinction between the thesis (the truth) and the hypothesis (what can be allowed in given circumstances) which had been used in Pius IX's reign to save that Pope from the consequences of his own more intransigent remarks. He had little difficulty in reconciling himself with the French Third Republic or even with part of Bismarck's programme in his Kulturkampf, and he could have reconciled himself with Italy. But he did not choose to. He maintained to the full his clerical boycott of Italy because he did not think Italy would survive. Here he miscalculated, but it was a mistake easily made. Many shrewd observers were sceptical of the future of this new-fangled and disparate kingdom which had been put together by mutually antagonistic forces between 1860 and 1870. And the Pope had special cause to be sceptical for had not Rome, throughout the centuries, seen a succession of political régimes in the peninsula, all of them transitory? This was the third time, within the nineteenth century, that the Pope had lost his political position; why should he not recover it, as he had in 1815 and in 1850?

Towards the end of Leo's reign, when the new Italy acquired increasingly reliable diplomatic support from Germany and Austria, Leo realized he had been wrong. But he was now a very old man. He would have to leave it to his successor to adjust matters, to get on to terms with an Italy which now seemed likely to survive.

And his successor St Pius X did begin the work of political reconciliation; but he did so very guardedly, and he never abandoned the principle that the loyal Catholic must look to the Church before he exercised his vote. He was not much interested in politics, and was free from his two predecessors' concern for the papal states; the existence of Italy, as such, did not bother him. What did concern him, deeply, were the intellectual and social movements which he saw springing up around him, and which claimed to be independent of clerical control. Leo had seen the same thing – indeed the *Opera dei Congressi* through which lay Catholics, deprived of the vote, sought their own means at widely publicized congresses to influence public affairs, was becoming a formidable force by the end of his reign and one towards which Leo was inclined to be indulgent. But Pius saw that this congress activity was drawing Catholic social and intellectual movements in Italy right out of the control of the clergy, and he checked the whole movement by winding up the *Opera* altogether and replacing it by various forms of Catholic Action, which were under clerical control. In the same way, in his encyclical condemning Modernism, Pius X was at pains to set up a censorship which would kill "social Modernism", by which he meant any advocacy of a change in the social structure ordained by God. Though he relaxed the *non-expedit* by allowing Catholics to vote in certain areas where they could help to keep out the Socialists, his essential contribution was to put under papal control the independent, lay, Christian Democratic movement, which was developing at the congresses at the end of Leo's reign and which was looking for the chance to win political power. To Pius X, more than to any other modern pope, it seemed evident that Italian Catholics must take their social and intellectual as well as their political guidance from the Church. Leo had told them they must not vote because they must not recognize Italy. Pius told them they could vote, where he said they might, and provided they voted as he thought necessary. Italy was no longer the enemy; the enemies were laicism and Socialism. But the clerical control, inherited from Leo, though used in a different way, was more positive, and stronger in the hands of Pius X.

Pope John venerated this saintly predecessor. In doing so, however, he was venerating the memory of a man who, though linked by the bonds of sanctity, and by a similar humble background, had in fact been at the opposite pole to himself in his social outlook and in his authoritarian and conservative disposition. In his days as secretary to Bishop Radini Tedeschi of Bergamo Roncalli had been painfully aware of that devastating witch-hunt after Modernist heretics which was the result, in Italy, of the extreme terms in which St Pius X condemned intellectual and social Modernism, and of the machinery which he set up to ferret it out. As a result of the elaborate system of informing which had developed, men of the calibre of Radini Tedeschi had gradually withdrawn themselves from those clerical bodies which were supervising the affair and for showing insufficient zeal, had run into grave danger of bringing upon themselves the displeasure of Rome. The anxious months suffered by the Bishop of Bergamo, on this account, are recorded in Roncalli's life of him,[1] and we need not doubt that the biographer was at one with his Bishop in his feelings on the matter. He was careful to exonerate Pius X from any personal responsi-

[1] A. Roncalli. *Mons. Giacomo Maria Radini Tedeschi*, 3rd Ed. (Rome, 1963), pp. 149–52.

bility for the distressing consequences of his condemnations. All the same when later, as Pope, Roncalli said there had been enough condemnations, his mind must have run back to those dark days in 1911 at Bergamo, while he was brooding on the more recent activities of the Holy Office.

In spite, then, of a new acceptance of Italy *de facto*, but not *de jure*, under St Pius X, there was no acceptance by the Vatican of a lay, Italian, Catholic democracy independent of clerical control. The exasperated leader, in those days, of the Christian Democrats, Romolo Murri, who had dreamed of a new Catholic Italy (such as Vincenzo Gioberti had dreamed in the early days of the Risorgimento), rising on the ashes of the Piedmontese monarchical State, and independent of the clergy, was thwarted in his aims by Pius X, and in due course excommunicated for Modernism. The Pope had no liking at all for the idea of power passing to socially 'progressive' laymen, whether they were Catholic or no. He much preferred to go into alliance with the monarchy, or the Nationalists, and to make political arrangements with the astute premier Giolitti, with a view to keeping all sorts of radicals, whether Christian Democrat or Social Democrat, in their place.

And Pius XI, in his turn, after 1922, saw the problem in a similar light. But it was more difficult for him to maintain the clerical control because by the early nineteen-twenties the challenge from the Christian Democrats had become much stronger. This was because Pius X's successor Benedict XV (1914–22), perhaps the wisest, politically, of the modern popes, had abandoned all attempt to control the Italian Catholic vote after the First World War. As a result a lay, Catholic, Popular Party had sprung into being and in a mere three years had acquired, by 1922, more than a hundred seats in the Chamber, where it had become second in strength only to the Socialists. Had Pius XI, who succeeded Benedict in that year, chosen to give the support of the Church to the new party it could have been a formidable rival both to the Socialists and to the irregular Fascist *squadri* with which Mussolini was trying to make his own short cut to power. But Pius, and the hierarchy as a whole, disliked the Catholic Popular Party for its independence and for its social radicalism, and the Church tended to support the Nationalists, or the Liberals, or to stand aloof. Discountenanced by Pius XI, Don Sturzo, the Popular Party's leader, resigned, to be succeeded by Alcide de Gasperi. But already Mussolini had won power. As yet it was parliamentary power; the forms of the constitution were still preserved. It was still possible, in 1924, to replace Mussolini's government by constitutional means, but the only political combination which could hope to do it was a coalition between the two largest parties, the Socialists and de Gasperi's Popular Party. In short what (in today's parlance) was required was an *Aperta a Sinistra*, a Centre-Left or Catholic-Socialist coalition. De Gasperi was able to point to co-operation of this kind between Catholics and Socialists in Austria. But Pius XI was shocked by the idea. It seemed to him out of the question for a Catholic Popular Party to work with the Socialists. The Pope, the hierarchy, and the King preferred Mussolini to that. And since the decision rested with the King, the Fascist dictatorship was established, and the Catholic Popular Party, like the Socialists, was scattered abroad or went underground.

During these decisive events Roncalli was at Rome. He had been summoned there by Benedict XV, at the end of 1920, to help reorganize the work of the foreign missions. He also knew the new Pope, Pius XI, through his contacts with him at the *Ambrosiana* library at Milan. But he seems to have been little concerned with the dramatic political events in which the Vatican was involved. When faced later on, after he had become Pope, with similar proposals for a coalition government between the Christian Democrats and Socialists, he would eschew Pius XI's precedent and give the project his support; and the hierarchy in Italy would follow his lead. But this does not mean that in 1924 he had thought Pius XI was wrong. He had a great respect for Pius XI. We may be sure that he was repeating his own favourite motto, Caesar Baronius' *Obedentia et Pax*; it was the Pope's business not his; what the Pope decided would be best; it was not for him to judge. We know too from his diary that his mind was filled to overflowing in those critical days with other matters: "My whole spirit is absorbed with my new duties. It is my duty and my desire to remain without a glance, without a thought, without a wish for anything else."[1] "The

[1] *Il Giornale dell' Anima*, p. 203.

work of the Propagation of the Faith is the breath of my soul and of my life. For that my whole being, always: mind, heart, speech, pen, prayer, labour, sacrifice, night and day. . . . "[1] "Anything which does not belong to the honouring of God, the service of the Church, the good of souls, is incidental for me, and without importance."[2]

He was thus a busy and a preoccupied man at the time when Mussolini came to power. Besides his work for the Congregation for the Propagation of the Faith, which took him travelling around Europe, he was also a professor of patristics at the *Apollinare* (the Pontifical Roman Seminary) which kept his mind on the early centuries of the Church and on the eastern Mediterranean. Less than most rising Italian ecclesiastics would he be likely, at this date, to be concerning himself with Italian affairs. They were the concern of the Italian bishops. In March 1925, at the early age of fourty-three, Roncalli became an Archbishop, but his See was *in partibus infidelium*, the titular Archbishopric of Aeropolis, and the purpose of this honour bestowed upon him by Pius XI was to strengthen him in his new post as Apostolic Visitor to Bulgaria. Not until 1953, when Pius XII made him Patriarch of Venice, would Roncalli be working again in Italy; in Bulgaria, in Turkey, in France, Italian politics became to him something remote; to few Italian ecclesiastics of his position can they have seemed so remote as they did to Roncalli. The formal ending of the *dissidio* between the papacy and Italy in the Lateran Treaty of 1929, the growing tension between Pius and Mussolini in the early 'thirties, the Abyssinian and Spanish wars – he might, as the Pope's representative, be expected to say something about Pius XI's attitude on these matters, but his essential work was quite remote from them. In any case: *Obedentia et Pax*.

But then, suddenly, at the end of 1944, Roncalli was thrust right among the problems raised by the resurgence of Christian Democracy in the west when he was sent to the Paris of de Gaulle, of the Free French, of the Resistance. To the leaders of the Christian Democratic Party at Paris (the *Mouvement Républicaine Populaire*, or MRP), men like Robert Schumann and Georges Bidault, the idea of any dependence of a Catholic political party upon the clergy was merely laughable;

[1] *Ibid.*, p. 204.   [2] *Ibid.*, p. 212.

they belonged to a lay movement which had relied upon its own efforts and which had never been taught to believe that it should accept political control from bishops; indeed the close relations of so many bishops with Vichy had made their politics particularly suspect to members of the MRP. These new leaders had been educated not by a clerically directed Catholic Action but by Bidault's paper, *L'Aube*; a large proportion of the French clergy were with them, but they did not lead them. During his period in Paris Roncalli was witnessing the kind of government de Gasperi had wanted for Italy in 1924, but had not been allowed by Pius XI to pursue, namely a coalition between a Catholic party and other parties, including anti-clericals of the Left, and independent of episcopal directives. When Roncalli became Pope he had had more experience of French than of Italian politics, his education in the problems of modern government in the west having been gained by watching the methods of the MRP. This may be one reason why, as Pope, he tried to keep the Church out of Italian politics, and why he was prepared to give his blessing to such political combinations as seemed necessary to the leftish Italian Christian Democratic leader Amintore Fanfani, whose political point of view had much in common with that of the French MRP leaders.

Italian politics, after the fighting was over, had this in common with French, that there was a natural tendency at first for all political parties, including the Communists, to co-operate in the immediate tasks of reconstruction, both local and national. Only gradually, as the policies of Stalin and Molotov destroyed the hopes of a continuation into the era of peace of the wartime co-operation between East and West, and as Moscow reasserted her authority over the western Communist parties, did the hostility harden between the Communist parties of France and Italy and all other political groups in the two countries. In Italy this brief period of collaboration and good will produced some startling results, in as much as the all-party convention, which drew up the Constitution of the new Italian Republic in 1947, agreed to re-affirm the Lateran Treaty of 1929 and the Concordat between Italy and the Holy See which had accompanied it. In this way the Communists shared in accepting the sovereignty of the Vatican State, recognized that Catholicism was the religion of the great majority of the Italian people, and accorded it a limited, but privileged position in the public life of the country and in education, while the Papacy accepted the principle of the separation of Church and State, "each sovereign in its own sphere", and full toleration for all other groups. The Christian Democratic party, under the leadership of de Gasperi, claimed and insisted upon that independence from clerical control which Benedict XV had granted to the Popular Party (but Pius XI had gone far to nullify) and which the Christian Democrats in France were taking as a matter of course. On this basis de Gasperi won an overwhelming victory at the General Election of 1948 and was enabled to embark upon a programme of reconstruction which commanded wide support from the Left, although neither the Socialists nor the Communists were represented in his administration.

It thus seemed, momentarily, as though the perennial problem of nearly a century of Italian history had been solved, as though the Papacy had at last been reconciled with Italy in the sense that she was willing to allow Italians, whether Catholic or no, to determine their political destiny without the guidance or control of the Church.

But it was not to be. In the very year after de Gasperi's victory Pius XII issued his famous directive of July 1949 which made it an offence, for which the penalty was excommunication, for Catholics to give political support to Communists – i.e. to vote for them. The embargo was back again. It was a *non-expedit* once more. De Gasperi fought back, and was successful in resisting the endeavours both of Pius XII and of Professor Gedda (Head of Catholic Action) to persuade him to break with the anti-clerical elements in his own government, and to outlaw the Communists.[1] But at the next General Election, in 1953, the Italian hierarchy felt encouraged to throw the full weight of its authority behind the effort to prevent Catholics from voting either for the Communists or for any groups which might give them political support. They stopped short of *directing* Catholics to vote for the Christian Democrats, but they made their intentions sufficiently clear. In the following year de Gasperi died, and with his death there faded for the

[1] Cf the dramatic account of his interview with Pius XII in C. Falconi, *Gedda e l'Azione Cattolica* (Parenti, 1958), pp. 169, 170.

time being the vision of a Catholic party which should be truly independent of the directives of the Church.

His opponents claimed that by his political directives Pius XII was breaking the Italian Concordat which insisted upon the independence and sovereignty of Church and State, each in its own sphere; the Church, they insisted, had invaded the sphere of the State. His supporters replied that the matter was religious, because the Communists professed atheism and in eastern Europe, where they were in control, they were doing all they could to kill the life of the Church. Were they to be allowed to gain control in the west, and especially in Italy, and to deny there the rights of religion?

The whole argument served to reaffirm once again what a thousand years of European history had made evident, that it is not possible to distinguish clearly between the spiritual and the political spheres and that, in the absence of an effective umpire (such as the American Supreme Court), the stronger would prevail. Pius XII was reaffirming the traditional and entirely logical position of the Papacy, namely that the spiritual power is above the temporal power because a man's spiritual end is the purpose of his life and the temporal order only exists to help him to fulfil it. If, in the opinion of the Pope, a development in the temporal order threatened the spiritual well-being of Catholics (and Communism clearly did this) he could rightly call upon the faithful to resist it, as Pius IX had called upon them to resist Cavour, and later popes had insisted on controlling their relations with the government of Italy.

In an address of November 2nd, 1954, to the cardinals, archbishops, and bishops present in Rome[1], Pius XII reaffirmed, in striking terms, the superiority of the spiritual over the temporal power:

"The power of the Church is not bound by the limits of 'matters strictly religious', as they say, but the whole matter of the Natural Law, its foundation, its interpretation, its application, so far as their moral aspects extend, are within the Church's power ... even though to someone, certain declarations of the Church may not seem proved

[1] AAS, XLVI, p. 666. There is an English translation *The Authority of the Church in Temporal Matters*, National Catholic Welfare Conference, Washington, DC, from which I have quoted here.

by the arguments put forward, his obligation to obey still remains."
He went on to quote Pius X: " 'The social question and the controversies underlying that question . . . are not merely of an economic
nature, and consequently such as can be settled while the Church's
authority is ignored since, on the contrary, it is most certain that it
(the social question) is primarily a moral and religious one. . . . ' "
And not merely the social question but the political question. Pius XII
continues: " . . . there are problems outside the social field, not strictly
'religious', political problems, of concern either to individual nations,
or to all nations, which belong to the moral order . . . such are: the
purpose and limits of temporal authority; the relations between the
individual and society – the so-called 'totalitarian State' whatever be
the principle it is based on; the 'complete secularization of the State'
and of public life; the complete secularization of the schools; war, its
morality, whether it is licit, or illicit . . . .

"Common sense, and likewise truth, are contradicted by whoever
asserts that these and like problems are outside the field of morals. . . . "

On these matters, Pius XII insists, it is the duty of the Church not
merely to advise in private, but to proclaim: " . . . in the open, crying
'from the rooftops' . . . in the front line, in the midst of the struggle
that rages between truth and error, virtue and vice, between the 'world'
and the kingdom of God. . . . "

It is a striking address, and the most recent and complete statement
which we have of the traditional papal theory of ecclesiastical authority
over human society.[1] For Pius XII was not content merely to assert
the Church's right to pronounce on the great moral issues of the day,
or to interpret the Natural Law. He was careful to safeguard the
ecclesiastical right to Lordship over the political sphere generally. "Clergy
and laity," he insists, "must realize that the Church is fitted and
authorized . . . to establish an external norm of action and conduct for
matters which concern public order and which do not have their
immediate origin in natural or divine law. . . . " He recognizes the
existence of a revolt, on the part of the faithful, against this sort of

---

[1] An admirable short analysis of the traditional papal theory is to be found
in Dr Walter Ullmann's Aquinas Society paper, *The Medieval Papacy, St Thomas
and Beyond*, 1960.

political tutelage. "Not a few moderns ... wish to be treated as adults who are in full possession of their rights, and can decide for themselves what they must or must not do in any given situation. Let the Church – they do not hesitate to say – propose her doctrine, pass her laws as norms of our actions. Still, when there is question of practical application to each individual's life, the Church must not interfere; she should let each one of the faithful follow his own conscience and judgement. They declare this is all the more necessary because the Church and her ministers are unaware of certain sets of circumstances. ... But to be an adult and to have put off the things of childhood is one thing, it is quite another to be an adult and not to be subject to the guidance and government of legitimate authority. For government is not a kind of nursery for children, but *the effective direction of adults toward the end proposed to the State*."

I have put the last few words into italics because they provide the heart of Pius XII's teaching on this matter. It is a statement of the Church's claim to direct adults, politically, and to propose ends to the State. It defines the power by virtue of which Pius restrained the Italian voter, as his predecessors had restrained him. Since the Communists, like the nineteenth-century liberals, had a wrong view of the ends of the State it was found necessary to order Catholics to refrain from giving them political support as it had previously been found necessary to order Catholics, by the *non-expedit*, to refrain from using their vote at all.

Such was the politico-ecclesiastical position in Italy when Roncalli, grown accustomed to the freer atmosphere in France, sailed down the Grand Canal, in March, 1953, as the new Patriarch of Venice, the first Italian post he had held since he left his native Bergamo in 1920. We are told that Pius XII, aware that Roncalli was out of sympathy with the growing authoritarianism at Rome, was exiling him to a backwater, just as a few months later he would send Roncalli's friend Montini away from the Secretariat of State to Milan. Both future popes are spoken of as being at this time "under a cloud".[1] Whatever the truth about this (and there are, to say the least, alternative explanations

[1] Carlo Falconi *Pope John and his Council* (London, 1964), p. 76.

for both appointments) Roncalli, at Venice, found himself expected to adopt the full rigour of Pius XII's boycott of the Communists and Socialists, which was something he could not have done, even had he wanted, as Pius XII's representative in France. The papal ban on giving political support to the Communists had been of universal application, and had been intended to check the progress of the party in France as well as in Italy. But the French had long since lost the habit of following automatically the political directives given by their hierarchy, nor was their hierarchy always politically obedient to Rome. There was nothing left in France to compare with the political power of the Italian hierarchy, headed by the Pope, aided by a Catholic Action controlled by the bishops, and in alliance with a Christian Democratic party formally independent but in practice still obedient to episcopal directives. Pius XII might aspire to a political defence of the West, but there were few countries where he could hope to make his claim good besides Italy. Italy was the citadel that must never be surrendered. It was only when the Italians showed signs of rebelling against this tutelage (as they did when that over-zealous hammer of the Communists, the Bishop of Prato, was hailed in 1957 before a secular court to answer for libel) that Pius XII showed the real depths of his indignation and the wide interpretation which he gave to the rights of the spiritual power. The immense theocratic claims which Pius had made in his address at Rome in 1954, quoted above, were of merely theoretical interest to the members of his audience who came from America, France, Britain, or Germany. But the Italians could take them literally, because in Italy these claims might still be enforced. Abroad they were only the thesis; the hypothesis was different. In Italy they were actual.

Once established as Patriarch of Venice Roncalli became, for the first time, the Italian ecclesiastic. He gave no sign of being at variance with the political attitude of his master, the Patriarch of Italy. His writings and speeches[1] may still sound his own characteristic notes of friendship and understanding, but when they touch on secular matters they are hard to distinguish from those of other leading members of the Italian hierarchy. With his genius for adjustment, he had settled down

[1] Published in three volumes of *Scritti e Discorsi*.

to fulfil the functions expected of a senior member of the Italian Ecclesiastical Establishment; we even find him making the time-honoured thrust at tourists "for the most part from the north, who seem to have discarded at the frontier that sense of discipline and courtesy with which they clothe themselves at home",[1] imagining they are free to behave as they like on the Lido, or to enter St Mark's insufficiently clad.

It will come as a shock to anybody familiar with the Roncalli of the Balkans, of France, or of *Pacem in Terris*, to read his address of June 9th, 1956, at Venice, to Civic Committees (political pressure groups) of Catholic Action, following regional elections which had gone well for the Christian Democrats:

"The activity of the civic committees is to continue: this is the directive from above. This course of action is recommended by the results of the elections which confirm the advantages of fidelity and obedience on the part of Catholics.

" . . . As you know, I have been at Rome, where I have been meeting with high ecclesiastical personages who carry, like your Patriarch, a heavy responsibility.

"We shall pursue our path in accordance with agreed directives, firm and clear. You understand me. It is necessary to remain absolutely firm, true to our principles, to our doctrine, to our faith.

"On the ground of politics, or organization, it is possible to distinguish between Communism and Socialism.

"In the matter of principles it is not. Communism and Socialism have the same philosophy, and they are irreconcilable with Christianity. There is no possibility of agreement between Marxism and the Gospel. And we cannot sacrifice the gospel to Marxism.

" . . . It is necessary to know how to resist a pro-Socialist outlook which is spreading even in this country, and which withers up our resources; and it is necessary to know how to resist secularism. At first sight the danger which derives from this outlook may not seem grave, but it is. And if the Pope and the bishops say it is grave they have their reasons for saying so, and the faithful ought to listen to them. This is a matter of discipline, and you understand how serious that is. Two things matter in the Church: doctrine and discipline.

[1] *Scritti e Discorsi*, Vol. III, p. 159.

"Liberty of thought is all very well; personal opinions deserve respect; but within the agreed limits.

" . . . As always, the young people pretend to know more than their elders: they do not like to be warned: they do not care for advice.

"This is an old story, which will be repeated again for the elderly of tomorrow. What is precious, today and tomorrow, is experience, wisdom, discretion: above all it is conformity to the directives of the Church which, besides enjoying the grace of the Holy Spirit, has also at her disposal the experience of the centuries.

"Some think that Italians might take a lesson from what is happening in France. But in Italy, by the Grace of God, the situation is quite different and much better. There are no grounds for comparison.

"France had a concordat which was abolished. In Italy, besides the Treaty, there is the Concordat of the Lateran, an integral part of the new Constitution, which in religious and moral matters is the guarantee of order and peace.

"In the dangerous hour of battle and uncertainty, in an extremely delicate and difficult situation, navigation is dangerous, decision rests with the captain.

"Every man, then, to his post: let him who is to command command, him who is to obey obey. . . .

"You have understood me. When there is anything further to say it will be told you at the proper time. . . . "[1]

No doubt these members of Roncalli's civic committees, like others all over Italy, went away and did as they were told, thus helping to produce, in due course, the modest Christian Democratic success in the General Election of the spring of 1958, but helping also to perpetuate that estrangement of Catholics from other political parties which de Gasperi had eschewed, Pius XII had favoured, and Roncalli, as Pope, would attempt to heal. At this 1958 election the Italian hierarchy as a whole, following the lead of Pius XII, went into battle on behalf of the Christian Democrats in an all-out effort to keep out the Communists and Socialists. Ever since the affair of the Bishop of Prato, when Pius showed his feelings so clearly, the Pope had become in-

[1] *Op. cit.*, Vol. 2, pp. 435–37.

creasingly the target of attacks from the Left. In Italian eyes the quarrel had taken on a strongly personal flavour. Pius was hailed by his supporters as the champion of Catholic Italy against the enemy; but he was also subjected to personal attacks, in the anti-clerical Press, of a quite unaccustomed kind.

Roncalli would have been acting quite out of character if he had not rallied to the defence of a Pope so assailed. *Obedientia et Pax*. But *Obedientia* first. The lead had been given, his duty was clear, and he plunged into the political battle beside his brother bishops in defence of that Prince of the Apostles to whom they all owed obedience and devotion. On March 9th, as the electoral campaign gathered momentum, his attack thundered out from the ancient chancel of St Mark's. His special concern was to warn his hearers that they should recognize the Church's enemies, though they wore sheep's clothing, that they should beware of the false promises of those whose real aim was the ruin of religion. He was warning them not merely against her avowed enemies, the Communists, but against those other political groups, especially the Socialists, whose policies might play into the hands of the enemy:

" . . . a hostile wind has arisen, above all against the Church as a whole: her body of doctrine, her hierarchy, her history, and her divine mission in the world and especially in Italy. This wind mounts with unexpected violence, as occurs when the wild forces of nature are unchained.

"Against the Church I said, but further, it mounts especially against the very Person of the Supreme Pontiff and against the Bishops of the Church of God; indeed, without scruple, against her institutions of all sorts, for education, or assistance, in so insolent a manner as to make one ask whether the freedom of the Press – for it is the Press which spreads and gives credence to these distortions – has not come to be interpreted by some as none other than a liberty and right to offend, to lie against, to calumniate and to trample upon all that was sacred to our fathers and is still sacred to us and which we have the duty of defending even at the cost of life itself. . . . .

"Ah! my children! Beware of pacts and compromises, of understandings founded upon dreams, upon promises of respect for liberty made by those who trample truth, justice, and liberty under foot without scruple."[1]

His listeners could only conclude that it would be best to vote for the Christian Democrats, and to avoid political pacts with the Socialists.

This remarkable address, which goes on to build up a picture of Pius XII suffering insults as disgraceful as those suffered by Boniface VIII at Anagni, bears no resemblance to anything that Roncalli said after he had become Pope in the following November.

Obedientia et Pax. But when he had been elected Pope there was no longer any human being to whom he owed a duty of obedience. Absolved from *Obedientia* he was free to devote himself to *Pax*. Naturally for some months he allowed those who had been running the policy of the Curia to run it in their own way; so that the Holy Office was allowed, as we have seen, to renew, in April 1959, the boycott of the Communists and their friends. But further political directives ceased to emanate from the Pope, and when the crucial test came, in February 1962, with Fanfani's endeavour to form a Centre-Left coalition between the Christian Democrats and the Socialists, the hierarchy, in obedience to the Pope, mostly remained silent and allowed this political matter to take its own political course. It was thus that a coalition at last came into being of the kind which de Gasperi had urged more than thirty years before, as the only means of thwarting Mussolini, and to which moderate men had been looking since the Christian Democrats lost their over-all majority in 1953, but which Pius XII, like Pius XI, had refused to consider. Surrounded by the unaccustomed silence of the Italian bishops Fanfani and the Socialist leader Pietro Nenni shook hands.

Roncalli was now about to enter that last decisive year of his pontificate when he insisted that the Council had a message of peace and good will for all men. If he had ever himself believed in the value of political ostracism as a weapon for the defence of the Church he had ceased to do so now, and with *Pacem in Terris* he not only, in effect, lifted the ban on voting for the parties of the Left but he raised the fundamental question whether a political party's professed philosophy

[1] *Op. cit.,* Vol. 3, pp. 493–96.

really mattered very much. The fact that a movement derived from false principles, he pointed out, did not mean that it was incapable of good. The philosophical and the historical order were different. This suggested that those errors which Pius XII had so accurately diagnosed and so ineffectively pilloried were best ignored.

From the immediate standpoint of the political stability of Italy Pope John's new line did not prove a great success. Christian Democrats and Socialists proved too irreconcilable to maintain their coalition, entering the General Election in opposition to each other, and the voting showed a further decline in support for the Christian Democrats (the Pope's attitude was said to have cost the party anything from a million to four million votes) and a corresponding increase in the support given to the parties of the Left. The hierarchy took alarm and renewed its campaign on behalf of the Christian Democrats, and the only apparent result was the forming of a yet weaker Christian Democratic government, dependent upon the support of small groups from the Right and Centre, while the Socialists renewed their working alliance with the Communists. What Pope John had tried to do was to take the Church out of politics; but such a task was altogether too enormous to be accomplished in those last few months of his pontificate. To achieve it he would have needed first to free the Christian Democratic party leadership from clerical direction and second to free Italians from clerical control over their voting. He achieved the first, temporarily, when he freed Fanfani to form his Centre-Left coalition. And he took an important step towards achieving the second when he implied, in his encyclical, that it might be permissible to co-operate with the Socialists or the Communists. But the Italian bishops, as a body, were not with him in this matter, as may be seen from their political attitude at the time of the election, and their renewed efforts in November 1963, after the Pope's death.[1] Nor had Roncalli himself felt strong enough to set himself up in open opposition to them. *Pacem in Terris* might say that a false philosophy, professed by a party, was not in itself a sufficient reason to withhold support from that party, but it retained a very

[1] But their new appeal, published in the leading Italian papers on November 4th, 1963, was more ambivalent than their appeal of March 14th. *Pacem in Terris* had given some of them cause to reconsider their position.

significant saving clause which preserved the power of the bishops, when it said that "whether or not the moment for such co-operation (with those professing a false philosophy) has arrived, and the manner and degree of such co-operation in the attainment of economic, social, cultural and political advantages – these 'are matters for prudence to decide. . . . "[1] Catholics were still not free to follow their own choice in political matters because they must "observe the Church's social teaching and the directives of ecclesiastical authority. For it must not be forgotten that the Church has the right and duty not only to safeguard her teaching on faith and morals, but also to exercise her authority over her sons by intervening in their external affairs. . . . "[2] In short if, say, Cardinal Ruffini, Archbishop of Palermo, took the view, as he did, that collaboration between Catholics and Socialists in Sicily was a danger to the faith there, he was quite entitled to forbid it in his archdiocese, and must be obeyed. The Pope had clearly indicated his own view that the time had come when such political taboos could usefully be removed; but bishops were not necessarily bound to follow the Pope's lead, and he recognized their right to give political directives. In November 1963, when the possibility of a new Centre-Left coalition was under discussion, the Italian Episcopal Conference appears to have been acting on its own, rather than on papal initiative, in putting out a fresh warning against any action which might assist the purposes of atheistic Communism.

The indignation of the Press and the parties of the Right in Italy at the new "opening to the gospel" introduced by Pope John has already been discussed in the wider context of his relations with World Communism, Moscow, and mankind as a whole. But here, where we are concerned with Italian affairs, it is significant to notice that, since Pope John was now, rather crudely, identified with the Left, there arose from the Right new cries of warning that the Church must keep clear of politics, observing strictly the separation of powers laid down in the Concordat. Those very groups which had welcomed Pius XII's political ostracism of the Left, speaking of it as "a sign of the balance

[1] CTS p. 58.   AAS, LV, pp. 300, 301.
[2] *Loc. cit.*

and the traditional wisdom of the Church",[1] now began to speak about the dangers of clerical influence in politics and what was called "integral Catholicism" and questioned whether the Concordat had not left the Church too free to influence political affairs. Ironically the very men who had been most anxious to enlist the political support of Pius XI and Pius XII were now as anxious as the old anti-clericals of the Left to limit the political influence of the papacy. More than a century earlier Metternich, confronted by the unaccustomed spectacle of liberal policies at Rome, exclaimed that he had allowed for everything except a liberal Pope. The parties of the Italian Right were now finding themselves in the same dilemma.

This flurry in Italian politics serves only to underline how powerful and how accepted had become the steady opposition of the Church to the parties of the Left. The Church in Italy might no longer, since the Concordat, be established, but she was certainly assumed to be a reliable ally of the Establishment. But this alliance Pope John had betrayed. He had shown his faith in Fanfani, who wanted an alliance with the Socialists, and he had indicated that, in his view, it might be proper for Italian Catholics to collaborate with them or with the Communists. He had abandoned the direct attempt of the Papacy to control the Catholic vote in Italy, or the policies of the Christian Democratic party, and had shown a disinterest in influencing Italian politics such as had not been seen since Italy had been united.

Roncalli was no more anxious than anybody else in the Italian hierarchy to see the growth of Communism or of secularism in Italy; the 1963 elections were a shock to him as well as to the others. But he evidently thought it would be better, in the long run, to leave the Italians politically free. While as anxious as his predecessors to keep Italians within the Catholic obedience he doubted whether, with this aim in view,

[1] Cf the leading article in *Il Mondo* for March 26th, 1963. On May 8th the *Osservatore Romano* attempted a reply to the angry challenge of the right-wing *Il Tempo*, which had crudely put the question: was Pius XII right or was John XXIII? Italy needs to know. Laboriously the *Osservatore* tried once more to cover up for Pope John: the Adjoubei interview had been only "common courtesy", there was no new attitude towards the Communists, there "could never be a pact with error", and so on.

direct intervention in the political sphere was a good way for the Vatican to operate.

A more effective means of keeping Italians obedient had already been fashioned in the shape of the civic committees of Catholic Action, the body on which Pius X had lavished such loving care and which Pius XI had made the "apple of his eye"; even Mussolini had had to allow Pius XI to keep his control over Catholic Action. And Pius XII had been equally vigilant. In fostering Catholic Action these popes had, of course, been doing something much bigger than merely maintaining a political hold over Italy. Their concern was with nothing less than the spiritual welfare and the moral formation of Catholic Italians. Catholic Action embraces every sort of activity, from sport and entertainment to higher education and politics. Its members are zealous men and women, leading good Catholic lives, running clubs, schools, and hospitals, helping to keep the weaker brethren within the fold, and to bring back those who wander; they are men and women who have deserved well of Italy, as well as of the Church. But it is the political aspect of Catholic Action which is relevant to us here, because it is through its civic committees that the political influence of the hierarchy is most effectively exercised. So long as these civic committees are kept vigilant, and are responsive to episcopal direction, it does not really greatly matter whether the Christian Democratic party is, or is not, formally independent of the hierarchy, or even whether it is in power, since no Italian government is likely, for long, to walk out of step with the bishops. We had a glimpse of Roncalli handling Catholic Action leaders at Venice. If even he could so talk down to them we may be sure that these laymen are not, in general, lacking in respect for their ecclesiastical leaders; in the period following the Second World War, their energetic President, Professor Gedda, who was very close to Pius XII, brought them to a high pitch of loyalty.

So long as Catholic Action remains both virile and vigilant a return on the part of the Italian hierarchy, or the Vatican, to more direct methods of political control may not become necessary. If, however, a Communist-Socialist government were to be formed in Italy which showed itself determined upon interfering with Catholic Action, and upon a serious curtailment of the religious life of the country, a curtailment of the kind imposed upon Catholic Poland or Catholic Hungary, we may be sure that the leaders of the Church would react in such ways as they could, including those used by Pius XII, and no doubt even more drastically. The question is only how much political freedom can be allowed consistently with maintaining a Catholic way of life, public as well as private, cultural as well as domestic. On this Roncalli would have been at one with Pacelli. In short, the matter is rather one of method than of principle; on the latter all are agreed.

Pope John's reign was much too short for anybody to assert with confidence that he was seriously trying to lead the Italian Church into a new and more detached attitude towards politics. And even if he was, then it was also too short for him to do so effectively. But there is implicit in his teaching, and in his policies, a concept of "working with the enemy", of ignoring not only party labels but even religious and philosophical differences, in the mutual pursuit of the useful and the good, which was novel to Italian clerical thought and which, while it lasted, provided Italy with a political experience she had only previously enjoyed under Benedict XV.

It could be just the sort of experience, in the responsible exercise of power, which Italian politics need. Politics, the Church agrees, is the business of the layman, and it may prove advantageous, in the long run, to allow him to run them on his own responsibility, even at a certain risk. It may be that if the Italian Christian Democrats of 1904, or the Italian Popular Party of 1922, had been allowed to shape their own political destiny and pursue their own political programme it would in the end have been better for Italians, and also for the Church. It may be that if, in the nineteen-fifties, Italian (and other) Catholics had been left free to collaborate politically with their opponents, as Pope John later encouraged them to do, instead of being ordered to ostracize them, a more harmonious political society might have evolved in Italy, and elsewhere, and the spiritual as well as the political life of the West might have gained. There might even today be more believing Catholics for, as *Pacem in Terris* says, "collaboration with unbelievers may provide the occasion for their conversion to the truth."

We should certainly be careful not to exaggerate the distinction between Pope John's attitude in this essential matter and that of his predecessors. Even *Pacem in Terris* was very careful to preserve the ultimate ecclesiastical authority. In the sphere of the *thesis* there was no difference; Innocent III, Pius IX, Pius XII and Pope John were all at one in their belief that the ultimate authority, in human affairs, rested by right with the Vicar of Christ. The difference consisted in Pope John's attitude, not shared by his predecessors, that it was best for the Church to leave politics alone. His experience of the world, and especially his experience of France had taught him this, and although he was prepared, as Patriarch of Venice, to follow Pius XII's line, he developed, as Pope, a new one of his own. The Adjoubei interview, the dialogue with the Russian Orthodox, the Secretariat for Christian Unity, the acceptance of a responsibility towards the whole of mankind, the address to all men of good will, the collaboration advocated in *Pacem in Terris* – all these initiatives found their counterpart, on the narrower Italian stage, in Roncalli's refusal to try, any longer, to control Italy by political directives intended to exclude from power those outside the influence of the Church.

Whether he was right or whether he was wrong time alone can tell. It may be argued that the attempt of his predecessors, and of Catholic governments, to defend the Church by political means, in Italy and in so many Latin countries, has been a major cause of the survival there of a Catholic way of life, and of a Catholic cultural environment. We can respect the hundred and fifty years of patient resistance to the onslaught of the Jacobins and the successors of the Jacobins. Italy and Spain and Portugal and Malta are still today Catholic countries in a sense in which France, for all the enlightenment of her Catholic élite, is not, and this may be because the Church has not been afraid, in those countries, to keep a hold over the government, putting into political practice the principle that the spiritual power is supreme.

Most of the Italian cardinals and bishops are evidently impressed by the advantages of maintaining this kind of control. But the tendency of the times, and the spirit of the more vocal party at the Council, seem rather to lie with Pope John. It is no doubt much too early to talk, with some of the journalists, about the "end of political Catholicism", still less about the end of concordats. The Church has her own historic government, and her own historic diplomatic service (in which Roncalli played a notable part) and so long as that is so she will evidently reach understandings with other governments, giving her political advantages and safeguards, and these are called concordats. But it does seem likely that one result of the Council will be to encourage a rather wider freedom for the laity, and if this carries with it freedom for the laity in using its political vote, or more independence for Catholic Action, or a more genuine autonomy for Christian Democratic parties, then the Church will be moving in the direction towards which Pope John turned himself.

It is too soon to say. It may be that the liberal policies of the papacy in Italy, in 1962–63, will prove to be as short-lived a phenomenon as were the similar policies pursued on two earlier occasions when popes voluntarily relaxed their political hold over the peninsula, in 1846–48 and in 1919–22. But it is at least possible that ecclesiastical authority, both in Italy and more widely in the world, will work towards the goal envisaged in the concluding paragraphs of *Pacem in Terris*, and thus help to establish what that encyclical invoked, namely a political order "founded on truth, built up on justice, nurtured and animated by charity, and *brought into effect under the auspices of freedom*".[1]

[1] My italics.   CTS, p. 61.   AAS, LV, p. 303.

Epilogue

A CONTINUING REVOLUTION?

I have written of Pope John's revolution as though it were already a part of history. But, as every reader knows, this revolution is still with us, may indeed have only just begun. We are in the midst of a Catholic crisis of conscience – Karl Barth's 'event' – and none of us knows what the outcome will be. All we know is that Pope John opened a window, and that the episcopal view of the world was thereby both enlightened and extended. We do not know how this new view will change the policies of those who guide the Church. We cannot even be sure that the window will not be closed again.

The Johannine revolution has been carried forward at the Second Vatican Council. But what has happened to it? Where is it going? After the conclusion of the third session of the Council, in November 1964, it is especially hard to tell. If Pope John's revolution, as some believe, is already in retreat – if we shall one day look back on *Mater et Magistra* and *Pacem in Terris* and the summons of the Council, as on the early years of Pius IX (when Rome saw amnesties, and democratic liberties, and a free Press, all of which were withdrawn in the next decade) then Roncalli's work only has importance as herald of a new spring; it is not the spring itself. It will remain important that Pope John opened the window. But we shall have to recognize that he found no way of fastening it open; that it is tending to close again. His revolution will begin to look more like a *pütsch*.

To confident enthusiasts for the revolution such fears will seem unnecessarily pessimistic. Does not the so-called progressive party among the bishops enjoy a large majority? Has not the Council already achieved great results, with its liturgy decree, its constitution on the Church, and its ecumenical decrees? Has not Pope Paul promised to carry forward the work of his predecessor? Has not the so-called 'closed curial system' been shattered so that it can never be re-established? – and so on.

Clearly much has already been done, and more is likely to be done before the Council is concluded. But it is noticeable that the particular objectives of Pope John have hardly yet been forwarded at all. In his great addresses of September and October 1962, intended to provide the key-note for the first session, Roncalli insisted that the Council was to provide the world with a light to lead her towards unity, peace, and justice; that it was to be both an example and a guide to mankind. But even while Roncalli still lived the Council showed little inclination to become a light to lighten the Gentiles; and although he helped the bishops to overcome the efforts of the Curia to control their discussions, he did not succeed in turning their minds towards the world at large. At the end of the session, when he said good-bye to them, he warned them, most solemnly, that they would have to address themselves to the needs of the world, which they had not seen fit to debate. Then, to drive home his point, he published *Pacem in Terris*, almost literally with his last breath.

The bishops loved him, but they ignored him. Absorbed in the task of introducing the vernacular into the liturgy (not a Johannine objective) and still more in defining the title-deeds of their own powers, as successors of the apostles (a piece of left-over business from Vatican I), they postponed the vast task foremost in Roncalli's vision, the task of turning the Church outwards, instead of inwards, to the enlightenment and succour of the world, for the sake of the world, but for the sake, too, of the Church. Ignored during the second session, the *schema* on "The Church in the Modern World" did make a tardy appearance at the third. It proved to be a document of immense range, extending from the family to the world order, and obviously inspired in its teaching on economic social and political questions by the Johannine encyclicals. Apparently the work of that notable German redemptorist, Bernard Häring, one of the Council's experts, it alarmed the Archbishops of Washington D. C., and of Liverpool, by treating the use of nuclear weapons as always illegitimate, and the Archbishop of Westminster by speaking of contraceptive practices as though they belonged in the realm of private conscience. But the fathers, in general, welcomed it, seeing it as the natural counterpart to the proposed constitution on the Church. If that constitution defined the nature of the Church *ad intra*, this new one would expound her teaching and her mission *ad extra*. By adopting a *schema* of this sort the Council would thus have provided for a renewal of the life of the Church both within and without.

The indignation of the Archbishop of Westminster led him into a strong attack on the experts. Who were they to teach the bishops their job? The bishops should seek the guidance of those intimately involved in the day-to-day work of the world; it would be necessary to appoint a special commission to investigate such problems, which would need three or four years to complete its work. This view did not commend itself to the fathers, and they continued to debate the *schema*, which is to reappear, in a new form, at the fourth session. Whether a conciliar constitution on this wide field will be published before the Council dissolves, or whether some post-conciliar committee will produce a document which will be endorsed by the Pope, and perhaps by an 'Episcopal Senate', remains an open question. It also remains possible that neither development will occur. But to the student of Pope John it must be evident that, if nothing were done, or if the lead given were perfunctory, or obscure, then the kind of Council which he intended, and the kind of renewal of the life of the Church in the world which he had most closely at heart would have been abandoned.

By leaving all consideration of this vast field until its third session the Council has certainly not acted as Pope John expected it to act. But it is arguable that it has acted logically. It has chosen to give its main attention to a reconsideration of the nature of the Church and there were arguments to support such a course. Vatican I had left the picture unbalanced by defining the powers of the pope alone. It was important to redress the balance by asserting the principle of episcopal collegiality, not because the government of an absolute oligarchy of bishops is necessarily to be preferred to that of an absolute papal monarchy, but because the monarchy had come to mean the Curia, so that too much power had come to be assumed by men who in fact were only civil servants. Some decentralization was desirable, even though it might mean a more absolute government in some dioceses. Nor were the bishops the only ones to benefit from the Council's constitution *de Ecclesia;* the whole People of God were taught that they share in a common priesthood and a common prophetic office. Even laymen, though they are warned that they must continue to obey promptly the decisions of their pastors, are "entitled and sometimes even obliged to express their opinions on those things that concern the welfare of the Church" – an injunction which some lay writers had already seen fit to anticipate.

This constitution, *de Ecclesia*, is Johannine in spirit but, as Pope Paul emphasised to the third session, it changes nothing in the doctrine of the Church. Leaving the pope at the apex of the mighty pyramid it merely paints in some of the sub-structure, thus making the pope's elevation itself more intelligible. Perhaps more constitutions of the same sort will be needed at future Councils – will it not, for instance, be necessary some day to give fuller consideration to the special nature of the authority of the parish priest? But only indirectly, and in the course of time, can this constitution *de Ecclesia* contribute towards the *aggiornamento* for which Pope John looked. By associating the bishops more closely with the pope it may make the latter less dependent on the Curia. By making bishops less dependent on the Curia, and more reliant on the powers given to them by God, it may make for more realistic administration of dioceses, in accordance with local needs and opportunities. But clearly, by strengthening the hands of the bishops, it may facilitate some local tyrannies. It was found, in the middle ages, that the assumption of greater powers by the barons did not necessarily make for the freedom of the people. Sometimes the people's safeguard lay precisely in the strength of the monarch's centralised civil service. One can imagine dioceses, today, where *de Ecclesia* may not tend to promote the liberties of Catholics, or ecumenism, or any restatement of the teaching of the Church in terms of contemporary culture.

The decrees on ecumenism, already promulgated by the Council, are clearly to be welcomed by any sympathetic student of the endeavours of Pope John and of Cardinal Bea, even though it is a small ecumenical mouse that has emerged from the mountains of hope entertained in the great days of 1961-2. The hope then was that Catholic/Orthodox conversations, at the top level, would be initiated. But the Orthodox have willed otherwise. They seem to entertain renewed suspicions of Rome. Pope Paul's major encyclical, *Ecclesiam Suam*, for all its humility, its acknowledgement of past mistakes, and its spirit of charity, appears to have given offence by insisting on the Roman primacy. So the Council, denied the joy of giving birth to conversations, at the summit, has had to content itself with recommending local dialogues, and some measure of common worship (with episcopal permission). A separate decree on the Eastern Catholic Churches gives formal approval to the reception, in certain circumstances, of the sacraments by Catholics in Orthodox churches. In the ecumenical decrees there is a word of special commendation for the Anglicans, for the emphasis of many Protestant Churches on the bible, and for the Christian virtues nurtured by the many Christian communities. These decrees are marked by a very notable and new humility. Catholics are told "we must humbly beg pardon of God and of our separated brethren" for past offences, and the separated brethren are assured that they are forgiven for those they have committed against Catholics. To read these decrees after reading Pius XI's *Mortalium animos* is to enter into a new world of the spirit, and provides touching and eloquent evidence of the continued presence, at the Council, of the mind of John XXIII.

In all this there was a real and positive achievement; but the concluding stages of the third session were clouded by disappointment at the failure to bring to a positive issue the debate on Cardinal Bea's draft on the non-Christian religions, which contains an appreciation of the merits of the Hindus, the Buddhists, and the Moslems, a tribute to Judaism, and an exculpation of the Jews from guilt for the crucifixion. More serious was the failure to take a final vote on the *schema* on religious liberty. There is evidently curial opposition to this *schema* in its present form.

An impression exists that Pope Paul is more inclined to listen to the Curia, and less inclined to accept the majority or 'progressive' view of the bishops than was his predecessor. This impression arises from a series of incidents: from the amendments he inserted in the ecumenical decrees approved by the Council; from his refusal to yield to the pressure to bring the *schema* on religious liberty to the vote; from the emphasis he placed, in his concluding address, on the Marian chapter in the *de Ecclesia*. It was in this address that Pope Paul proclaimed Mary Mother of the Church, thus perhaps giving some measure of satisfaction to those many Italians, including Cardinal Ottaviani, who had wanted a separate constitution on the subject of Our Lady. The suspicion exists that special Italian considerations, even Italian political considerations, have once again begun to exert their traditional influence. Thus the Jesuit periodical *America* has said, editorially (December 5th, 1964) : "the Holy Father may well have judged that a vote on the religious liberty question just at that moment – rather than later, at the beginning of the next session – might have had some unsettling effect on the touchy Italian national elections, to be held two or three days later". (These were the regional elections in Italy.) If there were any grounds for such suspicions as these then it would mean that the times had indeed changed since Pope John was prepared to issue *Pacem in Terris* only three weeks before an Italian General Election, and thus to "dish the Christian Democrats". It would mean that matters were now being viewed in a more traditionally Italian and a less Johnninely world perspective.

However, it is too early to take alarm. We may expect Cardinal Bea's draft on the Jews, which so offends the Arabs, to be voted as an appendix to the *de Ecclesia*. We may expect a final and affirmative vote on religious liberty which will put the Council into line with *Pacem in Terris*. Crucial decisions will be taken at the fourth session, and the prudent purposes of Pope Paul, who is evidently anxious to keep open the bridges across the gulf dividing progressives from conservatives, may come to be better appreciated. It will be a great gain if he is successful in preventing an open split such as occurred at Vatican I.

What may prove ultimately more important than the issues dividing the Council at the end of the third session is the failure of the fathers to give sufficient serious attention to the cultural cleavage between the Church and the world. For the kind of *aggiornamento* of the Church which Pope John invoked must depend, in the long run, not so much on the way in which episcopal collegiality is worked out but on a matter nearer to the grass-roots, namely the education of the priests in their seminaries, and of Catholics generally in their schools and colleges.

For what is an *aggiornamento*? Essentially, literally, it is a "bringing up to date". And what does this mean? It means the Church doing what Pope John did, namely accepting, welcoming, sharing confidently and openly in the social, political, and cultural advances of the modern age, and especially in those many advances of the nineteenth and twentieth century at which she has been taught, in the past, to look askance. But she can only make this contact with the actual world if she is educated about it, if, for instance, her priests are taught modern history objectively, and without polemical intent, and are given a general education expressed in the idiom of the age.

Are the seminaries able to give an education that is modern and humane? One of the last, and perhaps the most important of the achievements of the Council of Trent was to set up that system of seminary education which has remained in being, remarkably little changed, ever since. It was thus that the details of the Faith, so fully defined by that Council, were transmitted to the young priest and his sound theological and philosophical formation were assured. Armed in this way, he went out into the world and combated, for some time with a marked success, the teachings of the Protestant reformers and later, in the nineteenth century, he tried to combat the ideas of the liberals, the 'men of progress', the socialists, the romantics, the philosophers, and the scientists – almost the entire culture of the age. Defying that culture, of which he was largely ignorant, the well trained priest reaffirmed the Faith in its traditional apparel; but his influence dwindled. The heart of the *aggiornamento* is nothing less than the re-entry of the Church into that world which she once led, but which she was driven to defy; it is her re-entry into living human culture, so that her message may again become intelligible and compelling. Clearly she cannot achieve this unless her priests are exposed to and educated in modern culture. Even were the Sacred Congregation of the Index to relax its vigilance; even were the fears and inhibitions that have blighted Catholic scholarship for centuries to be lifted altogether, there could still be no *aggiornamento* were the seminary to concern itself only with the dogmatic indoctrination of the future priest. For it is no longer possible to meet educated men and women – and they are becoming the majority – from the pulpit with a set of formulae, or with irate anathemas. It has become necessary to argue with them as reasonable beings and to lead them towards a Christian view of the human predicament, in its present form, a view that must be derived not only from dogma but also from some understanding of the nature of that predicament, which is unobtainable except by entry into the culture of today.

When, therefore, we read that Cardinal Bacci told the third session of the Council that he saw little need for a post-conciliar commission to consider necessary changes in the curriculum of the seminaries, because this matter could safely be left to the Roman congregation concerned, we may well begin to feel apprehensive about the fate of the entire *aggiornamento*. For we shall remember *Veterum sapientia*, with its injunctions that education in theology must continue to be given through the medium of the Latin language, and that the study of Greek be added; we shall remember that the Cardinal was closely associated with that encyclical; and we shall begin to wonder how it will be possible to find either the techniques or the time to educate intending priests humanely, liberally, and with sure knowledge, in the modern history, the simple sociology, the psychology, or the economics, without which nobody nowadays can even enter into reasonable dialogue about modern problems, still less guide others on the moral aspects of such matters. If the Church is to re-enter the cultural world, broadly and effectively, then it is obviously essential that her priests be brought abreast of that culture.

Much was said, at the third session, about the need for the moral formation of the seminary student: "to be a good priest one must first be a good man". But it is also necessary that he be an educated man, for a priest cannot avoid being a teacher; indeed he seldom tries to. It is not required of him that he be a specialist, except in theology; but he does need to be aware of the problems of today and the terms in which they are discussed. Without that sort of awareness of contemporary culture not only is he liable to be dismissed as irrelevant but the religious truth which he needs to convey may itself be sterilized because he cannot express it in a manner that is meaningful.

The debates on the seminaries, at the third session, did show a marked awareness of the need for change, though not a great awareness of the necessity for education about the modern world; the emphasis was placed upon the classics and upon philosophy (more difficult, to many students, than modern history and geography) and it seems to be assumed that a wider education, obtainable at a university, is only for the few. No doubt the university must remain for the few, but cannot the seminary incorporate something of the university's wider vision? One is left in some doubt whether, coming from a Catholic school, and finishing his education in the seminary, the priest of average intelligence is going to find it easy to relate his classical, philosophical, and theological lore to the actualities of modern life, even though he be helped, as is proposed, by some more psychology.

On the other hand the conciliar debate on the promotion of culture, while often content to point complacently to the cultural achievement of Christianity in the past, did at times break through the dense cloud that often divides the clerical idea of culture from the modern reality. Elchinger, of Strasbourg, asked for an "apostolate of intelligence", an end of dogmatic imperialism, and reminded the fathers that the world still awaited an acknowledgement by the Church of her mistake in condemning Galileo, and of the disastrous effects of the methods she used in fighting Modernism. Lercaro, of Bologna, asked how a true dialogue with contemporary culture could be achieved if those who speak in the name of the Church have had their minds formed by a programme of studies without contemporary relevance; their language is incapable of expressing the new ideas.

It would have been interesting, indeed, if the greater minds at the Council had seen fit to contribute to this fundamental debate, those few bishops, that is, who come near to Lercaro's ideal, which is the ideal of the doctor-bishop of a past age. For what is at stake is no less than the possibility of a renewal of Christian culture. Perhaps they felt they would be putting their heads into the clouds. It may, indeed, be extravagant to suppose, with Christopher Dawson, that there can once again be an age with a Catholic culture, an age in which the intellectual, artistic, and scientific framework in which the living human spirit moves is shaped by a renewed belief in the Christian revelation. At all events, the bishops did not see fit to give us such a vision, and a few came perilously near to expressing a nostalgia about a past that is past, a longing for what Professor Trevor-Roper has rightly ridiculed as a "re-entry into the womb" of medieval Mother Church.

Christopher Dawson entertained the hope, in his *Crisis of Western Education*, that the new Christian culture might be born out of the womb of the American Catholic colleges. This surprising confidence in the potential fertility of those worthy, but often conventional places arises from the undoubted fact that they represent the one extensive system of Catholic higher education in the modern world, so that he looks to them for a rebirth of Christian literature and history, art and philosophy. But they were founded with a much more modest purpose, namely to provide a general education for under-privileged Catholics, and Mgr John Tracy Ellis convincingly demonstrated in his *American Catholics and the Intellectual Life,* not only that they were relatively weak, intellectually speaking, but that they were particularly weak in humane, philosophical, and even theological studies, being strongest in their professional schools, such as medicine and law, which promote the careers of their students.

Not in existing colleges, nor indeed in ever more imposing pontifical institutes, enjoying episcopal patronage (and government), nor even at a General Council can we hope to find the key to a mystery which must wait upon God. Meanwhile culture has become both secularized and specialized, and it is no longer possible to envisage, as Newman was still able to envisage, a university, in the actual world, which is really abreast of modern thought and really Christian. All that is possible is to try to bridge the gap between the Church and the world by ensuring that they speak the same language, so that they may enter into dialogue. That initial step is necessary because, in the long run, the *aggiornamento* inevitably depends upon some growing together of religion and culture, so that religion may be realized, and able to express itself, and culture may not continue to be impoverished by a narrow secularism.

The Church cannot live effectively in the world save by clothing herself in the garments of the living contemporary culture, and that, again, is what *aggiornamento* means. It may, indeed, be more important that she should so clothe herself than that she should reform her government – though the two matters are, of course, related. For it is on the cultural side that Catholic awareness of the modern world has been most conspicuously lacking. The clergy have worked heroically in the slums. They have carried the Blessed Sacrament to the isolated villages. They have ministered to the unlettered native. But they have often been kept too distant from modern thought and teaching, and still further from a live aesthetic awareness.

Any easy optimism about the future of Pope John's revolution is clearly out of place when such vital matters as cultural and educational renewal, or the lead the Church should give to a tormented world, still remain in the melting pot of conciliar debate. There can be no confidence that a Council that has not yet chosen to endorse the principles of *Mater et Magistra* and *Pacem in Terris* has a message for mankind. Unless the fourth session, or post-conciliar commissions, effectively carry forward what has been begun there may not be a real *aggiornamento*, of the kind Pope John sought, and the Gentiles may be left without enlightenment.

We are told that the movement now started is irreversible; but it is hard to see why. We have, it is true, a useful broadening of authority, in principle, at the top of the ecclesiastical pyramid, but that is not, in itself, a guarantee of progress; moreover an able and experienced civil service, such as the Curia, could circumvent it. A few small steps have been taken towards ecumenism, but they might only lead out into the sand. A new and more generous mood exists but, like all moods, it is subject to reaction.

If the revolution fails, as fail it could, the failure would also in part be Pope John's failure, because it would mean that he had failed to give a sufficient lead to those elements in the Church which seek to renew her life and to bring her into effective asssociation, once again, with civilization. But if it moves forward, as we may all still hope it will, and a true *aggiornamento* takes place, rekindling both parish priest and laity, both seminary and school, and extending its light to the whole world, then the unique importance, in papal history, of Roncalli's short pontificate, is not likely to be disputed by historians.

Biographical Guide

THE RONCALLI PAPERS

One of the paradoxes about Angelo Roncalli is that, despite his reputation as a pastoral not a scholarly Pope, he left behind him a more considerable body of published writing of an unofficial kind than did any of his recent predecessors.

A. *His Writings on Church History*

His special interest was in Church history, from the earliest times right up to his own day. His published writings in this field include:

(1) His essay on Cardinal Baronius (1538–1607), the pupil of St Philip Neri, which he delivered as a lecture at Bergamo in 1907, and which was first published at Monza in 1908, a new edition being brought out in 1961: *Il Cardinale Cesare Baronio* (*Edizioni di Storia e Letteratura*). Baronius was a systematic historian of the first thousand years of Church history in the *Annales Ecclesiastici*, which he founded, and Roncalli's study of him, for which he found time while a student at Rome, stimulated his interest in history as well as helping to develop the characteristically gentle and humane quality of his own spirituality.

(2) His life of the bishop whom he served as secretary at Bergamo, Radini Tedeschi. This was first published in 1916 as part of a memorial volume in honour of the bishop who had died in 1914. It is now available in a third edition: *Mons Giacomo Maria Radini Tedeschi* (*Ed. di Storia e Letteratura*, 1963) thanks to the zeal of Roncalli's secretary, Don Loris Capovilla, who contributes a foreword and various relevant papers, including extracts from the diocesan paper of Bergamo, *La Vita Diocesena*, some of them written by Roncalli. The value of the book, for students of Pope John, lies in the light which it throws on the formation of his own mind while he was secretary and pupil (1905–14) of the bishop whose life he was writing.

(3) His writings on St Charles Borromeo. During his life as a priest at Bergamo (1905–22), as professor at the Seminary, and as secretary to the bishop, Roncalli developed a profound interest in the origins of the Bergamo Seminary between the years 1567 and 1575. It was stimulated by his study of the quantity of documents he unearthed at Bergamo and at Milan, and it remained with him throughout his life, so that he returned to it on his holidays from Bulgaria or from Istanbul. These studies resulted in his publishing, with the help of his friend Don Pietro Forno, the papers relating to the Saint's apostolic visitation to Bergamo in 1575: *Atti della visita Apostolica di S. Carlo Borromeo a Bergamo nel 1575* (Firenze, Ed. Olschki, 1936–39). In 1939 he also published an interesting concise account of the early foundation of seminaries in Italy, arising from the decisions of the Council of Trent, with special reference to the Bergamo seminary, in his *Gli Inizi del Seminario di Bergamo e S. Carlo Borromeo* (Bergamo, 1939).

B. *His Spiritual Diary*

The diary which he kept intermittently from the age of fourteen until the last year of his life was published, by his own permission, almost immediately after his death, again by the zeal of Don Loris Capovilla: *"Il Giornale dell'Anima" e Altri Scritti di Pietà (Ed. di Storia e Letteratura)*. A first and second edition appeared in March and April 1964. With the diary were published a number of prayers, a few letters, and various personal papers such as Roncalli's Will. The diary is strictly a spiritual document, being an examination of the state of his own soul, fullest, and most interesting, for his early years as a student, brief and more intermittent for the years from the First World War onwards. Apart from the earliest ones, the entries were mostly made while he was on retreat. English translation Dorothy White (Chapman 1965).

C. *Collections of his Speeches and Letters*

(1) Before his election as Pope.

Various addresses and letters belonging to Roncalli's life as Papal

Nuncio at Paris were collected and published by Capovilla: *Souvenirs d'un Nonce. Cahiers de France* (1944–53) (*Ed. di Storia e Letteratura*, 1963). The addresses are mostly formal, and of little interest; the letters are often valuable.

A larger and more important collection was made of his letters and speeches as Patriarch of Venice (1953–58): *Scritti e Discorsi*, 3 Vols. (Ed. Paoline, 1959).

(2) After his election as Pope.

His formal allocutions, encyclicals, etc, as well as many of his less formal addresses will be found (mostly in Latin) in the *Acta Apostolicae Sedis*, Vols. L to LV, for the years 1958–63. A fuller collection, published first in Italian, in the *Osservatore Romano*, can be read, in French, in *La Documentation Catholique*, the useful fortnightly published by the *Maison de la Bonne Presse*, 5, Rue Bayard, Paris 8e. (See also *Informations Catholiques Internationales*, 163 Boulevard Malesherbes, Paris XVIIe). His major encyclicals were translated and published as pamphlets by the Catholic Truth Society (London) and the National Catholic Welfare Conference (Washington, DC) and others in the USA.

SOME WIDER READING ON POPE JOHN
ON THE FIRST SESSION OF THE COUNCIL,
AND ON THE BACKGROUND
OF CHURCH AND STATE IN ITALY

ARADI, Z, with MICHAEL DERRICK and DOUGLAS WOODRUFF: *John XXIII, Pope of the Council*, Burns and Oates, 1961 (Still the best book in English on the life of Roncalli up to the end of the year 1960)

BEA, AUGUSTIN, CARDINAL: *The Unity of Christians,* Geoffrey Chapman, 1963 (Some of the Cardinal's public speeches)

BOSWORTH, W: *Catholicism and Crisis in Modern France,* Princeton, 1962

CALVEZ, J-Y : *Église et Société Économique*
Vol I (with Perrin, J) *l'enseignement social des papes de Léon XIII à Pie XII, Aubier*, 1959
Vol 2, *l'enseignement social de Jean XXIII, Aubier*, 1963

CONGAR, Y : *Report from Rome: The first Session of the Vatican Council*, Geoffrey Chapman 1963

FALCONI, C : *Gedda e l'Azione Cattolica*, Parenti, 1958
Pope John and His Council, Weidenfeld and Nicolson, 1964 (A detached, critical, but penetrating diary of events during the first session of the Council, translated by Muriel Grindrod)

GOZZINI, M : *Concilio Aperto*, Vallechi, 1962 (A "progressive" Italian commentary, fourth edition October 1963)

JEMOLO, A C : *Chiesa e Stato in Italia negli ultimi cento anni*, Einaudi. New edition, 1963, of a classical exposition of the subject, bringing the survey down to the times of Pope John

KAISER, R : *Inside the Council*, Burns and Oates, 1963 (A commentary which reflected the popular mood at the time of the First Session).

KÜNG, H : *The Council and Reunion*, Sheed and Ward, 1961
The Living Church, Sheed and Ward, 1963

LAZZARINI, A : *Giovanni XXIII*, Herder, Rome, 1958 (One of the better accounts of Roncalli's life before he became Pope)

RYNNE, XAVIER: *Letters from Vatican City*, Faber, 1963 (The best account in English of the First Session of the Council)

TEDESCHI, M : *I Pericoli del Concilio*, Milan, Longanesi, 1962
La Chiesa dopo Giovanni, pub. by "Il Borghese" for pseudonymous author "Lo Svizzero", 1963. (Two examples of the Italian Right Wing opposition to Pope John and to the Council with which Borghese publications are associated.)

VITO, F, and others: *I Nuovi termini della Questione Sociale e l'Enciclica Mater et Magistra*, Milan, Vita e Pensiere, 1961

WEBSTER, R: *Christian Democracy in Italy* 1860–1960, Hollis and Carter, 1961. (An excellent account of the subject.)

WENGER, A: *Vatican II, Première Session,* Éditions du Centurion, 1963 (The best account of the First Session of the Council and of its background.)

Index

INDEX

Ad Apostolorum Principis (letter to Chinese bishops, 1958), 111

Ad Petri Cathedram (Encyclical, 1959), 102, 112, 120 note

Adenauer, Chancellor, 131

Adjoubei (Kruschev's son-in-law), 87, 153, 154, 155, 157, 158, 188 note, 191

Agriculture, 49–52, 80, 156

Aid (economic), 29, 72–78, 130, 136

Alexis, Patriarch of Moscow, 141, 142, 147, 148

Ambrose, Saint, 7

Ambrosiana, library at Milan, 11

America (Jesuit paper), 200

Antony of Padua, Saint, 7, 12

Apollinare, Roman Seminary, 11, 163, 175

Aradi, Z., 211

Assumption, definition of, xiv

Atheism, 131, 155

Athenagoras, Patriarch of Constantinople, 98, 107, 141, 142, 148

Aube (French political paper), 19, 176

Augustine, Saint, 117

Auriol, Vincent, President of France, 19

Bacci, Cardinal, 117, 118, 202

Bakunin, 41

Balzan Peace Prize, awarded to Pope John, 153, 154

Baronius, Caesar, 11, 12, 174, 209

Barth, Karl, 110, 195

Bea, Cardinal, 101, 104, 110, 122–8, 130, 132, 134, 135, 141, 142, 198–200, 211

Benedict XV, 13, 168, 173, 174, 177, 190

Beran, Archbishop of Prague, 111, 144

Berlin Wall, 130, 143

Bidault, Georges, 18, 19, 175, 176

Bismarck, 87, 171

Bombs, nuclear, 67, 71

Borghese, Il, Italian paper, 158 note

Boris, King of Bulgaria, 16

Borovoi, Vitalyi, Russian Orthodox Observer at Vatican Council, 143

Borromeo, Saint Charles, 11, 12, 14, 210

Bossuet, 56

Bosworth, W., 211

Brahmins, 125, 126

Buddhists, 125, 126, 199

Byron, 163

Calvez, J.-Y., 212

Capovilla, Mgr, 9, 209, 210, 211

Catholic Action, 13, 21, 120, 129, 171, 177, 181, 182, 189–90; 192

Cavour, 32, 87, 178

Christian Democrats (Italian political party) xii, 21, 39, 150, 157 note, 159, *early struggles for recognition*, 172–8; *under Pius XII*, 177–85; *under Pope John*, 185–90; 192, 200

Ciappi, Father, 117
Cicero, 12, 117
Clement XIV, 39
Colonialism, 29, 72–78, 91, 155
Communists xi, xii, xiii, 4, 21, 35, 38, 39, 44, 53, 63, 65, 67, 68, *co-operation with Catholics*, 69–71, 88–90, 155–60, 185–92; 73, 86, 87, 110, 111, 112, 113, 133, 140, 144–50, 153, *and Pius XII*, 177–85
Concordat (Italian), 176, 177, 178, 183, 187, 188
Congar, Y., 212
Contraceptives, 79, 196
Coptic Church, 69
Cuba, Crisis of 1962, 147–9
Curé d'Ars, 115 note.
Curia, the Roman, 57, 93, 103, 104, 105, 106, 110, 116, 119, 149, 154–5, 166, 185, 195–9
Cyril, Saint, 128

Dante, 12
Darboy, Archbishop of Paris, 32, 38
Dawson, Christopher, 203
de Ecclesia, Constitution promulgated at Second Vatican Council, 195–8, 200
de Gasperi, Alcide, 174, 176, 177, 183, 185
de Gaulle, 18, 175
Democracy, Pope John's faith in, 52–58
Derrick, Michael, 211
Disarmament, 79
Divini Redemptoris (Encyclical, 1937) 37
Divino Afflante Spiritu (Encyclical, 1943), 94

Ecclesiam Suam (Encyclical, 1964), 125, 198
Ecumenism, decrees of Second Vatican Council, 198–9, 205
Elchinger (Coadjutor, Strasbourg), 203
Ellis, Mgr John Tracy, 204
Engels, 89

Faber, Father, 3
Falconi, Carlo, 21, 152, 180 note, 212
Fanfani, Italian Premier, 158, 176, 185, 186, 188
Fascists, 44, 53, 63, 86, 173, 174
Felici, Archbishop, 105
Fellini, film producer, 108
Feltin, Cardinal, Archbishop of Paris, 114
Fiordelli, Bishop of Prato, 146, 181, 183
Fisher, Dr., Archbishop of Canterbury, 108, 110, 121, 123, 124

Galileo, 203
Garibaldi, 169
Gedda, Professor, 177, 189
Gibbons, Archbishop of Baltimore, 42
Gioberti, Vincenzo, 173
Giolitti, Italian Premier, 173
Giornale d'Italia, 157, 158
Gizenga, Congolese leader, 132
Gladstone, 32
Gomulka, President of Poland, 152
Gozzini, M., 212
Gregory XVI, 27, 28, 29, 30, 31, 38, 39, 40, 56, 59, 85, 89, 169
Gronchi, Ex-President of Italy, 154

Halecki, O., 68 note
Häring, Bernard, 196
Harmel, Léon, 42
Heenan, Archbishop of Westminster, 3, 4, 124, 196, 197
Hindus, 127, 133, 199
Hitler, 34, 35, 55, 87
Hoover, President, 52
Humani Generis (Encyclical, 1950), 91, 94

Iakovos, Orthodox bishop, 142
Immortale Dei (Encyclical, 1885), 27
In Mortalium Animos (Encyclical, 1928) xiii note
In Questo Giorno (Pius XII's Christmas Message, 1939), 65
Index of Prohibited Books, 120, 201
Innocent, 111, 191
Izvestia (Moscow paper), 144, 153

Jedin, Hubert, 62
Jemolo, A.C., 212
Jesuits, 39
Jews, 58, 133, 199
John XXIII: *passim*

Kaiser, Robert, 3–5, 212
Kemal, Mustapha, President of Turkey, 16
Kennedy, President, 131
Ketteler, Archbishop of Mainz, 42
Knox, Ronald, 33
Kolonitski, P., Russian Editor, 152, 153
Kotliarov, Vladimir, Russian Orthodox Observer at Vatican Council, 143

Kruschev, xi, 38, 87, 130, 131, 143, 152, 153, 155, 157
Küng, Hans, theologian, 118, 122, 212

Lactantius, 117
Lamennais, 59 note
Lateran Treaty (1929), 31, 166, 167, 175, 176
Lazzarini, A., 212
Lenin, 89
Leo XIII, xiii, 13, 27, 28, 35, 36, 37, 38, *and Rerum Novarum* 40–44, 46, 48; 55, 58, 59, 74, 86, 88, 90, 91, 93, 102, 117, 139, 154, *his attitude to Italy,* 168–71
Lercaro, Cardinal, 203
Liturgy, 115–19, 195
"*Lo Svizzero*", pseudonym, 100 note, 110 note, 212
Lombardi, Father Riccardo, 21

Manning, Archbishop of Westminster, 42
Marx, Karl, 41, 87
Mater et Magistra (Encyclical), xii, 13, 41–60, 63, 72, 74–82, 91, 92, 1?, 127, 129, 131, 136, 137, 151, 60, 165, 195, 205
Mazzini, 41, 74, 163–7
Merry del Val, Cardinal, 8?
Methodius, Saint, 128
Michelangelo, 145
Mindzenty, Cardin? ?'s letter,
Mirari Vos (Gre? ?yclical, 1937) 1832), 27, 30
Mit Brennende? 37
Molotov

Mondo, Il (Italian paper), 158 note, 188 note

Montalembert 31, 89, 140, 163, 166

Montini, Cardinal (later Paul VI), 22, 101, 102, 141, 142, 180, 195, 198–200

Mortalium Animos (Encyclical, 1928) xiii note, 199

Moslems, 58, 125, 126, 127, 133, 199

Mouvement Républicaine Populaire (MRP), 175, 176

Munificentissimus Deus (Apostolic Constitution, 1950), xiv

Murray, John Courtney, S. J., 31 note

Murri, Romolo, 173

Mussolini, 35, 63, 68, 87, 167, 173, 174, 175, 185, 189

Mystici Corporis (Encyclical, 1943), 91, 94

Napoleon I, 85

Nenni, Italian Socialist leader, 156, 185

Neri, Saint Philip, 11, 209

Newman, Cardinal, 204

Nicodemus, Russian Orthodox Arch-bishop, 142, 144, 148, 152

Abbiamo Bisogno (Encyclical, 37

Ortho...
Ortho...rch (see also Russian 97–99, ... rch), 15, 16, 68, *failure to s*... 124, 126, 135, 141–3; 148, 19...*ers to Council,* *of Rome*, 198... *d suspicions*
Osservatore Romano 97, 98, 117, 134, 1...
...aper), 211 ...ote,

Ottaviani, Cardinal, 82, 103, 120, 134, 149, 150, 153, 158 note, 200

Pacem in Terris (Encyclical), xi, xii, 30, 53–82, 88, 91, 92, 110, 131, 152, 155–60, 165, 182, 185–8, 190–2, 195, 196, 200, 205

Parente, Archbishop, 105

Pascendi Dominici Gregis (Encyclical, 1907), 36, 92

Pax Romana, 68 note

Peace Corps, 74

Perrin, Father, Worker-Priest, 113

Pétain, 18

Paul VI, see Montini, Cardinal

Pius VI, 39, 86

Pius VII, 28, 62, 85

Pius IX, 5, 27, 28, 30, 31, 32, 34–40, 55, 56, 59, 64, 85, 88, 92, 103, 119, 164–71, 178, 191

Pius X, 5, 13, 20, 36, 37, 38, 40, 56, 64, 86, 88, 92, 120, 127, 168, *opposes* *Christian Democracy*, 171–3; 179, 189

Pius XI, xiii, 5, 11, 14, 15, 16, 28, 31, 36, 37, 38, and *Quadragesimo Anno*, 40–48; 52, 55, 59, 63, 84, 86, 89, 90, 110, 112, 154, 156, 167, 168, *his Italian policy*, 173–7; 185, 189, 199

Pius XII, xii–xiv, 3, 4, 5, 17, 18–22, 27, *pessimism of*, 32–39; 40, 43, 45, 46, 48, 49, 52, 55, *on Women*, 59, 60; 63, *on Peace*, 64–69; 72, 73, 75, 81, 82, 83, 84, 86, 88, 89, 91, 102, 106, 110, 111, 112, 113, 114, 117, 119, 140, 145, 153, 154, 156, 157, 159, 166–70; *his effort to control Italy*, 177–91

Pizzardo, Cardinal, 114

Population Problem, 78–80, 91

Princeps Pastorum (Encyclical, 1959), 120 note
Propaganda, Congregation of, 13, 15
Protestants, 58, 69, 97, 108, 123, 124, 126, 135, 199, 201

Quadragesimo Anno (Encyclical, 1931), 41–48, 90, 151
Quanta Cura (Encyclical, 1864), 30, 92

Radini Tedeschi, Bishop of Bergamo, 11, 13, 14, 109, 115, 119, 172, 209
Ramsey, Dr., Archbishop of York (later Canterbury), 124
Rerum Novarum (Encyclical, 1891), 13, 28, 40–44, 91, 93, 151, 170
Robespierre, 89
Roncalli, Angelo: passim
Roncalli, Ancilla, 20
Roncalli, Maria, 20
Roosevelt, President, 66, 137
Rousseau, 57, 89
Ruffini, Cardinal, 187
Russian Orthodox Church, 110, 141–9, 152, 191
Rynne, Xavier, pseudonym, 105, 212

Sales, Saint Francis de, 6
Sangnier, Marc, 19, 93
Saragat, Italian Socialist leader (later President of Italy), 157
Schumann, Robert, 18, 175
Secretariat for Christian Unity, 103, 110, 121–4, 128, 134, 146, 147, 191
Seminary education, 201–5
Sillon (French paper), 19, 93
Singulari Nos (Encyclical, 1834), 30
Slipyi, Archbishop of Lwov, 145, 146, 147, 152

Socialists, 21, 41, 43, 90, 112, 157, 174, Roncalli's opposition to, at Venice, 182–8
Stalin, 34, 35, 38, 66, 68, 69, 155, 176
Stepinac, Cardinal, 111, 113
Sturzo, Don, 174
Summi Pontificatus (Encyclical, 1939), 33, 36
Syllabus of Errors (1864), 27, 30, 31, 32, 37, 41, 170
Synod of Rome (1960), 97, 98, 100 note, 101, 108–9, 115

Tablet, the (London Catholic paper), 31 note, 152 note
Tardini, Cardinal, Secretary of State, 100, 102, 103, 104, 109, 117
Taylor, Myron, 66
Tedeschi, M., Writer and Editor, 158, note, 212
Tempo Il, Italian paper, 157, 158, 188, note
Tisserant, Cardinal, 134
Togliatti, Italian Communist leader, 63
Trevor-Roper, Professor, 203

Ullmann, Dr Walter, 179 note
UNESCO, 81
United Nations, xii, 37, 63, 64, 66, 67, 68, 71, 74, 81, 82, 155, 165
U Thant, Secretary-General of the U.N., 148

Valeri, Mgr Valerio (Nuncio), 18
Veterum Sapientia (Apostolic Constitution on Latin, 1962), 116–19, 202

Visser 't Hooft, Secretary-General of the World Council of Churches, 148

Vito, F., 212

Voltaire, 89

Webster, R., historian, 213

Wenger, A., Editor of *La Croix*, 100, 141, 142, 152, 213

Willebrands, Mgr, 122, 123, 141, 142, 144, 146, 147, 152

Women, Pope John on, 59, 60, Pope Pius XII on, 60

Woodruff, Douglas, 31 note, 211

Worker-Priests, 19, 113–15

World Council of Churches, 108, 123, 124, 135, 144, 152

Wyszynski, Cardinal, 145